Fireworks® 4
f/x & Design

Joyce J. Evans

CORIOLIS

President, CEO

Keith Weiskamp

Publisher

Steve Sayre

Acquisitions Editor

Beth Kohler

Product Marketing Manager

Patricia Davenport

Project Editor

Sean Tape

Technical Reviewer

Brian O'Donnell

Production Coordinator

Meg E. Turecek

Cover Designer

Jesse Dunn

Layout Designer

April E. Nielsen

CD-ROM Developer

Chris Nusbaum

Fireworks® 4 f/x and Design

Limits of Liability and Disclaimer of Warranty

Trademarks

The Coriolis Group, LLC
14455 N. Hayden Road
Suite 220
Scottsdale, Arizona 85260

(480)483-0192
FAX (480)483-0193
www.coriolis.com

Library of Congress Cataloging-In-Publication Data
Evans, Joyce J.
    Fireworks 4 f/x and design / by Joyce J. Evans.
        p.   cm
    Includes index.
    ISBN 1-57610-996-8
    1. Computer graphics. 2. Fireworks (Computer file) I. Title.
T385.E9823 2001
006.6'869--dc21   2001028383
                                                               CIP

Printed in the United States of America
10 9 8 7 6 5 4 3 2 1

 CORIOLIS

A Note from Coriolis

Thank you for choosing this book from The Coriolis Group. Our graphics team strives to meet the needs of creative professionals such as yourself with our three distinctive series: *Visual Insight*, *f/x and Design*, and *In Depth*. We'd love to hear how we're doing in our quest to provide you with information on the latest and most innovative technologies in graphic design, 3D animation, and Web design. Do our books teach you what you want to know? Are the examples illustrative enough? Are there other topics you'd like to see us address?

Please contact us at the address below with your thoughts on this or any of our other books. Should you have any technical questions or concerns about this book, you can contact the Coriolis support team at **techsupport@coriolis.com**; be sure to include this book's title and ISBN, as well as your name, email address, or phone number.

Thank you for your interest in Coriolis books. We look forward to hearing from you.

Coriolis Creative Professionals Press
The Coriolis Group
14455 N. Hayden Road, Suite 220
Scottsdale, AZ 85260

Email: **cpp@coriolis.com**

Phone: (480) 483-0192
Toll free: (800) 410-0192

Visit our Web site at **creative.coriolis.com** *to find the latest information about our current and upcoming graphics books.*

Other Titles for the Creative Professional

Dreamweaver® 4 f/x and Design
By Laurie Ulrich

Flash™ 5 f/x and Design
By Bill Sanders

Flash™ 5 Cartoons and Games f/x and Design
By Bill Turner, James Robertson, Richard Bazley

Flash™ ActionScript f/x and Design
By Bill Sanders

Photoshop® 6 In Depth
By David Xenakis

Illustrator® 9 f/x and Design
By Sherry London

Painter® 6 f/x and Design
By Sherry London and Rhoda Grossman

Adobe InDesign™ f/x and Design
By Elaine Betts

This book is dedicated to my loving and supportive family who helped remove much of the pressure of writing on a tight schedule.

❧

About the Author

Joyce J. Evans is a dynamic communications professional with a lifetime of experience in instructional design and human interaction. With over 10 years of experience in education, tutorial development, and Web design and usability, she faces every challenge with a genuine concern for the user. Joyce currently writes Web reviews, tutorials, and articles for *Web Review*, *DT&G Graphic Design*, *The Internet Eye*, and *Art Today*.

Joyce also maintains the Idea Design Web site (**www.je-ideadesign.com**), a Web design studio she founded and designed. In conjunction with the ID Bookstore and other clients, she keeps herself very busy in the online development world. Authoring *Fireworks 4 f/x and Design* has given Joyce the opportunity to use all of her skills, from basic writing and tutorial development, to advance interface design and information architecture. She also contributed the Fireworks 4 section to *Dreamweaver 4: Complete Reference* (Osborne/McGraw Hill).

Acknowledgments

First and foremost, I want to acknowledge that I am who and what I am today because of my God who keeps the promises in His word and continually opens doors of opportunity, which I gladly walk through.

I couldn't have brought this book in on time without the help and support of my loving family. I especially want to thank my husband who did most of the shopping and cooking, and reminded me to eat. Also my appreciation goes to my children who were very understanding (I'm sure the increased allowance had nothing to do with it) of losing a mom for several months and who helped out with the housework and kept me supplied with coffee.

I'd like to thank Jeffrey Roberts for the interface designs and the animations he supplied. It helped to have the designs done in the vector and animation chapters, so I could concentrate on the teaching instead of the designing. Also thanks go to Japi Honoo who graciously allowed me to use her techniques for producing the great-looking gel button in the special tutorial project in Appendix D.

I'd like to thank Scott Hamlin for taking time out of his busy schedule to write the foreword to this book. Running the Eyeland Studio Web site, which specializes in Flash, he understands the importance of a tool such as Fireworks for producing graphics suitable for Flash.

My appreciation also goes out to Fred Showker of **Graphic-design.com** and Allen Harkleroad of *The Internet Eye* for publishing my reviews and tutorials for the past year and a half. And a special thanks goes to Molly Holzschlag for allowing me write for *Web Review*.

It's been a pleasure working with the crew at Coriolis who worked so hard to get this book to press in a timely manner. Thanks go to Sean Tape, my project editor, who was always patient with my many questions and Bill McManus, my copy editor, who asked great questions, especially, "what is— it?" Because this is my first book I had a lot to learn, and I honestly believe that Bill helped me become a better writer with his superb copyediting and attention to detail.

And thanks to everyone else at Coriolis who made this book possible: Beth Kohler, Senior Acquisitions Editor; Michelle McConnell and Chris Nusbaum for their work on the CD-ROMs; April Nielsen and Laura Wellander for their work on the Color Section; Meg Turecek, the Production Coordinator; and Patti Davenport, Product Marketing Manager.

—*Joyce J. Evans*

Helping out with this book has been one of the best experiences of my career. Working closely with Joyce has been a dream. I would like to thank her for allowing me to help and for providing the all-important critical eye when needed.

Also, I'd like to take this opportunity to thank my parents. Without their support for over 35 years, I'm sure I'd be flipping burgers somewhere, instead of heading my own freelance consulting design firm. And let's not forget "the wife" Rachelle.

—Jeffrey Roberts
   Contributor of interface designs and animations

Contents at a Glance

Table of Contents

Foreword

Only a few short years ago, Web designers were lucky if they could find a few Web-oriented graphic utilities for doing things like Web animations and image mapping. Image optimization was practically impossible and generating HTML tables and JavaScript rollover events were often multiday jobs. Today, tasks such as these are all but automated by programs like Macromedia's Fireworks 4.

The Web has long since demonstrated key advantages over the printed page, and as the Web has grown in sophistication, so have the demands on the Web designer. Fortunately, Macromedia has responded with an accelerated development cycle for tools like Fireworks, Flash, and Dreamweaver. In years past, popular desktop publishing program upgrades often took several years, but new Internet technologies crop up almost daily, making even an annual development cycle feel like a delayed reaction. On the other side of that is the Web designer who is forced to stay current with as many of these technologies as possible to remain competitive.

Perhaps, in the end, this is why programs like Macromedia Fireworks are so valuable. By reducing some of the most commonly required Web-design tasks from multiday prospects to a matter of 15 to 20 minutes, Web designers are ultimately freed up both to keep up with the industry trends as well as to focus more on design and less on the technical issues of implementing the design. While there's always a learning curve that comes with a new version of a program like Macromedia Fireworks, there's also, thankfully, books like *Fireworks 4 f/x and Design* to help us learn the new features and capabilities as quickly as possible.

Joyce Evans has done a remarkable job of clearly and concisely uncovering the capabilities of Fireworks 4. *Fireworks 4 f/x and Design* doesn't resort to the fluff and nonsense so common in books these days. Rather, Joyce systematically covers the techniques and features in Fireworks 4 that are of real value to professional Web designers. *Fireworks 4 f/x and Design* will allow you to quickly dispense with learning the tool and return to what you get paid to do: design Web pages.

J. Scott Hamlin
director, Eyeland Studio, www.eyeland.com
author: *Flash 5 Magic* (New Riders Publishing)

Introduction

I'm thrilled that you are taking the time to read this page. Whether you've just purchased this book or you are thinking about it, I want to tell you why I've written *Fireworks 4 f/x and Design* and what you can expect from it. But first, let me give you some information about Fireworks 4.

About Fireworks 4

Fireworks was originally developed by Macromedia to do superior image editing in preparation for Internet presentations. Today, Fireworks 4 is the premier image-editing program for serious Web designers. One of the main benefits of Fireworks is that you can optimize your images to gain smaller file sizes, resulting in faster loading times for the user. A new feature in version 4 called Selective JPEG Compression allows you to have two different quality settings within the same image and/or slice.

Many other enhancements and new additions to Fireworks 4 will help streamline your production time, such as the new Pop-Up Menu Wizard, which produces great-looking menus in a fraction of the time it would take to do it manually in Dreamweaver. The animation controls are easier than ever to use, and you'll love how simple it is now to make disjointed rollovers (arrays) using the new drag-and-drop function.

Which Fireworks Book Is Right for You?

A handful of Fireworks books are on the market right now, but how do you begin to select which ones to buy?

Fireworks books fall into several categories. Some books are for absolute beginners, those who are unfamiliar with any kind of graphic program. These books usually contain many images, which are great for the new user. Other books are reference books, such as the *Fireworks Bible*. Due to the all-embracing nature of reference books, they are not true competitors of this book. Another category of book is the "studio" book. *Playing with Fire* (due to be published about the same time as this book) is the first studio book for Fireworks. The studio type book usually features the work of various designers/artists and is used primarily for inspiration although some techniques may be taught.

So, what approach does this book take? Actually *Fireworks 4 f/x and Design* takes a bit of every category and a lot of "none of the above." I picked a wide (but by no means exhaustive) range of techniques. I have covered both vectors and bitmaps in great detail as well as the new features of Fireworks 4.

Who Needs This Book

A professional designer, student, hobbyist, or teacher could benefit from this book. Although it isn't written for the new user of a graphics program or someone totally unfamiliar with Fireworks, it can be easily used by anyone who is comfortable with the basics of Fireworks or the features of other graphics programs. The *f/x and Design* series of books are written for the intermediate to advanced user. Because the word "intermediate" is such a nebulous term, it's difficult to say what is intermediate. What one person may think is basic, another person may believe to be intermediate; it's all in the interpretation. Because of this range of expertise, all the projects and exercises are written with precision details.

f/x and Design Philosophy

This *f/x and Design* book will help you gain a better understanding of Macromedia's Fireworks 4 intermediate and advanced features. You will learn how to use all the vector and bitmap drawing and editing tools, as well as how to produce several complete interfaces using the many different kinds of navigation you can employ in Fireworks 4. You also will use transparency techniques to make seamless image compositions as well as to make tonal corrections to images.

Because the best way of learning is doing, the techniques taught are quickly reinforced with real-world projects. Each step in each project will have been taught prior to the project. If a technique is explained in more detail in another chapter, then a reference is given so you can get more details about that technique if needed.

As I noted earlier, it's impossible to know exactly the level of expertise an intermediate user has gained, and so all steps necessary to produce a project are listed, no matter how basic. The end result is an intermediate to advanced technique presented in a manner that a broad range of users can understand.

How This Book Is Structured

The *Fireworks 4 f/x and Design* book is not just a project or a studio book of projects, although it contains over 60 projects. You'll be taught the majority of the tools and functions in Fireworks, and you'll then use those techniques by doing the projects. If you have a basic understanding of Fireworks or any other image editing program, you can master Fireworks with this book.

The projects in *Fireworks 4 f/x and Design* do not use starter files—files that have most of the work completed—but rather give you the original files to allow you to complete real-world projects. Every image in the Color Section is a representation of something you can actually do in this book, not something someone else did and included for inspiration only. Every image or piece of clipart used in a project has been made available for your use. I have obtained special permission to include all the source images for you on this book's CD-ROM, as well as some great freebies and demos.

Because I wanted to illustrate Fireworks techniques with real-world projects, I have included complete interfaces and Web pages for the projects in this book. Parts of several projects are made in different sections throughout this book to illustrate a specific technique. When the project is assembled, references are made to the chapter where each portion was made. If you'd rather not make certain parts of a design from scratch—no problem—the image file is included in each of the chapters resource folder, ready for your use. Some of the projects are actual working Web sites; you can't get more real-world than that. The only thing not included are copyrighted fonts. The fonts used in the projects are for display purposes only; you can substitute any font you'd like. The fonts used are always mentioned in case you want to use or purchase the same font.

Great care and effort has been taken to give you the best book possible. I've enjoyed writing this book tremendously and hope you enjoy it as well.

Feel free to keep in touch. I have a companion Web site to this book at **www.je-ideadesign.com/fireworksbook.htm**, where any updates will be posted, as well as new tutorials.

Chapter 1

Layers and Beyond

In this chapter, you will review the new features of Fireworks 4 and delve into the Layers panel. You will compare and explore the power of blending modes to enhance images. Finally, the batch processing techniques presented later in the chapter will help you to automate many tedious tasks.

What's New in Fireworks 4

If you have worked with Fireworks before, you are probably anxious to know what the newest additions are and how they can make your work more productive. The most notable addition is the Pop-up Menu feature. The other two vital improvements are the Selective JPEG optimization and the drag-and-drop rollover functions. The majority of the new features in Fireworks 4 will be discussed at more length in the chapters that discuss each particular topic. Here is a quick overview of the new features.

Macromedia User Interface

The visual interface of Fireworks has changed to become compatible with Dreamweaver 4's interface, making working with both applications seamless and familiar. You can also now customize your own keyboard shortcuts, or even use the shortcuts from Photoshop, Freehand, Illustrator, or Fireworks 3. The new Launcher Bar at the bottom of the document window offers quick access to many commands and looks the same as the Dreamweaver 4 icons.

Pop-up Menu Feature

By using the new Pop-up Menu feature, even a novice can generate a pop-up menu. (If you like to have complete control, and don't mind editing the Java-Script, you can always edit the code and customize the menus.) You can control whether the menus are HTML or image based, and you can add URLs all without writing a single line of code. You can also customize the look of the menu by using styles. In Chapter 7, you will make a pop-up menu.

Drag-and-Drop Rollovers

The new drag-and-drop feature allows you to use rollover behaviors to produce complex interactivity, even if you are a novice. Rollover behaviors include replacing one image with another, displaying another image when the mouse cursor hovers over a "hot" area (one with a behavior attached), and setting what is displayed in a browser's status bar. The drag-and-drop technique is much easier than adding behaviors through the Behavior panel. (See Chapter 7 for a full step-by-step description.)

Masking and Layers Panel Enhancements

With a new thumbnail preview of every object, selecting multiple objects is extremely easy to do from the Layers panel. The stacking order of layers and objects can be changed by simply dragging and dropping them to a new location. There is even a representation of image masks which can be clicked on and edited—all from within the Layers panel—instead of having to go through menus for access. The gradient handles are readily available once you click the mask icon.

Refined Photoshop Import and Export

With improved layer mask handling, Photoshop files, even Photoshop 6 files, can now be opened in Fireworks.

Live Animation

Fireworks has improved the animation user interface tremendously. With the Live Animation feature, you can use VCR-like controls to reposition, redirect, reanimate, and preview your animations across multiple frames, without ever leaving Fireworks. Now, you can set the start and end location of your animation directly on the screen. The improved Object panel shows the number of frames, the scaling, the rotation, and the opacity, making editing extremely convenient.

Batch Process

A step-by-step Batch Processing Wizard helps you to set up and execute batch processes, which can even include commands. You can specify specific files or whole folders for processing, and specify which action to take—Export, Scale, Find and Replace, or Commands. With the ability to assign a naming scheme for the batch, you can determine which files have been changed and even export them into a specific folder.

Roundtrip Table Editing with Dreamweaver

With this new version, you can edit and update HTML code, JavaScript code, and images from Dreamweaver and pass the file back to a colleague using Fireworks while maintaining the integrity of any custom code.

Export Controls

You can customize how your images are named using your own auto-naming conventions. You can also specify where the image slices are exported to.

Selective JPEG Compression

This feature is really an important new addition. With it, you can use two different compression settings within the same JPEG slice, allowing you to get the best possible image at the smallest possible file size. In Chapter 6, you will see how a JPEG slice is optimized at 80 percent quality; but parts of the image are, well, frankly, not so good. These parts can now be optimized at 100 percent quality, while keeping the file size within an acceptable range. This feature alone will make the Fireworks 4 upgrade worth its price.

Now that some of the new features of Fireworks 4 have been introduced, it's time to start using the program, beginning with the Layers panel.

Layers Panel Refresher

Because layers are such a vital part of the workflow in Fireworks, this section covers some of their most important features. Some of the functions you will learn are how to add, delete, lock, and arrange your layers. If you are extremely familiar with the Layers panel, you may want to skip this section.

The layers in Fireworks serve as the "file cabinets" for your documents. You organize all the pieces of a document in a layer, which is analogous to a folder in a file cabinet. If you have worked with layers in other applications, you will discover that Fireworks handles layers differently. Whereas other applications put each individual object on its own layer, in Fireworks multiple objects can be placed on one layer and edited individually. This feature really saves time, because you don't have to scroll through a multitude of layers searching for the item you want to edit. What's really great about being able to put more than one object on a layer is that you can work in the same layer with related items and simply click an object if you want to select it.

Figure 1.1
The Layers panel.

The Layers panel in Fireworks 4, shown in Figure 1.1, has two new icons added at the bottom: Add Mask is a quick way to add a mask to a document you want to alter, and New Bitmap Image is the shortest route to getting a blank canvas on which to paint a new bitmap image. The functions of these tools will be discussed in more detail in Chapter 5.

The Web Layer

The Web layer is a special layer that always remains on top—you can't delete, duplicate, rename, or move it. It is very unique in its function; it stores slices you produce when you cut up your document for exporting and hotspot areas you define in image maps. (The Web Layer contains only slices and hotspots.) Slices and hotspots are Web objects; their only purpose is to receive a behavior, such as a mouse click, which in turn triggers an action or event, such as a rollover, a pop-up menu, or maybe a pop-up window. When you're assigning rollover functions and working with animations, objects will be on different frames. What is done to an object on one frame won't transfer to other frames. In contrast, the contents of the Web layer are always shared across all frames, so you only have to set the behavior once.

Stacking Order of Regular Layers

Whenever you generate a new document, by default it will have a Layer 1, which is a regular layer to hold your objects until you add another layer. Each layer in Fireworks may contain many objects. Each time you add a new object, it is placed on top of the previous object by default. To change the stacking order of your objects within a layer or between layers, do the following:

Refined Photoshop Import and Export

With improved layer mask handling, Photoshop files, even Photoshop 6 files, can now be opened in Fireworks.

Live Animation

Fireworks has improved the animation user interface tremendously. With the Live Animation feature, you can use VCR-like controls to reposition, redirect, reanimate, and preview your animations across multiple frames, without ever leaving Fireworks. Now, you can set the start and end location of your animation directly on the screen. The improved Object panel shows the number of frames, the scaling, the rotation, and the opacity, making editing extremely convenient.

Batch Process

A step-by-step Batch Processing Wizard helps you to set up and execute batch processes, which can even include commands. You can specify specific files or whole folders for processing, and specify which action to take—Export, Scale, Find and Replace, or Commands. With the ability to assign a naming scheme for the batch, you can determine which files have been changed and even export them into a specific folder.

Roundtrip Table Editing with Dreamweaver

With this new version, you can edit and update HTML code, JavaScript code, and images from Dreamweaver and pass the file back to a colleague using Fireworks while maintaining the integrity of any custom code.

Export Controls

You can customize how your images are named using your own auto-naming conventions. You can also specify where the image slices are exported to.

Selective JPEG Compression

This feature is really an important new addition. With it, you can use two different compression settings within the same JPEG slice, allowing you to get the best possible image at the smallest possible file size. In Chapter 6, you will see how a JPEG slice is optimized at 80 percent quality; but parts of the image are, well, frankly, not so good. These parts can now be optimized at 100 percent quality, while keeping the file size within an acceptable range. This feature alone will make the Fireworks 4 upgrade worth its price.

Now that some of the new features of Fireworks 4 have been introduced, it's time to start using the program, beginning with the Layers panel.

Layers Panel Refresher

Because layers are such a vital part of the workflow in Fireworks, this section covers some of their most important features. Some of the functions you will learn are how to add, delete, lock, and arrange your layers. If you are extremely familiar with the Layers panel, you may want to skip this section.

The layers in Fireworks serve as the "file cabinets" for your documents. You organize all the pieces of a document in a layer, which is analogous to a folder in a file cabinet. If you have worked with layers in other applications, you will discover that Fireworks handles layers differently. Whereas other applications put each individual object on its own layer, in Fireworks multiple objects can be placed on one layer and edited individually. This feature really saves time, because you don't have to scroll through a multitude of layers searching for the item you want to edit. What's really great about being able to put more than one object on a layer is that you can work in the same layer with related items and simply click an object if you want to select it.

The Layers panel in Fireworks 4, shown in Figure 1.1, has two new icons added at the bottom: Add Mask is a quick way to add a mask to a document you want to alter, and New Bitmap Image is the shortest route to getting a blank canvas on which to paint a new bitmap image. The functions of these tools will be discussed in more detail in Chapter 5.

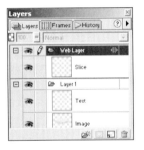

Figure 1.1
The Layers panel.

The Web Layer

The Web layer is a special layer that always remains on top—you can't delete, duplicate, rename, or move it. It is very unique in its function; it stores slices you produce when you cut up your document for exporting and hotspot areas you define in image maps. (The Web Layer contains only slices and hotspots.) Slices and hotspots are Web objects; their only purpose is to receive a behavior, such as a mouse click, which in turn triggers an action or event, such as a rollover, a pop-up menu, or maybe a pop-up window. When you're assigning rollover functions and working with animations, objects will be on different frames. What is done to an object on one frame won't transfer to other frames. In contrast, the contents of the Web layer are always shared across all frames, so you only have to set the behavior once.

Stacking Order of Regular Layers

Whenever you generate a new document, by default it will have a Layer 1, which is a regular layer to hold your objects until you add another layer. Each layer in Fireworks may contain many objects. Each time you add a new object, it is placed on top of the previous object by default. To change the stacking order of your objects within a layer or between layers, do the following:

1. Open a new document, by selecting File|New.

2. Near the bottom of the toolbar in the color section, click the Paint Bucket color well and select a red color.

3. Select the Rectangle tool from the toolbar and draw a rectangle filled with red.

4. Change the fill color to blue by clicking the Paint Bucket color well and selecting blue.

5. To access more than just the Rectangle tool, select another shape tool. Click and hold down the little arrow at the bottom of the Rectangle tool icon; a pop-up menu will appear, displaying other options. Draw another shape filled with blue.

6. Open the Layers panel by pressing F2 or choosing Window|Layers. As Figure 1.2 shows, the blue shape on Layer 1, which was added last, is on top, and under the blue shape is the red shape that was drawn first.

Note: The only reason you are drawing different shapes with different colors in this exercise is to be able to recognize the shapes easier in the Layers panel. The icons in the Layers panel show small representations of each object. If you'd like the icons to appear a bit bigger, click the right-pointing arrow and choose Thumbnail Options. You have four sizes from which to choose, or you can choose to have no icon shown.

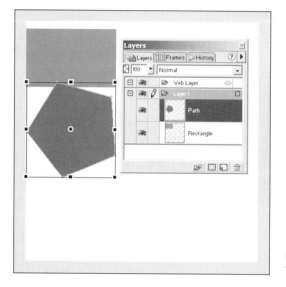

Figure 1.2
The stacking order of two layers.

7. Click the blue object called Path (Path is the default name of every object drawn—except objects drawn with the Rectangle tool, which use the default name of Rectangle—until you specifically rename it) and drag it below the red rectangle object. The red object now is on top of the blue object. Either save this practice document now or keep it open for the next exercise.

Managing your layers becomes quite easy when you have the ability to move objects around and put them on layers with unique names. For instance, if you have a navigation bar, all the buttons and objects associated with it can be together on one layer, keeping them organized in a group so you can easily locate them in a multi-layered document.

Showing/Hiding Objects

Figure 1.3
The show/hide icon.

To show or hide objects or whole layers, click the eye icon (see Figure 1.3) of any object or layer. If the eye icon associated with the object is visible in your document and you click it again, it will toggle the visibility off. The same technique works for whole layers.

Using the Opacity Settings

The Layers panel has opacity settings that can be adjusted for each object on the layer independently. By adjusting the opacity of an object, you will be able to see through it to varying degrees. To adjust the opacity of the shapes drawn in the last exercise, take the following steps:

1. Using the shapes from the previous exercise (or draw two new shapes with different colors), click the blue shape and drag it on top of the red rectangle. To lower the opacity, locate the opacity slider, which is to the right of the blend modes box and below the Layers tab on the far right; it usually contains the number 100. Simply click the down arrow and drag it to the desired setting; try 60%.

2. Draw two more objects and repeat step one with a different opacity setting; try 30%.

You can adjust the opacity not only for every layer, but also for each individual object on a layer.

Adding Layers

The New/Duplicate Layer icon has changed in the Layers panel; it is now a yellow folder instead of the black and white page icon used in version 3. To add layers, follow these steps:

1. Open any image by selecting File|Open.

2. Click the New/Duplicate Layer icon.

Duplicating Layers

Duplicating layers couldn't be easier. With the layer selected that you want to duplicate, simply click the right-pointing arrow and select Duplicate layer. You will be given the option of how many layers and where you'd like them added—before or after the current layer, or at the top or bottom of it. Duplicating layers is a great way to save layers as backups before you edit extensively.

One other option exists for duplicating layers: Select the layer you want to duplicate and Edit|Copy and Edit|Paste into a new layer.

Deleting a Layer

Deleting layers can be done in any of three different ways:

- Highlight the layer or object you want to delete and use the Delete key on the keyboard

- Click and drag the layer or object on top of the trash can icon

- Click the layer or object to delete and click the trash can icon

You may find the last option the easiest to use.

Locking Layers

To lock a layer, click the box to the left of the layer's name. After it is locked (indicated by a padlock, as shown earlier in Figure 1.3), you can't alter anything in this layer, and you can't even select it.

To lock or unlock all the layers, click the right-pointing arrow in the Layers panel and choose the appropriate action.

Renaming a Layer

To rename a layer or an object, double-click the layer or object name and rename it in the dialog box that pops up.

Copying Objects

If you want to copy objects from one layer to another, hold down the Alt or Option key while dragging the object to the new layer. Another option is to copy (Edit|Copy) and paste (Edit|Paste).

Layer Editing

Layer editing, by default, enables you to work on all layers simultaneously. (This is the opposite of how Photoshop works.) There are times, however, when you will want to change the default behaviors of layers. For example, when working on objects that appear on just one layer, you may want to lock the other layers so you don't accidentally alter them, or you may want to hide them from view to avoid unnecessary distractions. Perhaps, you want the objects on one layer to appear on all your layers.

Locking or Hiding Layers

Hiding layers or locking them makes all layers unavailable for editing, except the one you want to edit. If you hide layers, you don't have to lock them because hiding a layer also locks it. The difference between the commands is that locked layers will still be visible, even though they can't be edited. To hide or lock a layer, follow these steps:

1. To hide the entire layer, click the right-pointing arrow in the Layers panel and choose Hide All.

Note: Another way to hide or lock other layers is to click Commands|Documents|Hide Other Layers or Commands| Documents|Lock Other Layers.

2. To lock all the layers or unlock all the layers, click the right-pointing arrow in the Layers panel and select Lock All or Unlock All, respectively.

Single-Layer Editing

If you want to work on only one layer in Fireworks, you need to lock all the layers except the one you are working on, or choose Single Layer Editing mode.

To use Single Layer Editing mode, click the right-pointing arrow and select Single Layer Editing. Now, you can only select or edit objects on the current layer. You can still see objects and other layers, but you can't alter them.

Sharing a Selected Layer

The sharing of a selected layer comes in really handy when you are producing animations. If you need objects or images to appear on all frames, you use this option. You simply select the object, click the right-pointing arrow in the Layers panel, and choose Share This Layer. You will use this option in Chapter 8.

Blending Modes

Blending modes baffle many designers. The blending modes are used when you want to achieve special effects, such as darkening, lightening, adjusting the hue and saturation, and so on. In the simplest terms, blending modes change the appearance of pixels on one layer as they are "blended" with the pixels of another layer. The result is based on calculations Fireworks makes on the values, which are associated with the pixels. The values used in the calculations depend on the blending mode chosen; it could be hue, RGB values, brightness, or the transparency of the pixels. The calculations Fireworks makes are mathematical ones that are similar for each blending mode. For example, the multiply mode used on two images is calculated by multiplying the brightness values for each of the three color channels: red×red, green×green, and blue×blue. (RGB is what Fireworks uses.) The formula used is base color times blend color divided by 255. It is divided by 255 to keep the result within the values of 255; anything higher is not possible. If you are mathematically minded, you'll understand the concept; if not, just try out all the different modes to see the results.

The following sections describe the various blending modes that are available to you from the Mode options box, which usually says Normal.

Normal

Normal mode is what you are using when no blending mode is applied. The pixels on the top layer simply hide any pixels below them. Normal mode does not affect any pixels in the layer below it. Lowering the opacity settings on the top layer may appear to change the pixels on the layer below it, because it gives the impression that additional color information has been added to the lower layer, but this is not the case.

Multiply

When you apply Multiply mode to your top layer, you will notice that it appears quite a bit darker than either of the layers individually. This mode reproduces what you would see if you were to put two transparencies on a light board, one on top of the other. The best way to see how Multiply mode blends the pixels of two layers is to try it out.

Note: Multiplying any color with black produces black, but if you multiply any color with white, no change in tone occurs.

PROJECT Using the Multiply Mode

For this project using blending modes, the blendingmodes.png file is supplied on this book's CD-ROM. Comstock provided the use of these images for your practice from its Scenic Overlooks CD-ROM collection.

1. From the menu bar, choose File|Open, navigate to the book's CD-ROM, and open blendingmodes.png in the Chapter 1 folder (see Figure 1.4).

Select and move objects

Figure 1.4
A scene before applying Multiply mode.

2. Looking at the Layers panel (press F2), notice that layer 1, waterfall, is on top of the background, which is sand. Don't be concerned that you can't see the sand. To experiment with Multiply mode, select the waterfall layer.

3. From the Layers panel, click the down arrow and choose Multiply. See how dark it just got? This would be great if you were looking for a nighttime effect. Notice how the bottom layer affects the top layer even though you can't see any of the underlying layers. The two layers have had pixels blended by certain Fireworks calculations.

4. The desired effect of this exercise is the illusion that a waterfall exists in this desert. From the Opacity option in the Layers panel, with the waterfall layer still selected, change the opacity to 50 percent. You can type "50" and press Enter; it's quite difficult to get exact numbers using a slider. You will also need to press the Enter or Return key for the opacity to be applied.

5. For the illusion to be pulled off, the image obviously needs work, but it looks quite interesting already: water coming from the sand, bushes growing, and even some mountains in the background that were not there. Now try 60 percent; that looks better yet, and more realistic (see Figure 1.5).

Figure 1.5
A scene with Multiply mode applied at 60 percent.

You can close the image now and reopen for the next mode or return the waterfall layer to 100 percent and Normal mode, whichever method you prefer.

Screen

Screen mode is the opposite of Multiply mode. Screen mode produces tones that are lighter by inverting the foreground color and then multiplying it with the background color. Imagine what your image would look like if you were to paint it with diluted bleach.

> **Note:** When you screen any color with black, no change in tone occurs, but if you screen with white, it produces white.

PROJECT Screen Mode Applied

To see how the Screen mode affects two images, follow these steps:

1. Open gradient.png from the Chapter 1 folder on the book's CD-ROM. (Using gradient fills will be discussed in Chapter 2.)

2. Open any image you like. A winter scene is used here. Click your image and drag it into position on the gradient. To drag, simply use the pointer tool and click and drag from one document to the other. Your image will automatically be placed on top of the gradient.

3. From the Layers panel, click the down arrow and choose Screen. Notice the hazy effect on the left side. If you recall, the white of the gradient is under that side. A portion of the black tree was left on the right side to demonstrate that when the image is placed over black, no change occurs, but where white is on top of white, the image remains white. Figure 1.6 shows the result.

Figure 1.6
Screen mode applied to a scene.

4. Try changing the opacity to about 70 percent; this produces what looks like a dark and dreary day. With Screen mode, the lower the opacity, the darker the image. Try 50 percent mode.

Darken

When Darken mode is used in grayscale, the results are quite predictable. The pixels on the top layer that are lighter than those on the bottom layer become invisible, but if they are darker than the pixels below them, no change occurs.

But, if you use Darken mode on a color image, the results are very different. When Darken is applied as the blending mode for colors, the brightness of the values for all the color channels (red, blue, and green) is evaluated. For example, if the value of the bottom layer is a darker blue than the top layer, the bottom layer remains and the other pixels disappear. This same procedure applies to the other two channels. The resulting color is a composite of the values of both layers. In a nutshell, Darken mode compares the top layer and the bottom layer and keeps the darkest brightness values.

PROJECT Applying the Darken Mode

In this exercise, a black-and-white image is used, because it would be futile to demonstrate the effects of Darken with color when this book uses black-and-white illustrations. To see how this mode works, follow these steps:

1. Open the gradient.png file and the burlap.png file from the Chapter 1 folder on the book's CD-ROM. The burlap.png file was made using a Pattern fill in Fireworks (using the Pattern fill tool is discussed in Chapter 2).

2. Drag the burlap.png file on top of the gradient.png file; see Figure 1.7.

3. From the Layers panel, click the down arrow and choose Darken mode. The results can be seen in Figure 1.8.

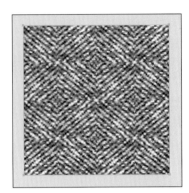

Figure 1.7
A grayscale pattern before
Darken mode is applied.

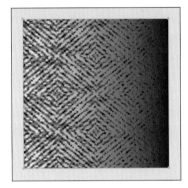

Figure 1.8
Darken mode applied to a
black-and-white pattern.

To get a better idea of what Darken mode can do, apply the steps from the preceding exercise to a few color images. One sample called blendingmodes3.png is included in the Chapter 1 resources folder on this book's CD-ROM. It can also be seen in the Color Section.

Lighten

Lighten mode basically is the opposite of Darken mode: The foreground and the background colors are compared, and only the lightest colors are kept (see Figure 1.9).

Figure 1.9
The same burlap pattern with
Lighten mode applied.

Difference

Difference mode, without getting too technical, causes the pixels of the bottom layer to appear to be inverted depending on the brightness value, which is calculated in each channel. Try the following steps to see it in action:

1. Open the blendingmodes.png file from the Chapter 1 folder of the book's CD-ROM.

2. Click the waterfall layer and select Difference mode. Try adjusting the opacity to about 60 percent.

Hue

Hue mode combines the hue value of the top layer of pixels with the luminance and saturation values of the bottom layer of pixels. This effect is most noticeable when the values of the layers used are quite different.

Saturation

Saturation mode combines the saturation value of the top layer of pixels with the luminance and hue values of the bottom layer. This mode is rather dull, but check it out as you try the different blending modes.

Color

Compared to Hue and Saturation, Color mode is the most interesting. Color mode blends the hue and saturation values of the top layer of pixels and combines the result with the luminance of the bottom layer of pixels. Try using Color mode for colorizing grayscale images.

Luminosity

Luminosity mode is the reverse of Color mode. The resulting color is the hue and saturation values of the bottom layer and the luminance of the blend layer. This combination produces colors that are darker and much more intense than they were originally.

Invert

When you apply Invert mode to the top layer, the foreground colors are replaced with the inverted background color. Follow these steps to see how the Invert mode looks:

1. Open a new document and draw a rectangle filled with green.

2. Click the New layer icon and draw a rectangle filled with red, overlapping the green layer.

3. With the red layer selected, choose Invert from the blending modes drop-down panel (see Figure 1.10).

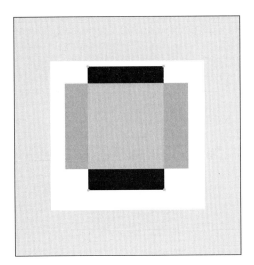

Figure 1.10
Invert blending mode applied to
two layers.

With Invert applied, the intersecting area is purple, the edges of the red that are not touching the green are black, and the edges of the green layer that do not touch the red remain green. Try it and see the effects you can produce. It may also help in deciding on color combinations to use in your projects.

Tint

When you apply Tint mode, gray is simply added to the bottom layer; no pixels are replaced, but a gray tint is added to the existing colors:

1. Use the same colors as you did in the preceding Invert example.

2. With the top layer selected, choose Tint mode.

The area where the red and green intersect turns to a medium-brown color (see Figure 1.11).

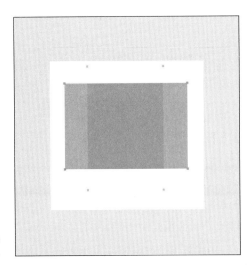

Figure 1.11
Tint blending mode applied to
two layers.

Erase

Erase mode erases to the canvas color.

Project Log

The Project Log, used to monitor the Find and Replace functions, is accessed by choosing Window|Project Log. To do a search and replace, you need to select the right-pointing arrow and choose Add Files To Log; then click the first down arrow and choose Search Files (see Figure 1.12). A panel appears in which you can select from your hard drive which files to add. When you click a folder with files in it, you have two options. You can add individual files by clicking them and then clicking the Add button, or you can choose to Add All. Click Done when you are finished. You will now see a list of the files you chose in the Project Log.

Now, when you do a search with the scope set to Files, any files with alterations are listed by name, frame number, date, and time. You can verify a change, or reverse it, by opening the file from the Project Log. To open a file, click its name or select it, and then click the Open button.

Now that you have been introduced to the panels, it's time to learn a wonderful time-saving tool: batch processing.

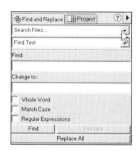

Figure 1.12
The Find And Replace/Project Log panel.

Batch Processing

When you have repetitive tasks to accomplish, you can manage your time better by using batch processes. The more tasks you automate, the more time you'll have to do fun stuff, like producing great graphics.

Some of the things you can do with batch processing include converting files to another format, converting files to the same format but with different optimization settings, scaling exported files, and finding and replacing text, colors, URLs, fonts, and non-Web216 colors (more on this in Chapter 2). You can also rename files by adding a prefix or suffix.

To begin a batch process:

1. Choose File|Batch Process; you will be presented with a screen giving you access to your files. Choose a file, files, or an entire folder. If you want to use the files you added to the Project Log, then put a checkmark in front of Project Log. If you have an image open that you'd like to include, put a checkmark in front of Include Current Open Files.

2. After you select the files you want in the batch process, the Batch Process dialog box appears (see Figure 1.13).

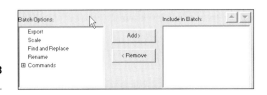

Figure 1.13
The Batch Process dialog box.

Note: If you choose Add Files from the Project Log, the files won't appear in the list of files that are being processed; but don't fret, because they are indeed being processed. Current open files won't appear either. If you have a file open that hasn't been saved, then the latest version won't appear in the batch process. In fact, the process will stop and ask you to save; if you do, the process continues, but if you don't, it stops.

3. To select the processes you want to run—Export, Scale, Find And Replace, Rename, or Commands (run a command from the Command menu)—select all the options you want and click the Add> button to add the option to the Batch Process side (the right).

4. To remove a batch option, select it from the right side and click the <Remove button.

5. Each batch process option has its own submenu of choices. If you choose Export and add it to the batch process, the Batch Process dialog changes with the options available as seen in Figure 1.14. The Edit button gives you access to the full range of export options.

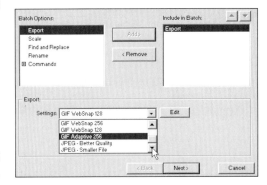

Figure 1.14
The Batch Export dialog box.

PROJECT Running a Batch Process on a Folder of Images

The scaling option that is found in the Batch Process dialog box is commonly used to scale thumbnails, which is what you will do in this project:

1. Choose File|Batch Process.

2. From the Batch Process dialog box, navigate to your CD drive, open the Chapter 1 folder from the book's CD-ROM, and open the color folder. Click Add All, and then click Next.

3. Because you are going to be changing the size of these color images, click the Scale option, and then click the Add> button to include this command in the batch process. The dialog now changes. Click the down arrow in the Scale dialog (bottom) and select Scale To Size. You are now presented with an arrow indicating width; type in "20", and at the arrow indicating height, type in "20".

4. Back in the Batch Options, select Export and click the Add> button. In the Export Settings area, select GIF WebSnap 128.

5. In the Batch Options section, choose Rename and click the Add> button. In the Rename area, click the down arrow, choose Add Prefix, and add whatever prefix you'd like to use to distinguish this process.

6. Click Next when you are done adding and setting your batch preferences. You are now presented with a dialog box of more options, such as where you want the output of the batch process to be saved, and even the option to save the whole batch process as a script for reuse. The options can be seen in Figure 1.15.

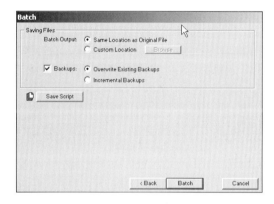

Figure 1.15
Options for saving batch processes.

7. Once you have selected all the options you need, click Batch. You will see a little dialog box showing the files being processed, and the results will be presented when complete.

You can now go back to your files and easily find the changed images because you added the prefix to identify them. It's easier still if you saved the files in the batch process to a separate folder. These little 20×20 color swatches will come in handy when you make a custom color swatch palette in Chapter 2.

Moving On

By now, you have been introduced to the new features in Fireworks 4, and you should be able to find and use all the layer tools and functions that the Layers panel offers. You have learned how to produce stunning effects using the different blending modes and how to automate tedious tasks using the Batch Process panel. In this chapter, you've learned how to manipulate your objects and layers to fit your workflow style.

In Chapter 2, you will discover some of the more intricate ways to accomplish stunning text effects like you've seen on professional Web sites on the Internet. You will also learn how to add special effects and control color.

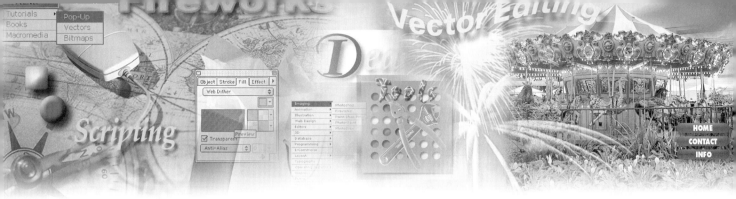

Chapter 2

Text with a Flair

In this chapter, you will discover some of the more intricate ways to accomplish stunning text effects like you've seen on professional Web sites on the Internet. You'll learn how to achieve color control, apply Live Effects, and use interesting patterns, textures, and gradients to produce text effects that grab the attention of your Web site visitors.

Using Text

Macromedia Fireworks 4 ships with plenty of tools that can be used to produce your own spectacular special text. You will find yourself using enhanced text frequently to add flair and pizzazz to your Web sites. In Fireworks 4, you can add Live Effects including shadows, gradients, strokes, and various fills, and you can place your text on a path. By using Web-safe colors, you can be assured that your audience sees the color of your design as you intended it to be seen.

In this chapter, you will be using enhanced text to produce company logos and banners. You will also learn how to make your own customized Web-safe palette of colors and how to customize your own gradient designs.

Transforming Text

To *transform* an object is to convert or change it into something different, and Fireworks 4 makes the transformation process a snap. You will find the process is also quite intuitive. In this chapter, you'll learn how to add strokes, fills, and effects—and other not-so-ordinary preset effects. You'll be amazed at how much flexibility you have in altering or transforming text. If you don't convert your text into an image or a bitmap, it remains fully editable, even after you twist it, turn it, and make it do all sorts of transforming contortions.

Many books devoted to the special effects of type are available, and many Web sites offer tutorials on producing these effects. Be careful, though, because with so many options, you can spend many hours just experimenting with these fun and functional tools, without really getting anywhere.

The first decision you need to make is which type of font to use in your project. This isn't as easy as it sounds. Go to any Web search engine and search for "fonts", and you'll be overwhelmed with choices. The use of the appropriate font is as important as the effects you apply.

This discussion assumes that you have used the Text Editor before (shown in Figure 2.1), and are familiar with its basic functions. You'll be pleased to

Figure 2.1
The Text Editor.

discover that in Fireworks 4, you can move text around in your document with the Text Editor open. Now, you can resize and make any font corrections in real time as you see the text on screen.

Converting Text to an Image

The process of converting text to an image is quick and easy, but why would you want to convert a text path that is completely editable into an image? The answer is simple: to add special effects. Many of the effects from the Xtras menu, including third-party plug-ins, often will work only on a bitmap image. To convert text into a bitmap image, follow these steps:

1. Select the text or object you want to convert into an image.

2. Choose Modify|Convert To Bitmap (or, on the keyboard, press Ctrl+Alt+Shift+Z for Windows, or Cmd+Option+Z for Macintosh).

The text is now an image and is not editable as text. Because it's an image, you can apply filters such as Gaussian blur, motion blur, and perspective shadow; these techniques are covered in more depth in Chapter 5.

Converting Text to a Path

Text is an object; by converting it to a path (any line containing at least two points), each letter becomes a separate path object. One reason to choose the Convert Text To Paths option is if you are sharing files with someone who may not have the same fonts on their machine. This ensures that the correct font is embedded within the file as a vector shape of the font. Keep in mind that this applies only for sharing files, not on the Internet. For use in a Web page, the font you use in a graphic is exported as an image, so it doesn't matter whether it's a path or not. Another reason to choose the Convert Text To Paths option is to have the ability to combine the text with other path objects or to alter the shape of the text. To change the shape of a letter, follow these steps:

1. Type a letter; make it large enough that you can see it well enough to distort it, as in the example shown in Figure 2.2.

2. Select the text, and choose Text|Convert To Paths (Ctrl+Shift+P/ Cmd+Shift+P). Notice how letters are converted into a path and are automatically grouped together.

3. Choose the Subselection tool (white arrow) and click your type to select it.

4. You can now see a bunch of little nodes; by clicking and dragging these nodes, you can alter your text. The *B* shown in Figures 2.3 and 2.4 was distorted by moving various points.

Figure 2.2
Large text to convert to a path.

Figure 2.3
Points on text converted to a path.

Figure 2.4
Text converted by modifying its points.

After you convert text to a path, it is no longer editable as text. That doesn't mean it can't be edited, though. As a path, you can reshape your letter or letters any way you desire. This technique is included in the project "Punching a Hole Through a Pattern with Text," later in this chapter.

Putting Text on a Path

Making your text do acrobatic feats around a path doesn't require any special training. Text doesn't have to conform to rectangular blocks, but can be attached to any path that you draw and still remain editable.

To put text on a path follow these steps:

1. Select the Pen tool or the Brush tool from the toolbar. Draw a curvy path that is open; in other words, don't close it by connecting the first and last points.

2. Select the Text tool from the toolbar and type some text anywhere in your document. The text in Figure 2.5 is Arial Black with a size of 22 points; everything else in the Text dialog box is left at the default setting.

3. To get the text to wrap around the curve, select the text and Shift+click to select the path as well.

4. Select Text|Attach To Path, and the text wraps around the curve. That sure was easy, but it doesn't look too good at this point. Notice in Figure 2.5 how some of the letters are at odd angles.

5. To edit the text, double-click the text to open the Text Editor. Highlight the text and adjust the alignment settings. Figure 2.6 shows the settings used for this example; the changes are nominal, but they did help the appearance. Figure 2.7 shows the result of these changes.

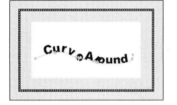

Figure 2.5
Text wrapping along a curve.

Figure 2.6
(Left) Text Editor settings.

Figure 2.7
(Right) Adjusted text along the curve.

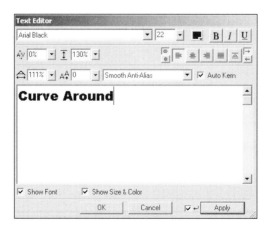

Changing the Flow of the Text

Text begins to wrap around at the first point you drew. If this placement isn't to your liking, you can alter the position of the text on the path by using any of these methods:

- From the Text Editor, choose the alignment you want, such as center, right, left, justified, stretched, horizontal, or vertical.
- Choose Text|Orientation and one of the options Rotate Around Path, Vertical, Skew Vertical, or Skew Horizontal.
- For the most control, use the Text Offset option in the Object panel. This enables you to use negative values as well as positive values to position the text. This option requires trial and error. Because you can press the Enter key after each change and see the result it makes, it's easy to keep trying different settings.
- Choose Modify|Transform|Numeric Transform. The choices you have in this dialog box are Scale, Resize, and Rotate. Then, you choose the percentage of change you want to occur; if you want just the height or just the width to change, be sure to uncheck the Constrain Proportions option.

6. It doesn't look quite right yet, so try another option. With the text selected, choose Text|Orientation|Vertical (see Figure 2.8). That looks pretty good, but just to experiment, try selecting Text|Orientation|Skew Vertical (see Figure 2.9). You decide which you prefer.

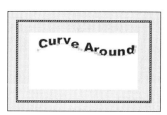

Figure 2.8
Vertical orientation applied to the text/path object.

You may wonder what happens if the text is too long for the path. Some programs will just bunch the ending text on top of itself. Fireworks 4 is much more intuitive than that. The text that won't fit on the length of the path drawn will wrap itself around the underside of the path following the same curve, as shown in Figure 2.10.

The results and settings for the alignment of the text will vary depending on the shape you are wrapping the text around. The best way to get the right look is to experiment with the alignment, offset, horizontal scale, baseline shift, leading, and kerning. Experiment away—after all, the changes won't take effect until you click OK in the Text Editor. Even if you click OK and accept the changes, you can always choose Edit|Undo if you change your mind.

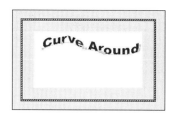

Figure 2.9
Vertical skew applied to the text/path object.

Editing Text on a Path

If you decide you want to change the text in any way, or to change the path that the text wraps around, then follow these easy steps:

1. Select the text and the path object and choose Text|Detach From Path.

2. Double-click the text to open the Text Editor and then make the necessary alterations.

3. Click the Subselection tool and then click the text and/or path you want to alter. The Subselection tool enables you to click and drag the individual points. (See Chapter 4 for more details on editing paths.)

Figure 2.10
Text repeated around the curve.

The path for the text or the curve can be either horizontal or vertical, and this option can produce some pretty interesting effects.

4. When you are done, Shift+click on the text and the path and choose Text|Attach To Path.

It's easy to experiment with the look and feel of text on a path when changes can be made this quickly. Try adding a few different curves to your design in both horizontal and vertical positions and place text on them.

PROJECT A Simple Company Logo Using Text on a Path

In this project, you will produce a logo using a photo object from Hemera's 50,000 Photo-Objects Premium Image Collection CDs. By using an image object and combining it with text on a path, you can produce a logo in a relatively short time by following these steps:

Figure 2.11
Text attached to the path before placement adjustments.

1. Open the image you would like to use for your logo. You can find the lizard.png file used in this example in the Chapter 2 resources folder on this book's companion CD-ROM.

2. Draw a curved path over the top of the image. The Pen tool was used in this example. To help smooth out the path, choose Modify|Alter Path|Simplify. (For more information on producing paths with curves, refer to Chapter 4.)

3. Select the Type tool, click on the canvas, and type the text "Lizard Design" into the Text dialog box. BinnerD was the font used in this example with a size of 20. To add color, click the color well, type in the Hex #990000 value, which is a burgundy color, and click OK.

4. Select the text and Shift+click to select the path as well.

5. Select Text|Attach To Path. Refer to Figure 2.11 to see the results so far.

Figure 2.12
Finished company logo.

6. The alterations in placement are going to depend on the font you use and the shape of the path. Open the Text Editor by double-clicking the text to make adjustments to the placement. Not a lot was needed for this logo; the text alignment was left and the horizontal scale was adjusted to 132 percent (see Figure 2.12). A background will be added to this logo in the "Gradients" section of this chapter.

PROJECT Placing Text on the Top and Bottom of an Ellipse

As you have seen, placing text on a path is quite simple. In this project, you will put text on the top and the bottom of an ellipse independently. To do this, the path has to be cut in half, forming two arcs, and then the direction of the bottom type has to be reversed:

1. Decide what image you would like to place in the center of your ellipse and open it; trans.gif, used in this example, is provided in the Chapter 2 resources folder on this book's CD-ROM. Then, choose Modify|Canvas Size. Increase the canvas enough to be able to draw a circle around the image and have room for the text. It's better to have it too big, because you can always crop the image when you are done.

2. To help draw the ellipse to fit around the image, choose View|Rulers. Click the Rulers checkbox if there isn't a checkmark there already.

3. To use guides, click and drag from the vertical ruler (you will see a green line as you drag) and place the line near the right edge of the image. Repeat for the other side.

4. Click and drag a horizontal guide line down from the horizontal ruler and place it on top of the image, leaving a little space so that the text doesn't touch the image. Repeat this step for the bottom of the image. The guides are to help you draw the path for the ellipse (see Figure 2.13).

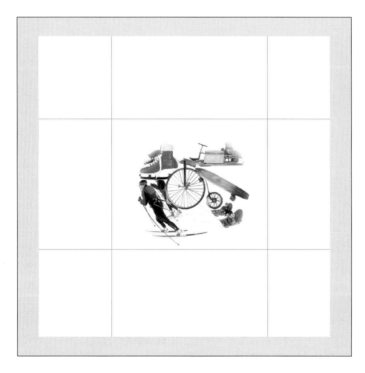

Figure 2.13
Guides in place for drawing the ellipse.

5. From the toolbar, click the Ellipse tool.

6. Place the cursor in the top-left corner of the guide intersection and drag a circle to the bottom-right corner of the guide intersection as seen in Figure 2.14.

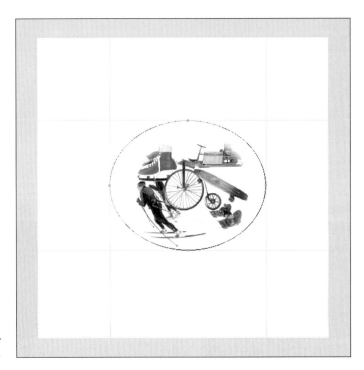

Figure 2.14
Paths prepared for the text.

Note: If you want to move the path you just sliced, click in your document to deselect the path. Now, select the path you'd like to move, and click and drag it wherever you'd like. Notice that you now have two open paths instead of one closed path.

7. Select the path with the Selection tool. From the toolbar, select the Knife tool. To cut a straight line, hold the Shift key as you slice horizontally. You can slice anywhere you want; it doesn't have to be in the center. The slice used here is a bit above the center because the bottom text is longer than the top text.

8. Type the text for the top; Ruzicka Freehand RomanSC, 36 point, bold is used in this example; use the font of your choice.

9. Open the Effect panel (Alt+F7/Option+F7) to apply any effects you'd like; in this example, a patterned fill was added. Open the Fill panel (Shift+F) and choose Pattern from the pop-up menu in the Fill category. Next, select the pattern by clicking the pop-up menu next to the Pattern Name box and choosing a pattern. (If you need a refresher on the Effect panel, see the following section.)

10. To add a bevel, click the Effect panel, click the down arrow, and choose Bevel And Emboss|Inner Bevel.

11. Shift+select the top text and the top ellipse, and choose Text|Attach To Path.

12. Double-click the text to make any adjustments needed. In this example, the horizontal scale is 205 and the leading is 130 percent.

13. If you want to change the text orientation, choose Orientation|Vertical.

14. If you were to attach the bottom text the same way as the top text, it would wrap around in the wrong direction, so flip it first. Shift+select the bottom text and the path, and choose Modify|Transform|Flip Horizontal.

15. The text now is on the inside of the path instead of the outside; to get the text on the other side of the path, you need to change the baseline shift (see Figure 2.15). Double-click the text, and in the Text Editor, set the baseline shift to a negative value of 75 percent of the font size. The font size for this bottom text is 28, so that was multiplied by 75 and made into a negative value. This value is typed in the box to the left of the Anti-Aliasing levels pop-up; it's got the two *A*s next to it.

> **Note:** If you were to flip just the text, it would start wrapping on the right side of the bottom ellipse instead of the left. This happens because text begins to wrap around at the first point of a path. When you split your path, the right-side node became the first point. By Shift+selecting the path and the text, you flip them both at the same time.

> **Previewing**
>
> When you enter a value in any of the panels, pressing Enter will accept the change. When you enter an offset value, press Enter; if it isn't enough or is too much, enter another number and press Enter again until you are satisfied.

> **Resetting Text**
>
> When you use your Text Editor again, the baseline shift will be at the negative value, so be sure to change it.

Figure 2.15
Baseline shift changed for the bottom text.

16. One problem still exists: The type is over to the left too far and needs to be repositioned. To reposition, Shift+select the text and the path, go to the Object panel, and enter a Text Offset amount (see Figure 2.16); an offset of 75 was used here to get the text positioned correctly.

17. To readjust the top text just a bit, select it and nudge it by using the left-arrow key on the keyboard. In this example, the arrow key was clicked two times, moving the text two spaces to the left.

18. To add a drop shadow, select the text, click the Effect panel, click the down arrow, and choose Shadow And Glow|Drop Shadow. A Shadow Distance of 5 and a Softness of 3 were used here. These settings were

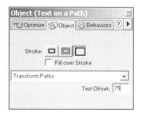

Figure 2.16
Offset applied to the text.

applied to the top and bottom text. To see the finished result, refer to Figure 2.17.

Figure 2.17
The finished company logo.

Editing Text with Transform Tools

Four transform tools are available in Fireworks 4: Scale, Skew, Distort, and Numeric Transform. These can be applied to any text object. By using these transform tools, text can be resized, rotated, slanted, and pulled out of shape—and still be fully editable.

Text can be transformed either as a path object or as a pixel image. The Transform As A Path option is the default, which produces much smoother edges that look less jaggy. Of course, in some instances, you may prefer the rough, jagged-edge look.

Skew

To skew text is to distort it; before skewing text, be sure to have the bounding box the same size as the text. The Skew Transform tool (see Figure 2.18) affects all of the text object, including the excess area in the bounding box. To skew text, follow these steps:

Figure 2.18
The Skew Transform tool.

1. Click the object to be skewed.

2. Click the Skew Transform tool.

3. Choose Modify|Transform|Skew.

4. You now have access to the points (see Figure 2.19). By dragging them, you alter the shape. To add perspective, click and drag a corner point; the result can be seen in Figure 2.20.

Figure 2.19
(Left) The text with control points.

Figure 2.20
(Right) The text with perspective.

Rotate

Rotating objects pivot from their center points. If you want to change the point of pivot, simply move the center point by clicking and dragging. Rotation can be applied manually or with preset settings from the menu bar. To rotate text, follow these steps:

1. Click the object to be rotated.

2. To rotate 180 degrees or 90 degrees, choose Modify|Rotate Canvas|180 degrees, 90 degrees CW, or 90 degrees CCW.

3. To rotate visually, select any of the Transform tools.

4. Move the cursor outside the area with the points and you will see the Rotation Pointer (see Figure 2.21). Simply click and drag in the direction you'd like to rotate. To constrain the rotation, Shift+click and drag.

Figure 2.21
The Rotation Pointer.

Distort

Distorting text is similar to using the Skew Transform tool, except that its points react a bit differently. To distort text, follow these steps:

1. Select the object you want to distort.

2. Click any Transform tool.

3. Drag points to adjust the shape.

Info Panel

When you need to make precise adjustments to an object's size and/or location, using the Info panel can save you a lot of time. The Info panel is where you can make numeric adjustments to objects.

To use the Info panel to read the X, Y coordinates of the width and height of a particular object, select it and read the results. To see the color or X, Y coordinates under your cursor, look at the bottom half of the Info panel—it changes as you move the cursor.

To make numeric adjustments, double-click the parameter you want to change and enter the new number. After each entry, press Enter or Return to activate the change.

From the right-pointing arrow, you can change the way the Info panel displays results. For instance, the color can be changed to HSB instead of RGB.

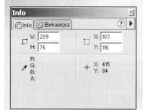

Using the Info panel.

Numeric Transform

Instead of dragging to make your transformations, you can do it numerically by following these steps:

1. Select the object to transform.

2. Select Modify|Transform|Numeric Transform (Ctrl+Shift+T/Cmd+Shift+T). From the Numeric Transform dialog box (see Figure 2.22), you can select Scale, Resize, or Rotate. If you deselect the Scale Attributes checkbox, any of the effects or strokes added won't scale with the object.

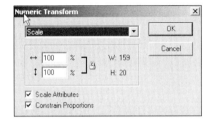

Figure 2.22
The Numeric Transform dialog box.

The Transform tools will come in really handy when you want to make special text effects or object effects for use in an animation. By simply rotating the text or by making it larger or smaller, you can produce interesting changes for an animation.

Effects

The effects in Fireworks are Live Effects; they can be edited even after you save the file and open it at a later date. The Effect panel even allows you to see exactly what effect has been applied and what settings were used. This feature is a great way to learn how an effect was achieved when someone shares their files with you, or if you forgot how you produced a certain effect.

Adding Effects

You will find yourself returning to the Effect panel often. It contains a variety of effects to enhance almost any project you design. For ease of use, you may want to leave the multi-tabbed panel containing the Effect panel, Stroke panel, and Fill panel open in your workspace. To open the Effect panel, choose Window|Effect:

1. Select the object you would like to add an effect to.

2. Click the Effect tab and, from the pop-up menu, choose the effect you would like applied. This menu contains the effects from the menu bar's Xtras category, plus Shadows And Glows and Bevel And Emboss. These two choices are ones that you may find yourself returning to often.

3. After you make a selection of Shadows And Glows|Drop Shadow, for example, you will be presented with a dialog box to set the distance of the shadow, the softness amount, the angle, and the opacity. The settings are similar for most effects.

4. Press Return or Enter, and the changes are applied.

Editing Effects

If you ever want to go back and change an effect or if you want to see how you achieved a certain look, all you have to do is open your PNG file and follow these instructions:

1. Click the object that contains the effect you would like to view or alter. If you have a hard time selecting the proper object, try selecting from the Layers panel.

2. After the object is selected, open the Effect panel (this works the same way for the Fill and Stroke panels as well). You will see a list of effects added with checkmarks next to them. To view what the object would look like without a certain effect, uncheck the effect. If you decide you don't want a particular effect, select it and click the trash can icon in the lower-right corner to delete it.

3. To view the specific settings of any effect, double-click the effect name. You now have access to the settings and can make any alterations here.

The ability to see the effects applied to any object and to change the settings is a terrific timesaver. If you have completed a project but haven't written down how you did it, you can reconstruct the entire object by clicking the various effects, strokes, and fills to see exactly what was done.

Strokes

The Stroke panel has 48 built-in strokes, but you can produce an infinite number of variations. Options such as color, strokes, patterns, textures, width, edge, softness, and so on can change the text effect slightly or drastically, to create a unique new look. To apply a stroke, you select your object and choose a stroke selection from the Stroke panel. Modifying a stroke requires a few more steps but remains quite simple.

Modifying a Stroke

You will now modify the stroke of a preset style that has been applied to some text. To follow along with this example, open the modify.png file found in the Chapter 2 resources folder on the book's CD-ROM:

1. If your Stroke panel isn't open (Figure 2.23), then select Window|Stroke (Ctrl+Alt+F4/Command+Option+F4).

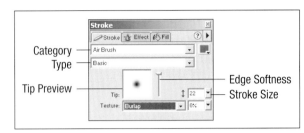

Figure 2.23

The Stroke panel.

Note: The stroke techniques you will be performing on text work the same way for any object.

2. Be sure the text you want to modify is selected. The text in Figure 2.24 has style 7 applied to it from the Styles panel. When it is selected, the strokes, fills, and effects applied appear in the Stroke, Effect, and Fill panels.

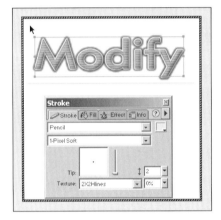

Figure 2.24

Text with a style applied.

Note: If you know the hexa-decimal number for the color, you can also type it in at the top of the color well.

3. To modify the stroke color, select the color change you want from the color well. In this example, green was chosen instead of the yellow stroke that the preset style added. (The yellow is just to the inside of the outside shadow.)

4. The Edge Softness slider changes how the stroke blends; change this if you want a softer edge.

5. To change the stroke's thickness, simply click the down arrow next to the thickness number or type in a number; two pixels is the setting being used here (see Figure 2.25).

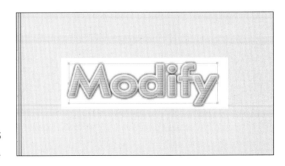

Figure 2.25

Text with the stroke modified.

Saving Strokes As Styles

You have probably experimented with strokes and saving styles by this point, so the review will be kept short. After you have completed your stroke and added any effects or fills, you can save your stroke as a style. To save any stroke effects as a style, follow these steps:

1. Click the Styles panel tab, click the right-pointing arrow, and from the pop-up menu choose New Style.

2. Check the features you would like saved for the style. For instance, when working with text, you may not want to save the font style, so just un-check that option. If you check Font, then when the style is applied, it

---

Stroke Tip Modifications

Before you leave the Stroke panel, take a look at some of the tip options. By double-clicking the Tip preview, you'll see three tabbed panels: Options, Shape, and Sensitivity.

The first figure (left) in this sidebar shows the Options panel. This is where you determine the percentage of ink to use for the initial stroke opacity, the space between brush stamps, the spray paint speed, the amount of texture, the soft-ness of the texture, how many brush tips to use, the type of edge effect, and the color variations. If you change the number of tips you'd like to paint with to more than one, the Tip Spacing and Variation options become available. The preview of the changes you've made will appear in the white area at the bottom of the Options panel. When you get the setting the way you like, click the Apply button to apply the changes to the selected stroke and then click OK.

The second figure (middle) shows the Shape panel. You have a lot of control here by altering the Size, Edge, Aspect, and Angle. When you get the shape just right, click the Apply button to make the changes to the selected stroke and then click OK.

The final figure (right) in the sidebar shows the Sensitivity panel, in which you can choose a stroke property such as Size, Ink Amount, or Saturation from the Brush Property pop-up menu. In the Affected By options, choose the degree to which sensitivity data affects your current stroke. Preview in the panel window and click the Apply button and then OK when you are satisfied.

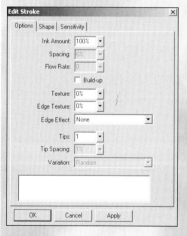

The Options panel.

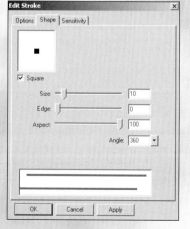

The Shape panel.

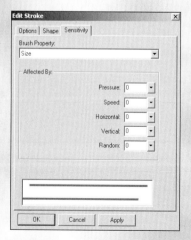

The Sensitivity panel.

will also use the font information. If it is unchecked, only the stroke, fill, and effects will be applied to any text or object.

3. Enter a name and click OK.

That's all there is to it. The new style will be added to the bottom of your Styles panel for use on any object.

Adding Texture to Strokes

Adding a texture to a stroke can really make an object pop out from the page. Fireworks 4 provides some textures that you can use. To apply texture, follow these steps:

1. Select the object you want to add a stroke to. From the Stroke panel, select a stroke from the Stroke category.

2. From the Stroke category, choose Texture.

3. Adjust the tip size to make it larger. A larger stroke will yield a better texture effect; size 20 or larger should work nicely.

4. From the Texture pop-up menu, choose a texture, and then set the opacity of the texture. If you don't see the changes occur on screen, then press the Enter (or Return) key after you choose each option.

To learn how to add custom textures, refer to the "Filling with Patterns and Textures" section at the end of this chapter.

The Stroke panel is one of the tools you will find yourself using over and over. It adds depth and detail to objects, making them pop out or seem to sink deeper into the page. You can achieve some pretty amazing effects using the Stroke panel.

PROJECT Enhancing an Image with a Unique Stroke

In this project, you are going to add special strokes around an image. Strokes can't be applied to an image, only to paths, so you need to make an adjustment to your image here. If you want to apply this effect to text, then skip Steps 1 through 4. To use a unique stroke, follow these steps:

1. Open a new image 400 pixels by 400 pixels; the color doesn't matter at this point.

2. Open the salad.png file located in the Chapter 2 resources folder in the book's CD-ROM, and then drag it onto your new document, placing it in the center.

3. Click the Pen tool in the toolbar. Click around the salad plate. The blue points in Figure 2.26 are the points that have been clicked. When you reach the first point, double-click it to close the path.

Figure 2.26
A path showing the points.

4. From the toolbar, select the Fill tool (see Figure 2.27) and change the fill to none (the circle with the line through it). Now you have a path and can still see the image below.

5. In this example, the color of the canvas was modified to complement the image. Select Modify|Canvas Color. Click the color well and take a sample with the eye-dropper from the pale part of the lettuce.

Figure 2.27
The Fill tool icon.

6. The scanlines.png file in the Chapter 2 resources folder on the book's CD-ROM includes a scanline texture that looks better with this effect than the scans texture that ships with Fireworks 4. Copy and paste scanlines.png into your Fireworks4/Configurations/Textures folder.

7. Open the Stroke panel (Ctrl+Alt+F4/Cmd+Option+F4), choose Air Brush from the Stroke category, and choose Textured from the Stroke name option. From the Texture name option pop-up menu, select scanlines (which you added to your texture file in Step 6), and use a percentage of 80 for the Amount of texture and a Tip size of 70. Press Return or Enter.

8. As Figure 2.28 shows, the lines go too far into the image. Click the Subselection tool from the toolbar and pull each point out until the lines are on the outside of the image. Figure 2.29 shows the new placement of the points.

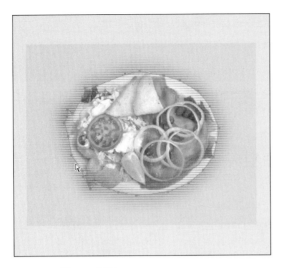

Figure 2.28

(Left) The stroke applied to the path.

Figure 2.29

(Right) The points pulled out, expanding the path.

9. The lines are too dark for this effect. With the path selected (check the Layers panel to be sure the path object is dark blue, indicating it is the selected object), click the down arrow next to the opacity number and choose 50 percent. To make another alteration, change the mode in the Mode box (it probably says Normal right now) and select the Tint blending mode. Now the effect is much more subtle. See Figure 2.30 for the final image.

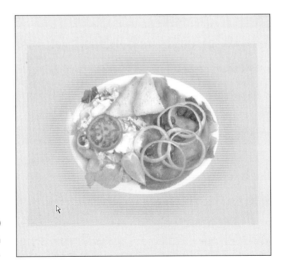

Figure 2.30

The completed image with scanlines applied.

 **Adding Pizzazz to Your Web Page Header**

The Stroke menu offers a multitude of innovative options. In this project, you use one of the unnatural strokes to produce a unique banner. The pizzazzbanner.png file used for this example is supplied in the Chapter 2 resources folder on the book's CD-ROM.

1. Open a new file (File|New) with dimensions of 400 pixels by 100 pixels and a canvas color of black.

2. Select the Text tool and type the word "Pizzazz" in your document. (The font used here is Trebuchet MS [use the font of your choice], Size 42, Color Black, Horizontal Scale 100 percent, Leading 115 percent, and Smooth Anti-Alias.) Click OK.

3. Open the Stroke panel by selecting Windows|Stroke (Ctrl+Alt+F4/ Cmd+Alt+F4), and from the pop-up menu, select Unnatural.

4. From the Stroke Name menu, choose Paint Spatter, type the color "#FF9900", enter a Tip size of 3, and press Enter to apply (see Figure 2.31).

Figure 2.31
Text with the Paint Spatter stroke applied.

5. A filter from Eye Candy 4000 (a third-party filter) that ships with Fireworks 4 is going to be applied next. Choose Xtras|Eye Candy 4000|Motion Trail. A dialog box opens stating that the image is going to be converted to a bitmap; click OK. Use these settings for the Motion Trail: Length 84, Opacity 88 percent and Direction 233. Click the checkmark to accept the changes.

6. The text is beginning to get some character now, but it is not distinct enough yet. Click the Text tool from the toolbar and enter the word "Pizzazz" again. The settings should be the same as when you last used the Text Editor, so simply highlight the text by clicking and dragging over it and change the color to #FF9900. Click OK.

7. Position the orange text on top of the black text. Open the Effect panel (Ctrl+Alt+E/Cmd+Alt+E) and select Shadow And Glow|Inner Glow. Use the following settings: Width 2, Softness 2, Color #FF6600, and Opacity 65 percent. Press Enter or Return.

8. From the Effect panel, choose Shadow And Glow|Drop Shadow and use the following settings: Distance 4, Softness 2, Opacity 65 percent, Color Black, and Angle 315. Press Enter or Return.

9. In the Layers panel, select both the text and the image object by Shift+clicking. Choose Modify|Group. Now your image can be moved and resized as one unit. Click the bottom-right point and pull upward to make the image a little bit smaller to fit on the banner.

Note: If you Shift+click and group and the objects still aren't grouped, check to see that you selected with the Selection tool and not with the Subselection tool.

10. This banner has an outer space background from Comstock's Exploring The Universe CD added to it. For more information on how to add backgrounds, see Chapter 5. The background image can be found in Chapter 2 resource folder named pizzazzbackground.png.

The banner is now ready for your company promotional material (Figure 2.32). It could also be used as an animated banner using special effects.

Figure 2.32
Pizzazz banner.

Colors

It's important to understand that monitors represent color as RGB—red, green, and blue. The hexadecimal system is the standard way to specify RGB color for use in HTML documents. Hexadecimal values are based on base-16 mathematics and not the standard base-10 counting system. The hexadecimal code never exceeds two digits, unlike the RGB values, which sometimes contain three digits, making the hexadecimal coding more uniform. You won't have to know how to actually convert RGB into hexadecimal unless you want to—just understand the difference in the numbers when you see them. You'll begin to see how the hexadecimal coding system works as you learn more about using Web-safe colors.

Note: If you want to sample a color and automatically convert it into a Web-safe color, simply hold the Shift key as you sample. Also, if you click in a color well and decide you don't want to change a color, you can press the Esc key on your keyboard to close the color palette.

A Web-safe color palette should be used when adding color to flat color images, such as backgrounds, text, logos, vectors you have drawn, and buttons. The Web-safe palette of 216 colors will display an image in the major browsers without dithering and will display the image the way you designed it. *Dithering* means to combine colors to produce alternate colors (not to be confused with the Web dithering option in Fireworks 4, which dithers Web-safe colors). Web-safe colors can be recognized by their hexadecimal numbers that contain three sets of 00, 33, 66, 99, FF, or CC. To make it easy to use Web-safe colors, Fireworks' default color picker in every color well is the Web-safe palette.

Using Web-safe colors isn't your only concern; you also have the problem of different platforms. Windows and Macintosh both have a different Gamma setting, which is used to keep midtones on screen from appearing too dark. The Windows system uses a setting of 2.2 (which is also standard for television) and the Macintosh defaults to a setting of 1.8. If you design on a Windows system, your images will appear brighter than on a Macintosh. To see how your work will look on the system that you don't have, choose View|Macintosh Gamma on a Windows system, or View|Windows Gamma on a Macintosh.

Finding Non-Web216 Colors

You can easily check an entire document or project log for Web-safe colors within Fireworks by using the Find And Replace feature. To begin the search, follow these steps:

1. Open the Find And Replace panel, shown in Figure 2.33, by choosing Window|Find And Replace.

2. Choose Search Files and locate a file you would like to check for Web-safe colors.

3. In the Find area, choose Non-Web216.

4. More options now appear. In the Apply area, you have the choice of applying the color change to just the Fill, Strokes, or Effects, to all the Fills and Strokes, or to All Properties. Click All Properties.

5. Click the Find button. The document you chose will now open, and the first area with a non-Web-safe color will be highlighted. Click Replace. If you want to automatically accept all the changes instead of one at a time, click Replace All.

This tool is quite a timesaver if you have a Web site you are upgrading for someone, or one that you want to convert to Web-safe colors.

Figure 2.33
The Find And Replace panel.

Customizing the Swatches Panel

Fireworks' default Swatches panel is the Web-safe 216 color Hexadecimal panel. You can change the colorspace, as described next, but be aware that when you open a document made in a different colorspace, the Swatches panel does not automatically change. The Swatches panel displayed is the last one you loaded, or the default if you haven't loaded any.

In the Color Mixer, you will find several other color swatches available: RGB, CMY, HSB, Grayscale, as well as the default of Hexadecimal. To customize the Swatches panel, follow these steps:

1. To open the Color Mixer (see Figure 2.34), choose Window|Color Mixer. Click the right-pointing arrow and choose the colorspace you'd like, or Shift+click in the color bar at the bottom for the different panels to cycle.

2. Be sure to deselect any objects, or they will be filled with the mixed color. Click the Stroke icon, the little pencil, and then move your pointer down to the color bar. When your mouse hovers over the color bar, your cursor becomes an Eyedropper tool with a wavy line. The wavy line appears when you are choosing a stroke color; if you click the

Figure 2.34
The Color Mixer panel.

Note: It appears that you can use only GIF or ACT files in Fireworks for the Swatches panel, but you actually can add another file type. You can force Fireworks to use Photoshop ACO files as well. From the right arrow in the Swatches panel, choose Add or Replace Swatches. When the dialog box opens to locate your file, go to the folder on your hard drive where you know a Photoshop ACO file resides. In the Find box, type "*.aco" and press the Enter or Return key. You can now see your ACO files. Choose the one you want and click Open.

little paint bucket and move the cursor over the color bar, a square box appears next to the cursor indicating you are choosing a fill color. Click and drag over the color bar to see the color well and the values change as you slide. When you release the mouse, the color well and the value settings are changed automatically.

3. If you have a custom color palette you would like to add, be sure it is a GIF file or an ACT file, and then click the Swatches tab; after doing that, click the right-pointing arrow, and from the pop-up menu, choose Add Swatches. Select the appropriate file and click OK. Adding swatches extends the existing palette. If you want to use just a saved palette, then choose Replace Swatches; when you choose Add Swatches, they are added to the bottom of the current panel.

As you can see, the Color Mixer adds a lot of flexibility in your color workspace. Click some of the other options in the Swatches panel and see what changes are made, such as being able to load just the Windows palette or just the Macintosh palette.

Web Dithering

When designing a Web site for the masses, you will want it to look its best for the widest audience possible. This is where the 216 Web-safe color palette comes into play. These 216 colors don't degrade on a monitor that can only utilize 256 colors. Many designers today are not as concerned about this problem as they were a few years ago, because more and more people are upgrading to better systems and monitors with better video cards, supporting millions of colors. However, good monitors are less expensive and more available in the U.S. than in many other countries that are online, so this reasoning does not necessarily apply to the global audience on the Web. The choice to use Web-safe colors is up to you, but keep in mind that a lot of new "consumers" are buying computers for the express reason of getting online. Many of these new users can barely use their mouse, much less check and change their monitor settings. Of course, if you know that your audience doesn't include people from other countries or new users, then you can skip this section.

Web dithering will expand your color palette greatly, and it will still be Web-safe. Dithering was originally used when all that was available was the GIF format, and photographs with millions of colors were being used for the Web and being viewed with monitors using 256 colors. The process of dithering involves taking two or more pixels of different colors and positioning them to produce a pattern. This pattern tricks the eye into seeing a different color. This technique works great with GIFs, but with photographs, you lose a lot of detail when many colors blend. The best path to take is to use the JPEG format for photographs and the GIF format for vectors and images containing few colors.

This technique of combining two colors or more into a new one is called dithering, or simply producing a hybrid-safe color—Fireworks calls it Web Dither. Web Dither contains two Web-safe colors in an alternating 2 pixel by 2 pixel pattern, producing a third color. With this technique, you now have 46,656 Web-safe "designer" colors. Don't worry, Fireworks provides you with a simple-to-use interface. To use the Web dithering feature, follow these steps:

1. Click the Fill panel; if it isn't open, choose Window|Fill (Shift+F7).

2. From the pop-up menu list at the top of the Fill panel, choose Web Dither (see Figure 2.35).

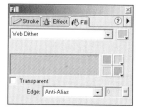

Figure 2.35
The dither pattern.

3. Notice that there are three color wells instead of one. The first one is the current fill color. Click the color well to choose a non-Web-safe color or type a Hexadecimal number. Another option is to use the Eyedropper tool to sample a color. The Eyedropper is automatically available when you click the color well. You can sample outside of your document, from the menus in Fireworks, or from another document. The color in the large area is the new Web-safe color that will be applied to your document.

4. To take this fill one step further, click the Transparent checkbox. If you export this file as a GIF or PNG with Index Transparency or Alpha Channel, you will have the illusion of a true transparent fill. The background will show through every other pixel.

Making Your Own Custom Colors

The 216 colors in the Web-safe palette generally make horrible backgrounds. So, if you want something other than the standard black or white or the 216 Web-safe colors, you need to mix your own. You can find these color files on

The Web Dither

You can see the two different colors side by side that Fireworks has chosen to pattern (the first two colors below the original color well), and then the reverse of these colors just below it. To see the Hexadecimal numbers, simply move your mouse over the color and the number will appear. Sometimes it's fickle, so simply move your mouse over again until you see the number. This is the pattern being used to produce the best match possible, which can be seen in the large color area. If the area you want to fill is selected, it will automatically fill with the new color.

You don't have to use the color that Fireworks has chosen to blend with; you can choose your own colors to mix if you are feeling adventurous. Fireworks 4 does a great job of automatically finding the best possible match to the color you want to be Web safe. If you move your mouse over the fill color from the Info palette, you will see two different RGB settings—one for each Web safe color used to achieve a new Web-safe color.

If you choose to set the Edge setting of a Web dither fill to Anti-Alias or Feather, the color will no longer be Web safe.

the CD-ROM in the Chapter 1 folder; they were used in the batch process explanation. You can use them to make your own palette of colors. To make your custom colors, follow these steps:

1. Select the Rectangle tool and draw a box about 20 pixels by 20 pixels—a good way to get an exact measurement is to adjust the size from the Info panel.

2. Open the Fill panel (Shift+F7) and from the Fill category choose Web Dither. Select the rectangle you drew, choose a non-Web-safe color that you'd like to make Web-safe, or type "Hexidecimal #99EBCC" into the first color well to the right of the Fill category; press Enter (or Return) to accept the color change. You can also sample using the Eyedropper tool from an open file or from your Fireworks screen.

3. Your object is now filled with the new Web-safe color (Web-safe, if you have Hard selected for the Edge). This is a lovely color, but you're going to make it lighter (save this image now for use in a custom palette). From the third color well, select white, #FFFFFF. All you did was add white to the current fill; choose File|Save As to save your new color.

4. To make a deeper green, choose Edit|Undo Fill.

5. Now you are ready to darken the shade. From the third color well, select a darker shade of green to mix with, such as #669966. Give it a unique name, and save.

6. Try some of these combinations:

   • With Web Dither fill selected, click the first color well and type in the non-Web-safe color #DCB17D (which Fireworks automatically mixes with #99FFCC and #99CCCC). Choose File|Save As and save. To make this color lighter, add white #FFFFFF to the third color well, choose File|Save As, and save. Try changing this color by changing the third color well to hexidecimal #FFFFCC, which adds a slight yellow hue, or try adding a light peach color to the third color well. Choose File|Save As to save the new color.

   • With Web Dither fill selected, click the first color well and type in the non-Web-safe color #05B9F6 (which Fireworks automatically mixes with 0099FF and 00CCFF); choose File|Save As. Now add white #FFFFFF and choose File|Save As. From the File menu, choose Edit|Undo Fill, and then change the third color well to #009900 and choose File|Save As.

Now that you've got the idea of how to produce your own custom colors, you can make your own custom color palette.

Making a Custom Color Palette

You've made your own custom color swatches in an earlier project; now you can use those swatches as a custom color palette. To make a color palette, follow these steps:

1. Open a new document with a width of 100 pixels and a height of 100 pixels.

2. Open each color image you saved in the previous exercise or get the ones you did in Chapter 1, in the batch process project (the Chapter 1 color folder on the book's CD-ROM).

3. Drag each color onto your new document, placing each color close to the other in neat rows. You can also Shift+click to select and choose Modify|Align|Center Horizontal.

4. Export the palette as a GIF file, give it a unique name, and put it in a folder where you will remember it. If you have Photoshop or another program that you often access color palettes from, that might be a good place to keep your own palette as well.

5. Open the Color Mixer by choosing Window|Color Mixer (F11) and click the Swatches tab. Click the right-pointing arrow and choose Add Swatches, or Replace Swatches. Browse to your saved GIF image.

Now you have your own custom Web-safe colors at your fingertips.

PROJECT Matching a Company's Logo Color

You will probably find yourself having to match some company's logo to put on the Web. If using Web-safe colors isn't an issue, then simply sampling the logo color and using it as the fill is all that is needed. But if a non-Web-safe color has been used, Web dithering is the best option. To convert a logo color into a Web-safe color using Web dithering, follow these steps:

1. Open an object that you want to match the color of, or open logo.png from the Chapter 2 resources folder on the book's CD-ROM, which is used in this example (see Figure 2.36).

2. From the Fill panel, click the down arrow and choose Web Dither.

3. Click the first color well and put your cursor, which is now the Eyedropper tool, over the color you want to match. The non-Web-safe color in the logo.png file is Hex #0D5C4A.

4. The new color is in the large area of the Fill panel, but this logo isn't a text object and isn't filled automatically. To change the color to the new Web-safe color, click the Magic Wand tool from the menu bar. Click the *I* and Shift+click the *D*.

Figure 2.36
The Idea Design logo.

5. From the toolbar, select the Paint Bucket tool (which now contains the new color) and click over the logo to fill.

Check the colors that Fireworks mixed together to produce a close match to the logo's color. Hex #666666 and #006633 were mixed together, and the result looks pretty close to the same color, except now it is Web safe.

Using Gradient Fills

A gradient is a blend of two or more colors. Gradients are often used to produce lighting effects to give the illusion of depth. They are also used as terrific backgrounds and as a fill for transparency masks when working with bitmaps (see Chapter 5). In this section, you will learn how to use gradient fills and how to edit them to suit your needs.

Filling with Gradients

You can add unique colorization to a graphic with the use of a gradient fill. Fireworks 4 ships with 11 types of gradients and 13 preset gradient color patterns. But, the number of alterations and variations is almost endless. The best way to describe the 11 types of gradients is to show you a small sample of each. Figure 2.37 shows a representation of each. From left to right, they are Linear, Radial, Ellipse, Rectangle, Cone, Starburst, Bars, Ripples, Waves, Satin, and Folds.

Figure 2.37
A representation of the gradient options.

To fill using a gradient, follow these steps:

1. Select an object you want to apply a gradient to.

2. From the Fill panel, choose one of the gradient options.

3. Choose the color combination you like from the Preset gradient color sets, or use the gradient that is the default. The default is a combination of whatever color your brush is and the color of the Fill tool.

4. You can adjust the Edge attributes in this dialog box; the choices are Anti-Alias, Hard, or Feather. If you choose Feather, you have the option to type in how many pixels you want the edge of your gradient to be feathered. (This is particularly important when you begin to use gradients in masks in Chapter 5.)

If your object is selected, it is automatically filled with the gradient. Test each of the presets and all the different gradient types to get an idea of how each one looks and performs.

Altering Gradients

This is where the real power of the Gradient tool becomes evident. Gradients can be customized by adjusting the pattern's center, width, and skew. To alter a gradient's position, follow these steps:

1. Follow the preceding steps for filling with a gradient. To alter the gradient's position, click on the object to make it active, and the gradient handles will appear.

2. To change the position of the gradient, drag the circular handle to adjust the gradient's starting point.

3. Move the cursor over the control handles until you see the rotate cursor. You can now drag the handles to a new location.

4. By dragging the square handle, you change the direction of the gradient (see Figure 2.38).

> **Note:** A gradient's control handles do not have to be constrained within the object. You can drag the round or square handles outside of the object area to achieve the desired effect; in fact, you can drag both handles completely off the object.

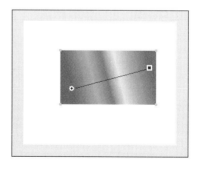

Figure 2.38
Using gradient handles to alter the gradient's look.

Editing Gradient Colors

Existing colors in a gradient can be changed, deleted, or moved around, or new colors can be added with ease. To make the changes, follow these steps:

1. Draw a rectangle to fill with a gradient style you like.

2. Click the Edit button in the Fill panel. You will see color swatches below the gradient representation. There will be a swatch for each color in the gradient and at the position that each color begins.

3. To change any of the colors, simply click the swatch and choose another color.

4. To add another color, place your cursor anywhere in the row containing the current color markers. You will see a + sign next to your cursor; click and then select the color by clicking the swatch.

5. To move the position of any of the colors, click and drag the swatch to the new location.

6. To delete a color, click and drag the swatch toward the bottom of the panel.

You have a lot of control when it comes to gradient colors. You can sample colors from other images with the Eyedropper tool—just as you can when selecting solid fills—to produce some interesting color combinations.

PROJECT Making a Gradient from a Photograph

Do you have an excellent photo with really great colors in it? If so, now you can make custom gradients using the colors in the photo. This is a great way to get a gradient with complementary colors without knowing a thing about combining colors. If you have a photo with the colors you want to use for another composition, making a gradient is much easier than removing foreground elements. To customize your own gradient, follow these steps:

1. Open the image you want to make the gradient match. In the CD-ROM's Chapter 2 resource folder, you will find sunset.png. This image is from the Comstock Vacations—Resorts CD-ROM. What better place to look for fantastic color combinations than in nature.

2. Open a new file 200 pixels wide by 100 pixels high with a white background.

3. Select the Rectangle tool and draw a rectangle over the white area of your canvas.

4. In the Fill panel, choose Cone for the Fill category, and then click Edit.

5. Figure 2.39 shows the placement of the color swatches. Figure 2.40 shows the numbered areas where the color samples were taken from. Click the first color swatch and, with the Eyedropper tool, get a sample from the brown area where number 1 is.

6. In the Edit panel, click below the color bar to add another color swatch. Click the swatch and sample the dark-gold area with a 2 on it in Figure 2.40.

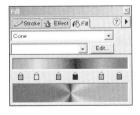

Figure 2.39
Color swatch placement for the gradient.

Figure 2.40
Numbered areas for color sampling.

7. In the Edit panel, click below the color bar to add another color swatch. Click the medium-brown area marked 3.

8. Repeat Step 7 for choosing color swatch numbers 4 through 6.

Isn't that a great gradient? If you want a different effect, then choose a different type of gradient or alter the position of the gradient. This gradient was changed to the Cone gradient type and added to the Lizard Design company logo from the text-on-a-path projects done earlier in this chapter. Figure 2.41 shows the logo complete with the customized gradient added.

Figure 2.41
A gradient added as the background of a logo.

Saving Gradient Colors

After you have meticulously produced a new gradient, you may want to use it again later. Unfortunately, saving a gradient in Fireworks does not make it available for another document; to save the gradient color, follow these steps:

1. To save a gradient that you have altered, choose Save Gradient from the right-pointing arrow in the Fill panel.

2. Name it, and click OK.

That was easy enough but not very useful except for in one document. A better way exists that enables you to use the gradient in any document:

1. When you are ready to save your gradient, open the Styles panel and click the right arrow.

2. From the pop-up menu, choose the New Style option; the New Style dialog box will open. Name the gradient, and choose which properties to save as a style. Click OK.

Your new gradient style has been added to the bottom of your Styles panel. Now, when you want to fill with your new gradient, you simply have to click the style.

Note: If you save properties such as text, then anytime this style is applied it will change the font, font size, or text style depending on which options you choose. If you want only the effects to be applied to any other text, then leave the text options unchecked.

Note: You are now going to be making a new gradient from scratch. What you see in the Edit panel is going to depend on what your stroke color and fill color are set to. The colors don't matter because you will change them all. See Figure 2.42 for the placement of the colors (a color image can be found in the Chapter 2 resources folder on the book's CD-ROM).

Figure 2.42

The color placement for the blue gradient.

PROJECT Designing a Company Logo Using a Gradient Fill

This is an example using a custom gradient fill, strokes, effects, clipart, and a flair:

1. Open a new document 400 pixels wide by 100 pixels high with a background color of Hex #003366.

2. Click the Text tool in the toolbar, and type the word "Fireworks". The font used in this example is Arial Black (or any heavy font), Size 53, Color Black, and Smooth Anti-Alias.

3. Open the Fill panel. From the drop-down list, choose Linear and then click the Edit button.

4. Click the first color swatch. In the Hex box, type "Hex #99CCFF", and then press Enter to accept the color.

5. To add a color, place the cursor below the color line and, where you see the second swatch in Figure 2.42, click to add a new color swatch. Click the swatch and type "Hex #FFFFFF", which is white.

6. Place the cursor in the third position and click to add a new color swatch. Click the color swatch and type "Hex #CCFFFF".

7. Place the cursor in the fourth position and click to add a new color swatch. Click the color swatch and type "Hex #6699CC".

8. Place the cursor in the fifth position and click to add a new color swatch. Click the color swatch and type "Hex #336699".

9. Place the cursor in the sixth position and click to add a new color swatch. Click the color swatch and type "Hex #000066".

10. This gradient is linear and it would look much better if it were horizontal instead of vertical. Drag the gradient handles until they are straight up and down, as shown in Figure 2.43.

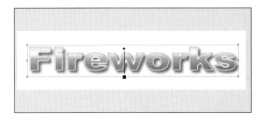

Figure 2.43

The correct placement of the gradient handles.

11. Now that the gradient is done, you need to make it a style so that it can be reused. Open the Styles panel (Shift+F11), click the right-pointing arrow, and from the pop-up menu, choose New Style. Enter a name and

click OK. The gradient is now available to add to any object. You can skip this step if you want to apply this gradient fill only to this object.

12. Add a stroke by opening the Stroke panel. In the Stroke category, choose Basic, Soft Rounded, Tip size 2, and type "#CCFFFF" for the color.

13. Next, add an inner glow. Click the Effects panel and, from the arrow pointing down, select Shadow And Glow|Inner Glow with the settings of Width 2, Softness 3, Opacity 75 percent, and Color #336699.

14. Add a drop shadow by clicking the down arrow in the Effect panel and choosing Shadow And Glow|Drop Shadow with the settings of Distance 7, Opacity 65 percent, Softness 6, Color Black, and Angle 315.

15. Add the lizard, found in Hemera's Photo-Objects 50,000 Premium Image Collection. The image is on a transparent background, ready to use. It simply needs to be resized. Open the image (hemeraslizard.png) and drag it into position. (Hemera made it available to you, and it is in the Chapter 2 resources folder.)

16. Open the flair.png file provided in the Chapter 2 resources folder on the book's CD-ROM or the flair you will make in Chapter 4. Drag it into position.

17. Click the Text tool from the toolbar and type ".com". The font used in this example is Arial Black, Size 18, Color White, and Smooth Anti-Alias. The finished logo can be seen in Figure 2.44.

You can change the gradient colors visually after you apply the gradient, or if you know the Hex numbers, you can substitute them in the instructions.

Figure 2.44
The finished Fireworks logo.

Filling with Patterns and Textures

Patterns and textures are commonly used to add depth and interest to objects. Fireworks 4 ships with some preset patterns and textures, but the real diversity comes from the ability to use almost any pattern or texture you have.

Filling with Patterns

The use of a pattern in a path object will increase the range of options you have as a designer, making flat, uninteresting objects come alive. Fireworks 4 ships with a small selection of 14 patterns. The Other option in the Fill panel opens the door to limitless patterns. You are limited only to what you can hold on your hard drive or on CD-ROMs. As long as an image is a 32-bit image in a file format of BMP, PNG, GIF, JPEG, TIFF, or PICT (for the Macintosh), then you can have an instant pattern. To use a pattern, follow these steps:

1. Select the object you want to fill.

2. From the Fill panel, choose Pattern from the Fill category.

3. From the Pattern name box, choose Other. Browse to an image file, select it, and click Open.

Patterns can be altered in the same way as gradients by moving the handles and rotation symbol. Another similarity is that pattern alterations cannot be saved for use in another document. If you really like the adjustments you've made to a pattern and think you would like to have it available for another use, then save it as a style.

Adding Textures

Textures can be added to any fill, modifying the brightness of the fill but not the hue. Texture files use the grayscale value of an image; you can also use any PNG, GIF, JPEG, BMP, TIFF, or PICT file as a texture. To add texture, follow these steps:

Note: To add your own texture files, simply place them in the Fireworks 4\Settings\ Textures folder. Unlike the Pattern option, any file you add will be available for other documents.

1. Select any object containing any fill, gradient, or pattern.

2. From the Fill panel, click the Texture drop-down arrow and choose one of the included texture files.

3. Adjust the percentage of opacity, which will determine the amount of the texture that is seen.

PROJECT Punching a Hole Through a Pattern with Text

After text is converted into a path, it can be used just like a cookie cutter. By placing the converted text on top of another path object, you can punch it out, leaving a see-through hole. You can produce some pretty neat effects with this process. In this project, you will punch a hole through an image so that the image placed below it can be seen:

1. Open a new image, 360 pixels wide and 500 pixels high, with a resolution of 72; the canvas color doesn't matter.

2. Select the Rectangle tool from the toolbar and draw a rectangle to fill the canvas. Place your cursor outside the canvas area and click and drag to cover the entire area.

3. From the Fill panel, select Pattern from the Fill category drop-down list, and then select Other from the Fill type drop-down list. Browse to the Chapter 2 resources folder on the book's CD-ROM and select water.jpg. The canvas will be filled with water. This image of water was found on Comstock's Vacations—Resorts CD-ROM.

4. The area is tiled and has four water images. Select the circle handle and drag up to the top-right corner to fill with just one image of the water instead of four.

5. In the Layers panel, be sure the water object is highlighted with dark blue, and from your keyboard, copy (Ctrl+C/Cmd+C) and paste (Ctrl+V/Cmd+V). You will see a copy of the water as a separate object on top of the first one. Keep this object selected.

6. From the Fill panel, select Pattern, then Other, and finally, browse to the sand.png image in the Chapter 2 resources folder of the book's CD-ROM. You can't see the water, but that is okay.

7. Type the text you want to use as a cookie cutter (Ctrl+Shift+P/Cmd+Shift+P). This exercise is using the word "Seaside", Font Arial Black, Size 60.

8. Select the text and choose Text|Convert To Paths. With the Subselection tool, Shift+click each letter.

9. To use this text as a cut-out to punch a hole, you need to ungroup the letters, and then combine them to form a composite path. To do this, select the text path and choose Modify|Ungroup (Ctrl+Shift+G/Cmd+Shift+G), and then choose Modify|Join (Ctrl+J/Cmd+J).

10. Shift+select the text and the rectangle, and choose Modify|Combine|Punch.

11. The hole is punched through the sand object, and the water object below the sand is visible through the cut-out text. Click the water object and position it below the cut-out text until you like the colors below the text (see Figure 2.45).

12. Select the text object by clicking the text. From the Strokes panel, choose Air Brush, Basic, Tip size 4, Color CCCCCC (dark brown).

13. From the Effect panel in the Add Effects Or Choose A Preset box, click the arrow which points down and choose Shadow And Glow|Drop Shadow Use the settings of Distance 4, Opacity 65 percent, Softness 3, Angle 315, and Color Black (000000). See Figure 2.46 for the final result.

Note: After you paste in an image, if it isn't visible, be sure the eye icon to the left of the object is turned on.

Note: Sometimes, it's difficult to select both objects if they are similar in size. Two other ways exist to select them both or to select multiple items. Select the object from the Layers panel and Shift+click each object to select them, or use the pointer tool and click and drag a box around the objects you want to select. You won't see the box except while you are dragging it, but you will notice the handles turn blue for all the objects you enclose.

Note: In this example, it is difficult to see the changes in real time on the canvas because so many points are on the path. To see clearly, deselect by clicking outside the image area. Then, reselect before applying or making changes to the effects or strokes.

Figure 2.45
A hole punched through
an image.

Figure 2.46
Seaside image with water
showing through the text.

Your design will determine which effects you add. You should experiment often. If you add an effect that you are not sure works, just go to the Effect panel and uncheck the options one at a time. You will see the change instantly in your design.

Moving On

You should now be an expert at producing all kinds of innovative text. You have learned how to work with text objects and how to enhance them. You have learned how to make custom gradients and how to use patterns to add interesting effects to your text. In this chapter, you have learned how to punch holes through one object to see another one through it, and how to tie all the effects together by actually producing logos and real-world projects.

In Chapter 3, you will master the vector tools, producing components for real-world projects, such as a game interface, a multimedia kiosk, and a sports calendar.

Chapter 3

Working with Vector Tools

This chapter describes how to use the vector tools, which are used to draw paths that can be manipulated and enlarged to any size without losing image integrity. You will learn to draw objects suitable for Web page use, and how to draw the components for a game interface, a multimedia kiosk, and a sports calendar.

Understanding Paths

In Fireworks, an object is also a *path* (a line segment with at least two points)—a vector graphic. Whereas bitmap images use *pixels* (see Chapter 5), a series of little squares with color, vectors use mathematical calculations. A path starts at X,Y and ends at A,B. Every path has at least two points to yield a line segment. A path can be open (a line) or closed (lines connecting). Because of the mathematical nature of vectors, they are very flexible. A vector object can be stretched to a larger height and width and still maintain its image integrity. As the object increases or decreases in size, Fireworks recalculates the math necessary to render a great-looking image. It's this quality that makes vector objects so popular for use in animations and Web page graphics. The ability to scale a vector drawing is also beneficial if you design a logo that you want to print. The logo can be scaled down for Web use and scaled up for print.

In the projects in this chapter, you will be making portions of a complete racing game interface, a multimedia kiosk, and a sports calendar, all of which you will combine in Chapter 4. To complete some portions of the interface, such as the rollovers, you are referred to other chapters in which more detail is given on the steps. (You should be able to complete the projects from the steps given in this chapter. The cross references simply provide more background information if it is needed.) For a sneak peek at the completed projects, you can find them in the Color Section of this book and in the Chapter 3 folders on this book's CD-ROM. The racing folder has gamecontrol.png, which is the "web racin" game interface. The multimedia folder has money.png showing the multimedia kiosk, and the sports folder has sports.png, which is the sports calendar.

Vector Tools

To use all the vector tools in Fireworks, you need to be in Vector mode. If you are currently in Bitmap mode (indicated by a blue-striped outline) and select a vector-only tool, such as the Pen tool, you will automatically be switched to Vector mode. But, if you choose to use a tool such as the Rectangle tool, which can be used in either mode, you will need to switch modes manually. The easiest way to switch to Vector mode is to click the red circle with a white X (the Exit Bitmap Mode button) at the bottom of your document window (see Figure 3.1).

The vector tools include the shape tools—Rectangle tool, Ellipse tool, Rounded Rectangle tool, and Polygon tool. Freeform vector tools also are available, which include the Pencil tool, Brush tool, and Pen tool. Every vector path object can have a stroke, effects, and fill applied to it. If you aren't familiar with the Stroke panel, Fill panel, and Effect panel, refer to Chapter 2; these panels are used extensively in this chapter and in Chapter 4.

Figure 3.1
The Exit Bitmap Mode button.

Using the Vector Shape Tools

The vector shape tools are some of the easiest to use. You will probably use tools such as the Rounded Rectangle tool on a regular basis for making buttons. Every object drawn with a vector shape tool always contains a starting point and an ending point, which plot the path of a line. With the vector shape tools, those points are automatically placed. You do have control over how the points are placed by editing them.

Applying Strokes

Vector paths can have a stroke applied to them. To apply a stroke, follow these steps:

1. Open the Stroke panel (Window|Stroke).

2. From the Stroke category, select a type, such as Watercolor.

3. Each stroke category has a submenu called Stroke Name and additional choices such as the stroke tip size and the option to add texture to the stroke. Make your selections.

4. If you require more control over pressure sensitivity, tip shape, and ink flow, double-click the Tip box (these options are used later in the chapter in the "Drawing a Dashed Line" project).

5. You can control where the stroke is applied in the Object panel (Window|Object). Ignore the Roundness setting (the degree of roundness of the rectangle's ends) for now; it is covered later in this chapter. Three stroke options appear below the Roundness setting:

   - Draw Inside Path
   - Draw Stroke Centered On Path
   - Draw Stroke Outside Of Path

   The Fill Over Stroke option is below these options. (This option draws a fill on top of the stroke.)

When you choose a stroke category and stroke name, your path's stroke is instantly changed on screen. This makes it easy to experiment with different strokes. Some settings, such as the tip size and when you type in a hexadecimal number, require you to press the Enter or Return key to activate the change.

More editing techniques for strokes are discussed in Chapter 2.

Besides containing starting and ending points, something else the vector shapes have in common is the method in which you can constrain the drawing shape. For example, if you want to constrain to a perfect circle or square, you press the Alt/Option+Shift keys and drag to draw. If you want to draw from the center out, press the Alt/Option key and drag to draw.

Ellipse Tool

The Ellipse tool can be used in both Vector and Bitmap modes. To draw an ellipse, follow these steps:

1. Select the Ellipse tool from the toolbar.

2. Click and drag an ellipse on your canvas.

3. If you want to set a specific size for your ellipse, open the Info panel (Window|Info) and enter the specific Height and Width measurements you want.

4. Add any strokes, fills, or effects you'd like.

5. If you want to edit the shape, notice that four points are automatically added to the ellipse you just drew (see Figure 3.2). The points control the shape of the object. Select the Subselection tool (white arrow) from the toolbar. Click and drag down on the bottom point of the ellipse you just drew. Figure 3.3 shows the result: an egg shape. As soon as you began pulling the point down, you probably noticed lines appear on the other points. These are control handles, which will be discussed in Chapter 4.

Rectangle Tool

The Rectangle tool can be used in both Vector and Bitmap modes. To draw a rectangle, follow these steps:

1. Select the Rectangle tool from the toolbar.

2. Click and drag a rectangle on your canvas.

3. If you want to set a specific size for your rectangle, open the Info panel (Window|Info), enter the specific Height and Width measurements you want, and press Enter/Return.

4. Add any strokes, fills, or effects you'd like. To apply strokes, open the Stroke panel (Window|Stroke). To apply fills, open the Fill panel (Window|Fill). And to apply effects, open the Effect panel (Window|Effect). The fill and stroke colors can be set faster from the Color section at the bottom of the toolbar. To set the stroke color, click

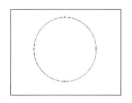

Figure 3.2
An ellipse with four points.

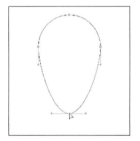

Figure 3.3
An ellipse with the bottom point pulled down.

Note: To constrain to a perfect square, press Alt/Option+Shift and drag to draw. If you want to draw from the center out, press the Alt/Option key and drag to draw.

the color well next to the pencil icon and type in a Hex number or choose a color. To set the fill color, click the color well next to the Paint Bucket tool and type in a Hex number or choose a color. (Hexadecimal numbers are discussed in detail in Chapter 2.)

5. If you want to edit the shape, notice that four points are automatically added to the rectangle you just drew (see Figure 3.4). Select the Subselection tool (white arrow) from the toolbar. Click and drag out the point in the lower-right corner. An error dialog box will open stating, "To edit a rectangle's points, it must first be ungrouped. Click OK to ungroup the rectangle and turn it into a vector?"

A rectangle in Fireworks is a group of four points, which is why the dialog box opens—the rectangle needs to be ungrouped so that you can manipulate just one point. The second half of the error message may lead you to think that you are not in Vector mode, but you are, so just click OK. Next, click and drag the lower point out; the results are shown in Figure 3.5.

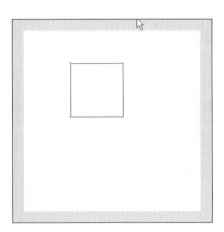
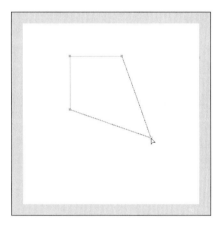

Figure 3.4
(Left) A rectangle with four points.

Figure 3.5
(Right) The rectangle with the corner pulled out.

PROJECT Making a Racing Flag

In this project, you will make a black and white grid to be used as a flag symbol in a racing game interface you will put together in Chapter 4. The completed interface can be seen in the Color Section. To make the grid using the Rectangle tool, follow these steps:

1. Open a new document (File|New). Type "288" in the Width box, type "144" in the Height box, and select white for the canvas color.

2. Select the Rectangle tool and draw a rectangle on the canvas (any size is fine). Click the Paint Bucket tool in the Color section of the toolbar and select white for the fill color. In the Info panel (Window|Info), type "286" in the Width box and "142" in the Height box.

3. In the Stroke panel (Window|Stroke), choose Pencil for the Stroke category, 1-Pixel Hard for the Stroke name, a Tip size of 1 pixel, and a stroke color of black. Position the black outline so that it is visible on your canvas.

4. Draw another little rectangle with a fill color of black. In the Info panel, type "36" for the Height and the Width settings. Position this rectangle in the very top-left corner.

5. A couple of guides will help you to position the black rectangles. To be able to pull guides onto the page, you'll need to have rulers visible. Choose View|Rulers, click in the ruler area, and drag a guide onto the canvas. You will see a green line as you drag. For horizontal guides, drag from the top ruler; for vertical guides, drag from the side ruler (see Chapter 6 for more details on using guides). Pull a guide from the left side to the right edge of the black rectangle.

6. Select the Pointer tool and move the black rectangle to the right of the guide you just placed. This is where the white part of the flag will be; you are putting the rectangle here temporarily as a marker. Pull another guide from the left side of your canvas from the ruler and place it to the right of the rectangle. These two guides will be enough to finish the flag grid. See Figure 3.6 for placement.

Figure 3.6
Placing the guides for the flag.

7. Move the black rectangle back to the top-left corner. Choose Edit|Duplicate (or press the Alt/Option key and drag) and drag the duplicate to the right of the second guide placed, leaving a blank, white area. Duplicate again and place the duplicate diagonally from the first rectangle, on the second row (see Figure 3.7 for placement).

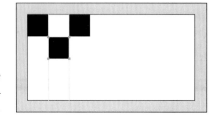

Figure 3.7
Three black rectangles placed for the flag.

8. Continue duplicating and placing the black rectangles on the diagonal to complete the racing flag. Save this image for use in a game interface. A copy (called flag.png) can also be found in the Chapter 3 racing folder on this book's CD-ROM. Figure 3.8 shows the rectangles being placed on the diagonal.

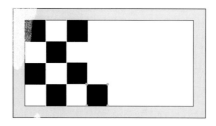

Figure 3.8
Black rectangles being added diagonally to the flag.

PROJECT Making a Control Bar for the Racing Game Navigation

You will make the control bar to place buttons on for the web racin' interface. To make the control bar to hold navigational buttons, follow these steps:

1. Open a new document (File|New) with a size of 200 pixels wide by 430 pixels high and a white canvas.

2. In the Fill panel, set the Fill color to None. Set the stroke color in the Stroke panel to black (Window|Stroke). Select the Ellipse tool, hold down the Shift key, and drag a circle onto the canvas. Place it somewhere near the top and center of the canvas.

3. With the ellipse selected, open the Info panel and set the Height and Width to 105.

4. If you don't have rulers showing in your work area, choose View|Rulers, and then drag a guide by clicking the left-side ruler and dragging a guide onto the canvas. Place one on each side of the ellipse you just drew.

5. Make a duplicate of the ellipse (Edit|Duplicate or press Alt/Option and drag). Select the Pointer tool and use it to move the duplicate ellipse near the bottom of the canvas, but leave room (about half an inch) for a good-sized drop shadow.

6. Select the Rectangle tool and draw a rectangle from the middle of the top ellipse to the middle of the lower ellipse. See Figure 3.9 for placement. To help align the rectangle to fit the ellipse perfectly, open the Info panel and set the Width to 105. Use the right and left arrow keys on the keyboard to nudge between the guides.

Note: Because the focus of this chapter is drawing the vector shapes, a style has been made for you with the gradient fill and effects. To learn how to make your own styles, refer to Chapter 2. You can find the style named Controlbar.stl in the Chapter 2 resources folder on this book's CD-ROM. To use it, copy it and put it in your Fireworks 4\Configuration\Styles folder. In Fireworks, open the Styles panel (Window|Styles), click the right-pointing arrow, and choose Import Styles.

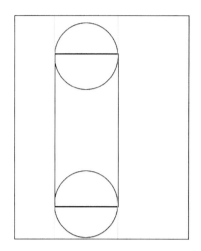

Figure 3.9

The alignment position of the two ellipses and rectangle.

7. Shift+select both ellipses and the rectangle and choose Modify| Combine|Union. If your shape isn't right the first time, just choose Edit|Undo and adjust the placement of the rectangle and repeat this step. Figure 3.10 shows the new shape.

8. All that is left is to finish with the fill and effects. To apply the controlbar style, open the Style panel (Window|Style) and click the style you just added. It will automatically be applied to the bar.

9. The only thing you'll have to change is the angle of the gradient. Figure 3.11 shows the gradient handles. To match the location of the handles, drag each one into position in your document. If you need more assistance in editing gradients, refer to Chapter 2.

10. Save this file for use in the completed game interface; a copy is saved in the Chapter 3 racing folder.

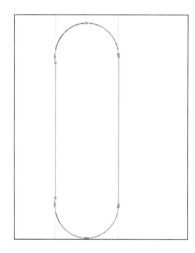

Figure 3.10

(Left) Two ellipses and one rectangle combined into one object.

Figure 3.11

(Right) The gradient handles on the control bar.

The buttons you will place on this bar need actions added to them. You can find complete instructions for making buttons that actually work in Chapter 7 in the "Navigation Bars" section.

PROJECT Making a CD Case

In this project, you will make a CD and its case. It is part of the multimedia kiosk that you will complete in Chapter 4. A copy of this file (cd.png) is in the Chapter 3 multimedia folder on this book's CD-ROM. To make the CD and case, follow these steps:

1. Open a new document (File|New) with a white canvas 320 pixels wide by 240 pixels high. Select the Rectangle tool and draw a rectangle. In the Info panel, type "20" for the Width (W) and "230" for the Height (H). In the Fill panel, choose Solid for the Fill and a color of black. In the Stroke panel, select Basic in the Stroke category, Soft Rounded for the Stroke name, a color of white, and a size of 1-pixel wide. This black rectangle is the side of the CD case.

2. Select the Line tool and draw a line from the top of the black rectangle to the bottom. Set the Stroke to Basic, Hard Line, 2 pixels, and a color of white. In the Info panel, set the Height to 230, which is the same height as the black rectangle. Press Alt/Option key and drag a copy; repeat three times. Using the Pointer tool, position all four white lines in the black rectangle. Figure 3.12 shows the placement of the lines.

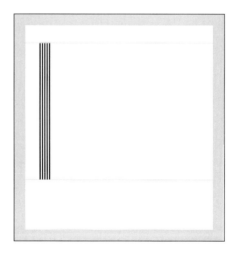

Figure 3.12
Four lines added to the side of the CD case.

3. Select the Rectangle tool and draw a rectangle. In the Info panel, type "245" for the Width and "230" for the Height. In the Fill panel, choose Solid and black as the color. In the Stroke panel, choose Basic, Soft Line, and 1 pixel, using white as the color.

4. Group the side of the CD case (the lines and the rectangle). To select everything on your canvas, use the Pointer tool to drag around the entire area and choose Modify|Group. Another way to select everything is to open the Layers panel, Shift+select everything you want to group, and then choose Modify|Group. In the Effect panel, choose Shadow and Glow|Drop Shadow and accept the default shadow. Figure 3.13 shows the group so far.

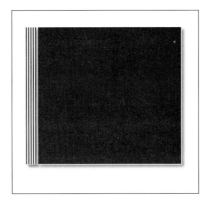

Figure 3.13
The CD case background.

5. To draw the CD, select the Ellipse tool, hold down the Shift key, and drag a perfect circle (don't worry about the size yet). In the Info panel, set the size to 208 for the Height and Width. Center the CD in the black area of the CD case. In the Fill panel, choose Linear for the Fill and Silver for the Gradient preset. Adjust the gradient to your liking. The only change made to this gradient was the position. To see the gradient used in this project, open the cd.png file located in the Chapter 3 resources folder on this book's CD-ROM. Click the CD part of the image, and the gradient handles will be visible, so that you can see the location used.

6. In the Stroke panel, set the color to white, use a Basic stroke, Soft Rounded, and 1 pixel. In the Effect panel, click the down-pointing arrow and choose Bevel and Emboss|Inset Emboss with a Width of 2 and a Softness of 2.

7. Select the Ellipse tool, hold down the Shift key, and drag a small circle for the center of the CD. In the Info panel, set the Height and Width to 70. In the Fill panel, set the Fill to black. In the Stroke panel, use a Basic stroke, Soft Line, and 1 pixel, with a color of white. In the Effect panel, choose Bevel And Emboss|Inset Emboss with a Width of 3 and a Softness of 3 (leave everything else at the default). Select the black circle and the CD, choose Modify|Align|Center Vertical, and then choose Modify|Align| Center Horizontal. Figure 3.14 shows the CD and its center.

Note: To have quicker access to commands such as Group, Ungroup, Join, Split, and Bring To The Front (and other alignment options), you can add another toolbar. Choose Window|Toolbars|Modify, and the bar will appear. If you want to dock it below the main menu, click and drag it below the main menu and it will stay there. Thereafter, when you want to use some of the Modify tools, they are one click away.

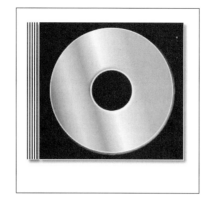

Figure 3.14
A CD with the center added.

8. To make the center look more like a CD case, you can borrow the spider web center, which you will make later in this chapter. Open webcenter.png, found in the Chapter 3 sports folder on this book's CD-ROM. Select any spine and delete it, and then delete every other spine. With the Pointer tool, draw a selection around the whole web center, and choose Modify|Group. In the Info panel, change the Height and Width to 45. Drag this version of the webcenter file onto the black center of your CD drawing. With these lines still selected, open the Effect panel and choose Bevel And Emboss|Raised Emboss with a Width of 3 and a Softness of 3. When you close the webcenter file, don't save the changes.

9. Draw one more little circle. In the Info panel, set the Height and Width to 23, and from the Fill panel, set the Fill to black. Center this over the white lines.

10. Select the Line tool and draw a line about 46 pixels high; make a duplicate (Edit|Duplicate) and use the down arrow on the keyboard to nudge the second line near the bottom of the CD. Select the Rectangle tool and draw a small rectangle (29 pixels wide by 15 pixels high), make a duplicate, and place one in each corner, as shown in Figure 3.15.

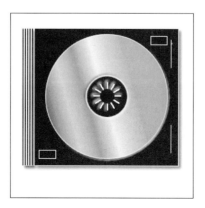

Figure 3.15
The finished drawing of the CD.

Deconstructing Fireworks Source Files

Any time a Fireworks source PNG file is provided, you can see the fills, strokes, and effects used (unless it's been converted to a bitmap or flattened). All you have to do is click the object you want to know about and then select the respective panels, as follows:

- *Fill panel*—If a gradient is applied, the type of fill will appear; click the Edit button and you will see the colors used and the positioning of each color. The gradient handles, which affect the angle and starting and ending positions of the fill, can be seen as soon as you click the object containing the fill.
- *Effect panel*—A list of the effects applied to the selected object will show. If you double-click each effect, the dialog box containing the settings used will open.
- *Stroke panel*—The stroke category, stroke name, color, and size of the stroke used, if any, are shown for the selected object.

---

11. Open feather.png from the Chapter 3 multimedia folder and drag it into place on your CD drawing. Select the Text tool, click on the CD, and, in the Text dialog box, type "Transitional Training". (The Font used in this project is Tahoma, 16 points; any color will do.) Click OK. From the Effect panel, choose Shadow And Glow|Drop Shadow; set a Width of 3, a Softness of 3, and an Opacity of 65%; and check the Knock Out option. Center the text on the CD. Save this file for inclusion in a multimedia kiosk, which you will put together in Chapter 4. Figure 3.16 shows the completed CD, including the clipart.

Figure 3.16
The finished CD, including clipart.

Rounded Rectangle Tool

The setting of the roundness of the rectangle may have baffled you if you read Fireworks' manual or help guide. The instructions are incorrect. The manual states that you should set the Roundness setting in the Tool Options panel before you draw the rounded rectangle. This is not accurate; the Rounded Rectangle tool does not have any tool options. The roundness is set in the Object panel after you draw the object.

Using the Rounded Rectangle tool is actually quite easy to do; just follow these steps:

1. Select the Rounded Rectangle tool.

2. Drag a shape on the canvas. You can set the size, height, and width in the Info panel (Window|Info).

3. To set the roundness, open the Object panel (Window|Object) and type in the amount of roundness your want or use the slider.

Another way to set the roundness is to press the up or down arrow on your keyboard repeatedly while you drag the shape. Using this technique provides no apparent benefit. It is not consistent in the roundness added; for instance, three clicks might be 61 percent this time and 91 percent the next time. When you repeatedly click the up arrow, roundness is added to the rectangle. The next rectangle you draw will maintain the roundness last used (unless it's 0, in which case it defaults to a roundness of 30). The next rectangle you draw (which will draw with the last roundness you used) will subtract from the roundness if you repeatedly click the down arrow. But, even counting the arrow clicks as you draw does not render the roundness with any consistency. Not only that, but roundness can be adjusted in the same way with the right and left arrows and with the 1 and 2 number keys of the keyboard, all producing the same inconsistent results.

PROJECT Making Horizontal Lines

In this project you make a horizontal line with a highlight and shadow, to be used in Chapter 4 when you finish the web racin' game interface. To make a horizontal bar, follow these steps:

1. Open a new document (File|New) and select a size of 570 pixels wide by 50 pixels high and a transparent background.

2. Select the Rounded Rectangle tool and drag out a rectangle the length of your canvas.

3. Open the Info panel (Window|Info). In the Width (W) box, type "567", and in the Height (H) box, type "12"; press Enter/Return.

4. Open the Fill panel (Window|Fill). In the Fill category, choose Solid, click the color well, type in the Hex #CC0000 (red), and hit Enter/Return. In the Edge box, select Anti-Alias.

5. To set the roundness of the rectangle, open the Object panel (Window| Object) and set the Roundness to 50.

6. Open the Effect panel, and from the Add Effects Or Choose A Preset box, choose Shadow And Glow|Drop Shadow. Choose a Distance of 7,

Figure 3.17

The beginning stage of a
horizontal line.

a Softness of 4, an Opacity of 65%, and an Angle of 315. Figure 3.17
shows the line so far.

7. To add a highlight, choose Edit|Duplicate. With the duplicate line still
   selected, open the Info panel (Window|Info), change the Height to 3,
   and press Enter/Return.

8. Open the Fill panel, change the color to Hex #CCCCCC, and press En-
   ter/Return. Be sure the Edge is set to Anti-Alias.

9. To set the roundness of the rectangle, open the Object panel
   (Window|Object), set the Roundness to 75, and press Enter/Return.

10. Open the Effect panel, and from the Add Effects Or Choose A Preset
    box, choose Shadow And Glow|Drop Shadow. Choose a Distance of 7, a
    Softness of 4, an Opacity of 65%, and an Angle of 315.

11. Position the highlight toward the top of the red bar and a few pixels
    to the right. To nudge the highlight a pixel at a time, press the right
    arrow key on the keyboard. The finished horizontal bar is shown in
    Figure 3.18.

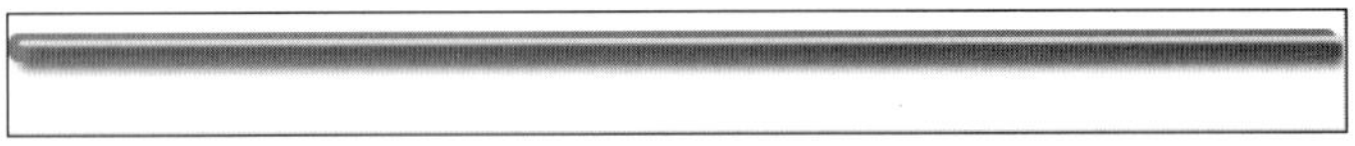

Figure 3.18

The finished horizontal bar.

PROJECT Making Tabs

You will be completing a sports calendar in Chapter 4. You can
see the finished project in the Color Section. The tabs that you design in this
exercise are the tabs that will be used in the sports calendar. To make simple
tabs suitable for navigation, follow these steps:

1. Open a new document (File|New). Select the Rounded Rectangle tool.

2. Double-click the Rounded Rectangle tool icon.

3. The Object panel will open. Type in or use the slider to choose a Roundness of 50, and select Draw Stroke Centered On Path.

4. Open the Fill panel (Window|Fill) and select Solid from the Fill category.
   Click the color box, type in the Hex #666600, and press Enter/Return.

5. To add a bevel, open the Effect panel (Window|Effect). From the Add
   Effects Or Choose A Preset box, click the down arrow and chose Bevel

And Emboss|Inner Bevel. In the Bevel edge shape box, choose Smooth, and type in a Width of 5 and a Softness of 3. Leave the Opacity at 75% and the Angle at 135. In the Button preset box, choose Raised.

6. Open the Stroke panel (Window|Stroke). From the Stroke category, choose Pencil. Click the color well and select white for the stroke color. In the Stroke name box, choose 1-Pixel Soft.

7. Choose Edit|Duplicate, two times. Select the Pointer tool and use it to move the tabs into position, as shown in Figure 3.19.

8. Select the Text tool and click on the canvas; Arial font with a point size of 12 was used in this project. Click the color well, type the Hex #FFFF00, and press Enter/Return. Type the word "Sept." Click OK.

9. Repeat Step 8, but type "Oct." instead. Repeat again and type "Nov."

10. Position the text on each tab until it looks right to you.

11. Save this project for use in the sports calendar.

Figure 3.19
The position of three tabs.

Polygon Tool

In Fireworks, you can draw equilateral polygons ranging from a triangle with 3 sides to a polygon with 360 sides. The Polygon tool also works in both Vector and Bitmap modes. To make a polygon, follow these steps:

1. Double-click the Polygon tool to access the Tool Options panel, shown in Figure 3.20.

2. The Tool Options panel is where you select the shape you want: Polygon or Star. If the Star shape is selected, an Angle option is also available. If you choose the Automatic option, the angle varies according to how many sides you have. The closer to 0 the angle is, the thinner the point is. The closer to 100 the angle is, the thicker the point is. To demonstrate this, choose Star for the shape with 12 sides and an angle of 10.

3. Drag and draw a star on your canvas (see the top star in Figure 3.21).

4. Double-click the Polygon tool again to have access to the Tool Options panel; change the angle to 90.

5. Drag and draw a star on your canvas (see the bottom star in Figure 3.21).

The Polygon tool always draws from the center out. If you want to constrain the shape to a 45-degree angle, hold down the Shift key and drag the shape.

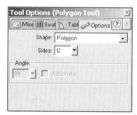

Figure 3.20
The Polygon Tool Options panel.

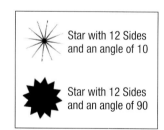

Star with 12 Sides and an angle of 10

Star with 12 Sides and an angle of 90

Figure 3.21
A star with 12 sides and an angle of 10 and the same star with an angle of 90.

Line Tool

The Line tool only draws a straight line with two points. If you want to constrain the line to a 45-degree angle, hold down the Shift key and drag the shape. The Line tool doesn't have any tool options. It can also be used in both Vector and Bitmap modes. To use the Line tool, follow these steps:

1. Select the Line tool from the toolbar.

2. Drag a line on the canvas by holding down the Shift key and dragging to draw a line at 45 degrees.

3. To change the size of the line, open the Info panel (Window|Info) and enter the height and width you want.

4. For transformation options, such as Scale, Distort, Rotate, and Skew, choose Modify|Transform and choose a Transform option, as shown in Figure 3.22.

Figure 3.22
The Transform options.

OBJECT Drawing a Dashed Line

If you draw maps or coupon cutouts, you will need to include dashed lines. In this project, you will make a dashed line and save it as a command to use again. To make a dashed line, follow these steps:

1. Click the Line tool and draw a line about two inches long. Before you release the mouse, press the Ctrl/Option key to constrain the line to a straight line.

2. Open the Stroke panel (Window|Stroke) and choose Random in the Stroke category.

3. In the Stroke Name box, choose Dots.

4. Double-click in the Tip box to open the Edit Stroke dialog box.

5. The first tab is Options. Set the Ink Amount to 100%, the Spacing to 250%, and Tips to 1.

6. Click the Shape tab. Enter a Size of 30, an Edge of 8, and an Aspect of 20, and leave the Angle at 360. Also check the Square option, unless you want to make a dotted line instead of a dashed line. Click the Sensitivity tab.

7. In the Brush category, choose Size. Change all the settings (Pressure, Speed, Horizontal, Vertical, and Random) to 0. Repeat this for every option in the Brush category. The result will look like the preview box in Figure 3.23. Click OK.

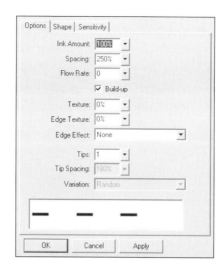

Figure 3.23
A single dashed line.

8. Your dashed line should now be applied to the line you drew. If it looks the way you like, continue to the next step. If it doesn't, go back to the Edit Strokes dialog box (double-click the Tip in the Stroke panel) and change the spacing and/or the size of the dash.

9. This step is optional. If you want to make a command, open the History panel (Window|History), Shift+select all the steps you see in the panel, and click the right-pointing arrow. From the pop-up menu, choose Save As A Command. Give it a name that you will recognize (it is named "road dashes" here). A copy of this command (also a dotted line and a shorter dash) is included in the Commands, Joyce folder on this book's CD-ROM. The command you just made and saved is automatically available for use from the Commands menu. If you want to use the ones included on the CD-ROM, you will need to copy and paste them into your Fireworks 4\Configuration\Commands folder.

Note: If you've made changes to the dash, or if you have redone steps as you've progressed in this project, you have to redo the project from the beginning because we are going to save the steps completed as a command. Step 9 leads you through making a command of the actions you took to make the dashed line. If you'd like more details on making commands before you continue, see Chapter 6.

PROJECT Drawing a Spider Web

Spider webs are popular on the Internet, and Fireworks makes them quite easy to draw. A spider web is also used in the sports calendar you will complete in Chapter 4. You will use the Line tool and Transform command, use the Ellipse tool, and borrow a simple animation trick (from Chapter 8) to draw multiple circles of varying sizes. To begin the spider web, follow these steps:

1. First, you are going to draw the spines of the spider web, as shown in Figure 3.24. Open a new document (File|New) with a canvas size of 300 pixels wide by 200 pixels high. Click the Custom option and choose black for the canvas color.

Note: This file, named webcenter.png, is also available in the Chapter 3 sports folder on this book's CD-ROM.

Figure 3.24
The spines of the spider web.

2. Select the Line tool and draw a horizontal line. The line color should be white; if it isn't, change the color in the Color section of the toolbar near the bottom with the pencil icon or from the Stroke panel. Click the color well and choose white. In the Info panel (Window|Info), enter a Height of 105 and a Width of 1.

3. With the line selected, press Ctrl+Shift+D/Cmd+Shift+D (clone), which places a copy of the line on top of the first one (don't use Duplicate, because the duplicate is not placed directly on top). Choose Modify| Transform|Numeric Transform, select Rotate, type "15" for the percentage of rotation, and click OK. Figure 3.25 shows the Numeric Transform dialog box.

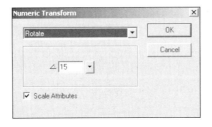

Figure 3.25
The Numeric Transform dialog box with the rotation options.

4. Repeat Step 3 until you have a complete circle of lines. If you prefer, you can bypass the menu bar by using the keyboard commands Ctrl+Shift+D/Cmd+Shift+D (clone) and Ctrl+Shift+T/Cmd+Shift+T (Numeric Transform dialog box). The previous settings will still be intact, so all you have to do is click the OK button.

Using Tween Instances

You could draw a series of circles in decreasing sizes by using the Numeric Transform command as you did in the first half of this project. But that way takes a long time. The fastest way to draw the multiple circles needed to complete the spider web involves using a technique normally used for animation, called *tweening*. Tweening is explained thoroughly in Chapter 8, but enough detail is given here to finish this project. This step in most drawing programs is usually done using a Blend command, which isn't available in Fireworks. The tween trick is a workaround that accomplishes the same end result a Blend command would.

If you'd rather not tackle tweening at this time, a spiderweb.png file is already in the sports folder on this book's CD-ROM, ready for use in the final project. If you are ready to give tweening a try and finish the spider web, follow these steps:

1. You can open a new document or work on the same canvas. Set the line Fill to white. The line color can be changed two different ways:

from the Color section near the bottom of the toolbar, you can click the color well next to the Paint Bucket icon and select the white square with a red slash in it; or, the fill can be set in the Fill panel (Window|Fill) to None.

2. Select the Ellipse tool. Hold down the Shift key and drag a perfect circle. In the Info panel, set the Height and Width to 105.

3. Choose Insert|Convert To Symbol and choose Graphic from the dialog box (you don't have to understand this for it to work; full details are given in Chapter 8). Figure 3.26 shows an instance (a copy) of the symbol on your canvas.

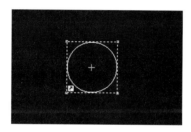

Figure 3.26
The ellipse turned into a symbol.

4. With the symbol selected, make a clone (Edit|Clone or Ctrl+Shift+D/ Cmd+Shift+D). In the Info panel, set the Height and Width to 15. Position this tiny circle in the center of the large one.

5. Select the larger circle and Shift+select the tiny circle. Figure 3.27 shows the two circles ready to be tweened.

6. Choose Modify|Symbol|Tween Instances. In the dialog box that opens, choose 6 Steps and don't check Distribute To Frames. Click OK.

7. With the Pointer tool, click and drag around the entire group of circles to select them all, and then choose Modify|Group. Place the group of circles on top of the circle of spines and behind them (Modify|Arrange| Send To Back).

Figure 3.27
The large and small circle instances ready to be tweened.

Save your new spider web. A copy of this file, called spiderweb.png, is in the Chapter 3 sports folder of this book's CD-ROM.

Vector Path Freeform Drawing Tools

The freeform drawing tools enable you to draw any shape you want. If you have a digital drawing tablet, now would be the time to use it. It's much easier to draw freeform lines with a drawing pen than it is with a mouse. A digital tablet is recommended in Appendix C.

Figure 3.28

The Pencil Tool Options dialog box.

Pencil Tool

The Pencil tool has a default stroke of 1-Pixel Hard. Unlike some of the tools that retain the last setting used, the Pencil tool has to be reset each time you use it if you want something other than the default stroke. The pencil stroke will always revert back to the default. The Pencil tool can be used in both Vector and Bitmap modes.

To see the Pencil tool options, shown in Figure 3.28, double-click the Pencil tool icon in the toolbar. The following list describes the options:

- *Anti-Aliased*—Puts a smooth edge on the lines you draw; this is particularly important if the lines are curved. Transitional colors are used along the edge of the object, blending the background color with the stroke color.

- *Auto Erase*—Macromedia describes this function as drawing the fill color over the stroke. It does, but only if you draw over the stroke after you've drawn it. This is a very strange feature; it works the same way as drawing a new path and applying a stroke.

- *Preserve Transparency*—Only works in Bitmap mode. It enables you to draw only in areas containing pixels, not in transparent areas with no pixels (see Chapter 5 for more on pixels).

To draw with the Pencil tool, follow these steps:

1. Select the Pencil tool from the toolbar.

2. Click and drag to draw with the Pencil tool.

3. If you want an open path, release the mouse when you are done drawing.

4. If you want a closed path, draw to the beginning of the line you drew and release the mouse.

Brush Tool

The Brush tool looks like paint or ink, but the result is still a path containing points. A path with the Brush stroke applied can be edited (see Chapter 4) like any other path. Strokes, fills, and effects can be added as well. The Brush tool can be used in both Vector and Bitmap modes. No Brush tool options (when you double-click the brush icon) are available in Vector mode other than Preserve Transparency.

To draw with the Brush tool, follow these steps:

1. Select the Brush tool from the toolbar.

2. Click and drag to draw with the Brush tool.

3. If you want an open path, release the mouse when you are done drawing.

4. If you want a closed path, draw to the beginning of the line you drew and release the mouse.

Pen Tool

With the Pen tool, you don't actually draw the line. You just define the points that make up the line, plotting out the points, if you will. It's similar to drawing a dot-to-dot picture. Each time you click, you put down a point (dot), and the next place you click adds another point. The line is automatically added between the points, thereby completing a line segment. The Pen tool is a vector tool only. If you are in Bitmap mode and choose the Pen tool, the mode will automatically be changed to Vector mode.

The Pen tool has two kinds of points: a Corner point, which has at least one straight segment, and a Curve point, which has at least one curved segment. To see first-hand the difference between these two types of points, follow these steps:

1. Open a new document (File|New) and use a size of 300 pixels by 300 pixels. Check to be sure the line has a color to it. In the toolbar near the bottom in the Color section, click the color well next to the pencil icon and choose a color.

2. Select the Pen tool and click the canvas; go straight across the page a few inches and click again. A line connects the two points you added. Continue clicking anywhere on the canvas. No matter where you click, the lines keep connecting the "dots."

3. Close your first practice document and open a new one (File|New); any size is fine, but 200 pixels by 200 pixels gives you a little room to practice in. Select the Pen tool and click the canvas; click again a few inches away, and then go down the page a bit and click and drag. See what happens as you drag? The line is curved, as shown in Figure 3.29. It takes practice to get used to working with a curved line.

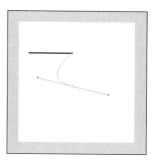

Figure 3.29
A path with corner points and a curved point.

When you draw with the Pen tool and drag to form curved points, Bézier control handles are added to the path. Control handles control the shape of the object. Chapter 4 explains in detail how to use these handles and actually uses them in projects.

A line in Fireworks that does not connect to itself to make an enclosure is considered to be an open path. To end an open path, double-click the last point. To end a closed path, click the first point added. The beginning point and the ending point are the same. If you happen to close the path by going beyond the first point, it won't be a closed path even though it looks like it is. That could affect your drawing, because a path that is not closed will not fill according to the shape you expect, and usually won't fill at all.

PROJECT Making a Jagged Line

With the help of guides, you can make an evenly spaced jagged line in Fireworks. To make a jagged line, follow these steps:

1. This exercise requires a bit of preparation before you begin. Open a new document (File|New) with a size of 300 pixels wide by 200 pixels high and a white canvas.

2. Check the pen fill color (the pencil icon near the bottom of the toolbar) and set it to black by clicking the color well and selecting black.

3. You'll need to use guides to produce a nice evenly spaced jagged line. Figure 3.30 shows the guide placement for this exercise.

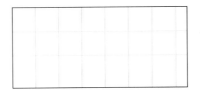

Figure 3.30
Guide placement for making jagged lines.

4. Select the Pen tool and click the second horizontal guide right at the beginning. Continue to add a point (click) on the intersection of each vertical and horizontal guide until you reach the end of the line. Double-click to end the line. See Figure 3.31 for an example of where the points should be placed.

Figure 3.31
Points added for the jagged line.

5. Select the Subselection tool (white arrow), click the second point (the first intersection), and drag the point up to the first line (see Figure 3.32).

Figure 3.32
The first point pulled on the jagged line.

6. Repeat Step 5 with every other point along the horizontal guide. Figure 3.33 shows the finished jagged line.

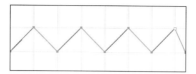

Figure 3.33
The finished jagged line.

Moving On

You should now be extremely comfortable working with the various vector tools. You now have an arsenal of different shapes and freeform tool techniques with which to draw your custom-made objects and line drawings.

Chapter 4 continues the subject of working with vectors. You will learn how to work with Bézier curves to add to the control that you have in designing custom shapes. You also will learn how to transform and edit the shapes you have drawn, by using the Vector mode editing tools. You will also finish all the projects begun in this chapter.

Chapter 4

Editing Vector Objects

This chapter describes how to use the Vector mode editing tools and how to manipulate Bézier curves to produce custom shapes. You will make a custom flair; finish the sports calendar, multimedia kiosk, and Web racin' game interface; and convert a bitmap logo into a scalable vector logo.

Bézier Curves

A Bézier curve (pronounced "bezz-ey-aye") is based on mathematical calculations. The name comes from Pierre Bézier, who in the 1970s formulated the principles on which most vector objects are now based. The theory is that all shapes are composed of segments and points. A segment can be straight, curved, or a combination of both straight and curved. A combination of two or more points joined by a line or a curve is referred to as a *path*.

A straight line is a line that joins two points using the shortest possible distance. A curved line is controlled by the position of the points and the control handles, which manipulate them. Figure 4.1 shows two paths with the same position of points; notice how different the same path can be made by manipulating the control handles.

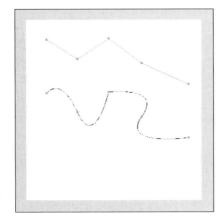

Figure 4.1

Two paths with the same position of the points.

After you draw a path, you can assign specific properties to it, such as fills, strokes, effects, and color. Paths can be *open,* wherein the beginning and ending points don't meet, or *closed,* wherein the beginning and ending points meet.

No limit exists to what you can do to a Bézier curve by adding, deleting, moving, and manipulating the points of a path; all of these techniques will be discussed in this chapter.

Drawing a Bézier Curve

To draw a Bézier curve, follow these steps:

1. Open a new document (File|New). Select the Pen tool and click anywhere on your canvas to set the beginning point of the path.

2. Move your cursor and click somewhere else on the canvas to set the second point of the path. Notice how a straight line automatically connects the points.

3. Move the cursor again and click to set another point, only this time hold the mouse button down and drag a bit in any direction. As you drag, a curve will form. You can click anywhere to place another point.

4. Double-click to end the path. Notice that a control handle is attached to the curve you formed, as shown in Figure 4.2.

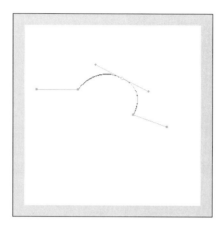

Figure 4.2
A path with a Bézier curve control handle.

Using the Control Handles of a Bézier Curve

After you've drawn a Bézier curve, you may want to make adjustments to it. To make adjustments with the control handles, use the Subselection tool and click a point on the path. When the cursor is near a point, it changes to a white arrowhead, which indicates the point can be selected. When you click a point, the solid square turns into a hollow square. Bézier handles are usually visible when you select a point that is a Bézier curve. To practice manipulating Bézier curves using Bézier control handles, follow these steps:

1. Select the Pen tool, click to place three points in a row, and then double-click the ending point of the path (see Figure 4.3).

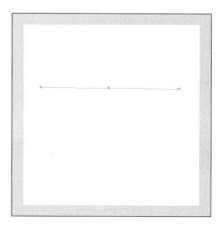

Figure 4.3
A line to practice Bézier curves on.

Note: To change a straight line into a Bézier curve, click a point with the Subselection tool, then hold down the Alt/Option key, and drag on a point. You will actually be dragging a control handle. To change a Bézier curve back into a straight line, select the Pen tool and click the point of the curve you'd like to be a straight segment; the curve segment of that point will become straight.

2. Select the Subselection tool. Click the middle point; it will turn into a hollow square. If no handles appear (which they won't on this straight line), press the Alt/Option key and drag the middle point down. When you release the mouse button, a control handle will be visible. Figure 4.4 shows what your curve should look like as a result of holding down the Alt/Option key and pulling down on the middle point.

3. Press the Alt/Option key on the same point and drag straight up. Figure 4.5 shows the results.

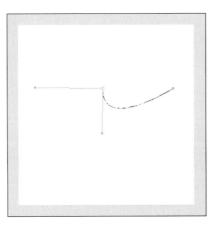 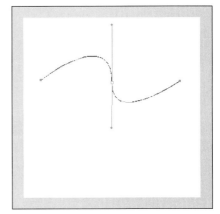

Figure 4.4
(Left) A Bézier curve added to the middle point of the practice line.

Figure 4.5
(Right) Two handles on the Bézier curve.

Working with Bézier curves takes practice to get a feel for what direction to pull and turn to get the desired shape. Practice by clicking and dragging the top control handle to the right and down. You can move it up, down, and all around.

Editing with the Pen Tool

In Chapter 3, you learned how to draw paths and how to connect the beginning and ending points. Sometimes, you will need to join multiple paths that you have drawn, or you may want to break apart a path. The Pen tool is used to join multiple paths, close a path, and continue a path you have drawn.

Closing a Path

If you try to fill a path object and nothing happens, or the fill doesn't go just inside the path, producing very strange results, your path most likely is not closed. If this happens, you need to join the path, or join multiple paths to close the path. To close a path, follow these steps:

1. With the Pointer tool, select the path you want to close.

2. Select the Pen tool, move your cursor over one of the end points of the path (when you are near the end point, a little *x* will appear in the

lower-right corner of the cursor), and click the end point once. A little arrow now appears in the corner of the cursor, indicating you can now select a closing point.

3. Move your cursor to the ending point and click it once. The path is now closed. You don't have to use only one point to close a path. If the ending point is not near, you may want to place points along the way and then select the ending point.

Continuing a Path

Adding to a previous path is quite similar to closing a path, except you don't have to close a path to add on to it. If you want to add on to a previous path, follow these steps:

1. With the Pointer tool, select the path you want to add on to.

2. Select the Pen tool, move your cursor over one of the end points of the path, and click the end point once.

3. Move your cursor to the next location in which you want to add a point and then click once; continue clicking to add points until you have the path you want.

Joining Paths

After you draw multiple paths, you can join them together using the Pen tool. This may sound like the same thing as closing paths, and it is almost the same procedure; the difference is that you don't have to close the joined paths. To join paths together, follow these steps:

1. With the Pointer tool, select the path you want to join.

2. Select the Pen tool, move your cursor over one of the end points of the path, and click the end point once.

3. Move your cursor to the end point of the other path you are connecting to and click once. You can combine as many paths as you like in this way.

Adding and Deleting Points

If you want a path to change direction, you need to add points to make it do so. You could use the Bézier tool to make a curve change direction, but you may not want a rounded curve. If you need to change direction but want a sharper turn, then you need to add points using the Pen tool. See the "Drawing a Control Panel" project later in the chapter for a good example of adding points. To add points to an existing path, follow these steps:

1. With the Pointer tool, select the path you want to add points to.

Note: You may also select the path using the Pen tool. To add or delete a point, you select the point by clicking it once with the Pen tool, which causes the + or – sign to appear, and then you click again to add or delete the point. You will also notice that while you move the Pen tool around, it appears attached to the end point (a line clings to the cursor); don't worry about this, because as soon as you click, the add or delete action continues as it should.

2. Select the Pen tool and click once on the path's line to add one point. If you want a curved segment with Bézier control handles, click and drag.

3. Repeat for as many points as you need. When you are done, select any other tool to end adding points.

When you use the Freeform tools, they often add more points than necessary to maintain the design's shape. The extra points don't hurt anything, but you may want to clean up the object some. Sometimes, the extra points can make a design look choppy or not as smooth as it should be. To remove points, follow these steps:

1. With the Pointer tool, select the path you want to delete points from.

2. Select the Pen tool. As your cursor passes over the point, you will see a minus sign on the right corner of the cursor. Select the point you want to delete by clicking it one time.

3. Another way to remove unwanted points is to choose Modify|Alter Path|Simplify and then type in how many points you want removed and click OK. Although this option doesn't give you precise control, it is a fast way to make simple changes.

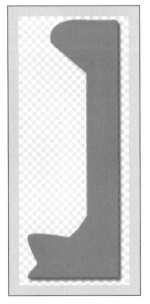

Figure 4.6
The completed control panel shape.

PROJECT Drawing a Control Panel

This project involves drawing a control panel to use in the multimedia kiosk that you began in Chapter 3 and will finish later in this chapter. Figure 4.6 shows what this control panel will look like when you finish this project. The completed panel is in the Chapter 4 multimedia folder and is called multicontrol.png. To draw the control panel, follow these steps:

1. Open a new document (File|New) with a width of 200 pixels and a height of 475 pixels, and a white canvas.

2. Select the Rectangle tool and draw a rectangle. In the Info panel (Window|Info), type in a Width of 165 and a Height of 460, and then press Enter/Return.

3. To get the shape you desire, it helps to have guides placed on the canvas. To set guides, the rulers need to be visible, so choose View|Rulers if they are not already in view. Pull a guide (click and drag) from the top or side of the ruler and drag it into position on the document. Figure 4.7 shows the placement of guides for this project.

4. Select the Subselection tool and click one of the rectangle's points. A dialog box opens, asking whether you want to ungroup the rectangle. Click OK.

Note: If you have a sketch or image you'd like to make into a vector path, open the file and drag it onto the canvas, and lock the layer in the Layers panel (refer to Chapter 1). After you place the guides, draw a path around the image, and manipulate the curves, simply delete the object you used as a guide.

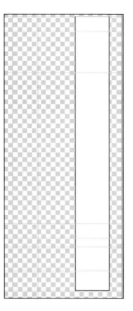
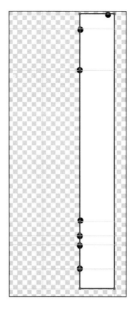

Figure 4.7
(Left) Guide placements for drawing the control panel.

Figure 4.8
(Right) The placement of the points added to the rectangle.

5. Choose the Pen tool and click to add points according to the placement in Figure 4.8. The black circles are not as large as shown here, nor is the outline of the rectangle that pronounced. They have been enhanced for this demonstration.

Figure 4.9
The top-right curve and the control handle placement.

6. To convert the corner point to a curved point, select the Subselection tool, click the rectangular path to select it, and then click the first point to the left of the top-right corner. Hold down the Alt/Option key and pull diagonally to the right. Figure 4.9 shows how the curve should look at this point.

7. With the Subselection tool, click the top-right corner point and move down the right side. You are pulling this point down far enough to line up the curve you just made with the top guide (see Figure 4.10).

Figure 4.10
The placement of the control handles for the right curve.

8. With the Subselection tool, click and drag the point on the left side of the second horizontal guide to the intersection of the second vertical guide. Press the Alt/Option key and pull up and to the right on this same point. Figure 4.11 shows how the angle should look.

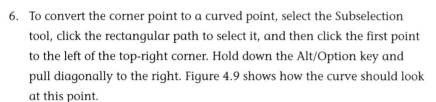

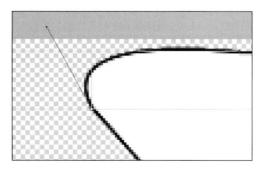

Figure 4.11
The placement of the control handles for the top curve.

9. Figure 4.12 shows a view of the bottom of the control panel. The *X*s mark where the points used to be. (The Xs are added so you can see where the points were.) Select each one with the Subselection tool and move it to the position shown in Figure 4.12.

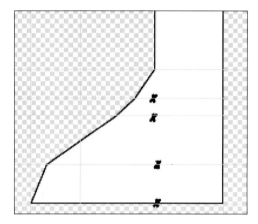

Figure 4.12
Moving four points for the center curve.

10. With the Subselection tool, select the bottom-left point, press the Alt/Option key (to add a curve), and pull up a little. Select the point just above the bottom-left point you just altered, and hold down the Alt/Option key (to add a curve) while you pull down a little. Figure 4.13 shows what the shape of the curve should look like.

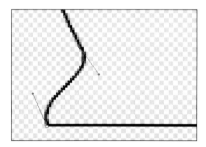

Figure 4.13
The bottom-left curve control handles.

11. Select the Pen tool and click where the circle is shown in Figure 4.14 to add another point.

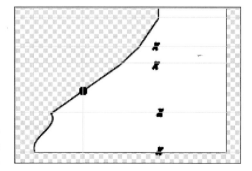

Figure 4.14
A point added to the bottom curve section.

12. Select the Subselection tool and move the new point according to the position in Figure 4.15. This figure also shows the position of the control handles. To get this position, press the Alt/Option key and pull up, and then pull down and a bit to the left on the second control handle.

Figure 4.15
The position of the moved point and its control handles.

13. To finish the design, select the Pointer tool and select the new shape. Open the Fill panel (Window|Fill), click the color well, and type in or choose Hex #006600 or any dark green color; if you type in a Hex number, you will need to press Enter/Return. After choosing a color, select Anti-Alias for the Edge. Open the Stroke panel (Window|Stroke) and select None for the Stroke. Open the Effect panel (Window|Effect) and choose Bevel and Emboss|Inner Bevel with a Width of 2, a Softness of 2, and an Angle of 121. The Bevel edge shape is Flat and the Button preset is Highlighted. Then, choose Shadow And Glow|Drop Shadow with a Distance of 5, a Softness of 3, and an Angle of 301. Figure 4.16 shows the control panel shape.

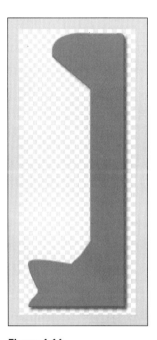

Figure 4.16
The finished shape of the multimedia control panel.

Reshaping Paths Using Path Operations

Combining, joining, intersecting, and punching holes in paths are all functions (also known as Boolean operations) you will probably find yourself using often. Many of the projects started in Chapter 3 couldn't be finished until this section because they each used one of these functions. You will see how many interesting shapes can be accomplished by using the path operations.

The combine options can be found by choosing Modify|Combine. The options are Union, Join, Intersect, Crop, and Punch. Figure 4.17 shows the result of the combine options applied to the same two ellipses. They are filled with effects that were added only for visual enhancement.

Union

The Union option is used when you want to merge two or more objects. This operation combines all the shapes into the outline of them all, and removes any overlapping areas. To use the Union operation, follow these steps:

1. With the Pointer tool, Shift+select each shape you want to merge.

2. Choose Modify|Combine|Union. An example of the Union operation is shown in Figure 4.17.

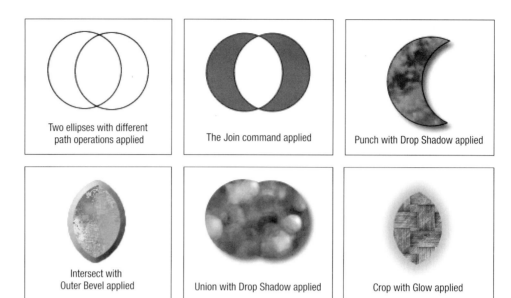

Two ellipses with different path operations applied

The Join command applied

Punch with Drop Shadow applied

Intersect with Outer Bevel applied

Union with Drop Shadow applied

Crop with Glow applied

Figure 4.17
The combine options applied to the same two ellipses.

Join

The Join operation isn't the same as connecting paths together into one continuous path using the join techniques with the Pen tool. The results of the Join operation can be seen in Figure 4.18. This example shows overlapping areas being joined, but you can select multiple shapes and join them into one path. This technique is used in the "Converting a Company Logo into a Vector Image" project, later in the chapter.

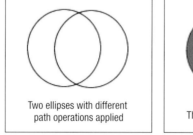

Two ellipses with different path operations applied

The Join command applied

Figure 4.18
The Join operation demonstrated on two circles.

To join paths together, follow these steps:

1. With the Pointer tool, Shift+select all the objects you want to join.

2. Choose Modify|Join.

3. If you don't like the result or if you want to split the join apart at a later time, choose Modify|Split.

Intersect

The Intersect operation works the opposite of Union. Whereas Union throws away the overlapping area, Intersect keeps it and throws away the rest. Figure 4.19 shows an example of the Intersect operation.

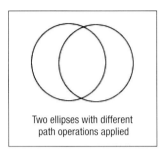

Two ellipses with different
path operations applied

Intersect with
Outer Bevel applied

Figure 4.19
Two circles with the Intersect
operation applied.

To intersect paths, follow these steps:

1. With the Pointer tool, Shift+select all the objects you want to intersect.

2. Choose Modify|Combine|Intersect.

Crop

The results of using the Crop operation look the same as the results of using the Intersect operation, as shown in Figure 4.20.

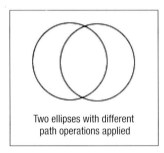

Two ellipses with different
path operations applied

Crop with Glow applied

Figure 4.20
Two circles with the Crop
operation applied.

To use the Crop operation, follow these steps:

1. With the Pointer tool, Shift+select all the objects you want to intersect.

2. Choose Modify|Combine|Crop.

Punch

Punch is probably the most fun of all the path operations, especially if you like to punch holes in things. You'll get to punch plenty of holes by the time you finish the projects coming up in this section. Figure 4.21 shows the results of using the Punch operation.

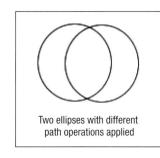 

Two ellipses with different path operations applied

Punch with Drop Shadow applied

Figure 4.21

Two circles with the Punch operation applied.

To use the Punch operation, follow these steps:

1. With the Pointer tool, Shift+select the object you want to punch and the object you are punching it out of.

2. Choose Modify|Combine|Punch.

PROJECT Making the Frame for the Web Racin' Game Interface

The frame is quite easy to make, and utilizes the Punch command. Figure 4.22 shows the finished project.

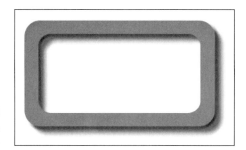

Figure 4.22

The finished frame for the web racin' game interface.

To make a frame, follow these steps:

1. Open a new document (File|New) with a size of 500 pixels by 500 pixels.

2. Select the Rounded Rectangle tool and draw a rectangle. In the Info panel, set the size to a Width of 325 and a Height of 175. Open the Object panel (Window|Object) and set the Roundness to 25.

3. Choose Edit|Duplicate, and then choose Modify|Transform|Numeric Transform. From the drop-down menu, choose Scale, uncheck the Constrain Proportions check box, type "85%" for the Width and "75%" for the Height, and click OK. In the Fill panel, change the color to something different than your larger rectangle so that you can see it. Using the Pointer tool, center the smaller rectangle in the larger rectangle.

To be sure it is centered accurately, Shift+select both rectangles and choose Modify|Align|Center Vertical, and then choose Modify|Align| Center Horizontal.

4. Shift+select both rectangles and choose Modify|Combine|Punch. From the Fill panel, use a Solid fill with the color Hex # 1B8A19, and then press Enter/Return. From the Effect panel, choose Bevel And Emboss|Raised Emboss with a Width of 4 and a Softness of 2. Then, choose Shadow And Glow|Drop Shadow with a Distance of 15 and a Softness of 4.

5. Save this file as frame.png for use in the web racin' game interface.

Making a Tools Poster

The main technique used in this poster is the Punch command. Figure 4.23 shows the finished project.

To make this poster for tools, follow these steps:

1. Open a new document (File|New) with a size of 200 pixels by 200 pixels.

2. Select the Rectangle tool and draw a rectangle to cover the entire canvas. Open the Fill panel (Window|Fill) and choose Cone in the Fill category and Copper in the Preset Gradient color sets.

3. In the Layers panel (Window|Layers), click the yellow folder icon to add a new layer. Select the Rectangle tool and draw a rectangle around the whole canvas. In the Fill panel, use a Solid fill with the color of Hex #996600, and then press Enter/Return.

4. Select the Ellipse tool, hold down the Shift key, and draw a constrained circle on the canvas. In the Info panel, set the size to a Height and Width of 21, and then press Return/Enter. In the Fill panel, change the Fill to White so that you can see the circle. Select the circle, press the Alt/Option key, and drag a copy, five times. Choose View|Rulers and pull a guide from the left side of the ruler to just inside the canvas, leaving a small border on the right; repeat for the left side. Drag another guide down from the top ruler, making a small top border, and repeat for the bottom border. With the Pointer tool, drag one circle to the top-left intersection of the horizontal and vertical guides. Place another circle at the bottom-left intersection. Arrange the rest of the circles anywhere in between. Shift+select all six circles and choose Modify|Align|Distribute Heights. Figure 4.24 shows the guide placement and the first row of circles.

Figure 4.23
The finished Tools poster.

Figure 4.24
The guide placement and first row of circles.

5. Deselect the line of circles by clicking anywhere on the canvas. Select one circle, press the Alt/Option key, and drag a copy, four times. Place one circle in the intersection at the top-right corner. Place the other four circles anywhere between the existing first circle on the left side and the last one you just placed in the top-right corner. Shift+select all six circles and choose Modify|Align|Distribute Widths, and then deselect by clicking a blank area of the canvas.

6. Place a guide under each of the circles going down the left side of the canvas. Shift+select the second through the sixth circles of the top row, choose Edit|Copy, choose Edit|Paste (a copy will be pasted on top of the selected circles being copied), and drag into position in the second row. Figure 4.25 shows the guides and the second row in place.

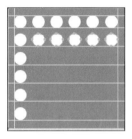

Figure 4.25

The placement of the remaining guides and the second row of circles.

7. Continue copying and pasting (or Alt/Option+dragging) the five circles into the rest of the rows. Deselect by clicking a blank area of the canvas. If you grouped anything while copying, then be sure to ungroup it.

8. This step takes a bit of time because you have to do it to one circle at a time. Shift+select one circle and the brown background, and choose Modify|Combine|Punch. Repeat this step for every circle.

9. When you finish all the punching, make sure the composite layer is still selected, go to the Effect panel, choose Shadow And Glow|Drop Shadow, and accept the default. Select the Text tool and click the canvas. In the Text dialog box, enter the text "Tools" and choose your font. This example uses the font Staccato55BT, a Size of 92, and a Leading of 60%. After you choose the options you want, click OK. In the Fill panel, choose Pattern for the Fill category, Illusion for the Fill name, and Anti-Alias for the Edge.

10. All that is left is to place the tools. The wrench and pliers are from the Hemera Photo Objects 50,000 Premium Image Collection and are in the Chapter 4 tools folder on this book's CD-ROM. Open each image and drag it onto the canvas. With the image selected, press the Q key and rotate each tool the way you want. The completed file is in the tools folder and is called punch.png.

Finishing the Multimedia GUI

You don't have much left to do to this illustration of an interface other than to put it together, make some punches, and add a button. Figure 4.26 shows the finished illustration of the multimedia GUI. Chapter 7 discusses various techniques to add interactivity. All the files needed for this project are in the Chapter 4 multimedia folder.

Figure 4.26
The completed multimedia GUI.

To finish this interface, follow these steps:

1. Open a new document (File|New) with a size of 600 pixels wide by 480 pixels high.

2. In the Chapter 4 multimedia folder, select the moneybackground.png file and open it. Drag it onto the new canvas and position it. Close the moneybackground.png file.

3. In the Layers panel, click the yellow folder icon at the bottom to add a new layer. Select the Rectangle tool and draw a rectangle to cover the canvas. In the Fill panel, choose Linear and the Preset Gradient color set of Emerald Green. Select the gradient layer. When the gradient handles appear, move them according to Figure 4.27. In the Layers panel, set the Opacity to 60% (the Opacity setting is in the top-left corner) and press Return/Enter (see Figure 4.28). This layer will add some color and lighting highlights to the background.

4. To add the buttons, holes, and text to the control bar, open the multicontrol.png file (made earlier in this chapter or available on the CD-ROM). Select the Ellipse tool, hold down the Shift key, and draw a circle. In the Info panel, change the Height and Width to 39 and press Enter/Return. Select the circle, press the Alt/Option key, and drag a copy of the circle; repeat until you have nine circles. Select one of the

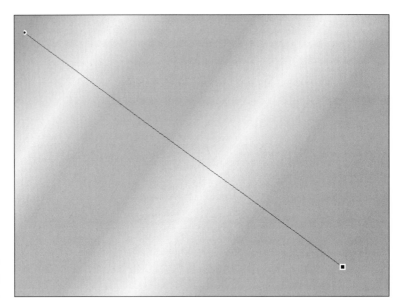

Figure 4.27
The gradient position of the new layer.

Figure 4.28
The Opacity settings in the Layer panel.

circles, change the Height and Width in the Info panel to 28, and press Enter/Return. Do this to a total of three circles. Make the last three circles a size of 25. You can place the nine circles randomly along the bottom of the control bar or use the finished image as a guide.

5. Select one circle at a time, Shift+select the control bar, and choose Modify|Combine|Punch; repeat for each circle. Notice that each punched hole automatically has a drop shadow added to it. The control bar has the shadow, and the shadow is applied to these openings as well.

6. For the buttons of the control bar, select the Rectangle tool and draw a rectangle on the control bar. In the Info panel, set the Height and Width to 24 and press Enter/Return. In the Fill panel, choose a Solid fill, choose a color of Hex #A16946, and press Enter/Return. In the Effect panel, choose Bevel And Emboss|Inner Bevel with settings of Flat, Width of 3, Softness of 3, and the Button preset of Raised. In the Stroke panel, choose Pencil, 1-Pixel Hard, and a color of black (Hex #000000). Select the button, press the Alt/Option key, and drag a copy; repeat until you have nine buttons. If you can't see the guides in this file, choose View|Guides|Show Guides; if you are using the multicontrol.png file, a guide is set up for the placement of the buttons. Place each button against the guide; put the top button into position (see Figure 4.26), the bottom button into position, and then place the remaining buttons anywhere in between the top and bottom buttons. Shift+select all the buttons and choose Modify|Align|Distribute Heights to get even spacing between all the buttons.

7. To finish the control bar, select the Text tool and click the control bar. In the Text dialog box, type the word "menu" in lowercase. In this project, a rounded font called AGSchoolbook Regular was used with a size of 18; the color is the same as the buttons, which is Hex #A16946. Press Enter/Return. Just past the color well, click the *U* with an underline to underline this word, and click OK. In the Effect panel, choose Bevel And Emboss|Inset Emboss, with a Width of 2 and a Softness of 2. Now drag the whole control panel onto the new document you are working on and position it according to Figure 4.26.

8. Select the Rectangle tool and draw a rectangle on your canvas. In the Info panel, set the size to a Width of 480 and a Height of 240. In the Stroke panel, choose Pencil, 1-Pixel Hard, and a color of black. Press Enter/Return. In the Fill panel, choose None for the Fill. In the Effect panel, choose Bevel And Emboss|Inset Emboss with a Width of 2 and a Softness of 2. Position this rectangle as shown in Figure 4.26.

9. Open the cd.png file (made in Chapter 3 or available in Chapter 4's multimedia folder); drag it onto the canvas and place it according to Figure 4.26.

10. Select the Text tool and click the canvas. In the Text dialog box, type "Basics of Money Management". The font used here is FlashDBol with a size of 16, Smooth Anti-Alias, and a color of Hex #A16946. Press Enter/Return and click OK. In the Effect panel, choose Shadow And Glow|Drop Shadow, and choose a Distance of 9, a Softness of 4, and an Opacity of 65%.

11. To finish this interface, open the moneyslice.png file and drag it onto the multimedia interface according to the placement seen in Figure 4.26. Then, open all three of the coin files and position them according to Figure 4.26.

Finishing the Web Racin' Game Interface

The finished web racin' game interface is shown in Figure 4.29. All the files you need for this project are in the Chapter 4 racing folder on this book's CD-ROM. To put this interface together, follow these steps:

1. Open a new document (File|New) using a size of 640 pixels wide and 400 pixels high.

2. Select the Rectangle tool and draw a rectangle around the entire canvas. In the Fill panel, choose Linear for the Fill, and in the Preset Gradient color sets, choose emerald green. With the Pointer tool, select the gradient background. Drag the square handle up near the top of

Figure 4.29

The finished web racin' game interface.

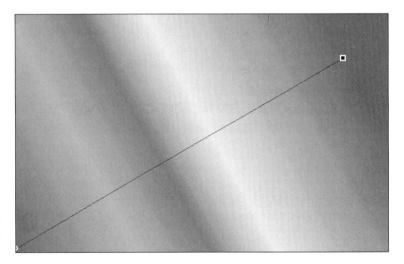

Figure 4.30

The gradient position of the background.

the canvas and the round handle to the lower-left corner; adjust the square to look like Figure 4.30. If you need more information on working with gradients, refer to Chapter 2.

3. You could use the background as it is, but for a softer look, you can use the Gaussian Blur filter (discussed in Chapter 5). Choose Xtras|Blur| Gaussian Blur. When the dialog box opens that says this operation will convert to a bitmap, click OK. Or you can apply the blur by opening the Effect panel and choosing Blur|Gaussian Blur. In the Gaussian Blur dialog box, type the number 20 and click OK.

4. To add some depth and character to the background, you will alter and shade the top-left corner of the interface. Select the Rectangle tool and draw a rectangle in the top-left corner of the canvas. From the Info panel, choose a Width of 420 pixels and a Height of 220 pixels. From the Stroke panel, choose Felt Tip, Thin, and a color of Hex #1D670C, press Enter/Return, and select a Size of 8. From the Fill panel, choose white for the Color so that you can see what you are doing.

5. Select the Pen tool and place the cursor over the bottom-right point. You will see a – (minus sign) in the lower-right corner of the cursor; click once to remove this point. Your rectangle will now be a triangle, as shown in Figure 4.31.

Figure 4.31
The rectangle turned into a triangle.

6. With the Subselection tool, click and drag the top-right corner to produce the curve, as shown in Figure 4.32. You may have to move the point to the right a bit. Adjust the curve until it is pleasing to you.

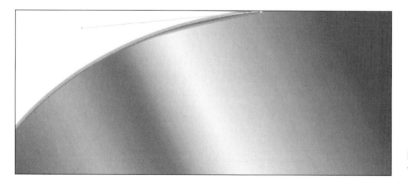

Figure 4.32
The triangle with a curve added.

7. To finish the top triangle, open the Fill panel, choose the Fill category of Bars, and click the Edit button. In the first color well (click it), type in the Hex #1D670C and press Enter/Return; in the last color well on the far right, click and choose black. You don't have to adjust the gradient at all.

8. Select the Text tool and click the document. When the Text dialog box opens, select a font. The one used here is FlashDBol with a Size of 32,

color Red, and Smooth Anti-Alias. The words to type are "web racin'". When you get a font and size you want, click OK. Press the Q key on the keyboard to get the transform handles, and pull the middle-right square on the right side to the right to stretch to a size that looks good or that looks like the sample. Select the middle-bottom square and pull up to "squash" the word a bit. From the Effect panel, choose Shadow And Glow|Drop Shadow, with a Distance of 7 and a Softness of 10. Click the color well, type in the Hex #333333, and then press Enter/Return.

9. With the Pointer tool, select the words *web racin'*, hold down the Alt/Option key, and drag to make a copy. In the Effect panel, double-click the Drop Shadow effect that is attached to this word. In the dialog box, put a check in front of Knock Out. Choose Modify|Transform|Free Transform. Pull, rotate, and skew until you get a position and angle you like. Use the Pointer tool to position the word.

10. In the Chapter 4 resources racing folder, open the horizontal.png file. This bar was made in Chapter 3. Shift+select the two objects, choose Modify|Group, and drag the horizontal bar into position below the red web racin' title.

11. This same bar is used for the red bars in the lower-right corner of the interface. Select the horizontal bar (not the highlight, just the red bar) and choose Edit|Duplicate. From the Info panel, change the Width to 131. In the Stroke panel, select Pencil and 1-Pixel Soft with a color of Hex #D8150D, and then press Enter/Return. Select the bar, hold down the Alt/Option key, and drag to make a copy; repeat until you have eight bars.

12. Arrange the bars at an angle in the right corner of the interface. Place the top bar and the bottom bar where you want them, with the other six bars in between. Shift+select all eight bars and choose Modify|Align|Distribute Heights to evenly space the bars. Then, choose Modify|Combine|Union to make all eight bars into one object. In the Fill panel, change the Fill to Linear and click the Edit button. Click the left color well and type in the Hex #D8150D. Press Enter/Return, click the right color well, and select black. See Figure 4.33 for the bottom horizontal bar placement.

13. Open controlbar.png (made in Chapter 3) and drag it into position (refer to Figure 4.29) in your interface. Next, open the flag.png (made in Chapter 3) and drag it into position (refer to Figure 4.29). Choose Modify|Transform|Distort and pull the transform handles until you have the flag positioned the way you like.

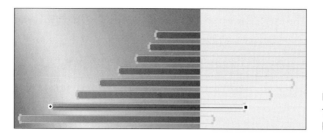

Figure 4.33
The placement of the bottom horizontal bars.

14. Open the Library panel (Window|Library), click the right-pointing arrow, and select Import Symbols. Navigate to the Chapter 4 racing folder and select racingbuttonsymbols.png. Click the Open button, click the Select All button, and click Import. The symbols can now be dragged from the Library panel onto your interface one at a time and positioned as shown in Figure 4.29. These buttons will be made in Chapter 7, where symbols and the Library panel are discussed in more detail.

15. The last item to bring into the interface is the frame. Open the frame.png file from the racing folder and put it into position. If you want to put a picture in the frame, go to Chapter 7 to see how to make this area of the frame interact with the buttons in the control bar.

PROJECT Finishing the Sports Calendar

Only one more shape needs to be made to finish the sports calendar. All the files needed to complete this project are in the Chapter 4 sports folder on this book's CD-ROM. The pieces of clipart are compliments of Hemera, and come from the Hemera Photo Objects 50,000 Premium Image Collection. Figure 4.34 shows the finished project; use this image as a guide in placing the individual components of the design.

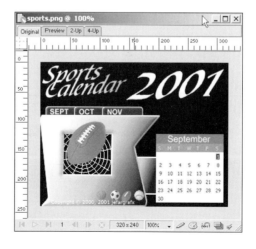

Figure 4.34
The finished sports calendar.

To finish the sports calendar, follow these steps:

1. Open a new document (File|New) with a size 320 pixels wide by 240 pixels high. Click Custom and choose black for the background. Select the Text tool and click in the document. In the Text dialog box, type the words "Sports Calendar". The font used in this example is BibleScrT, with a Leading of 60%, Smooth Anti-Alias, Size of 47, Bold, and Italic. The color doesn't matter. Any font you like will do. Click OK. Position the text in the top-left corner and choose Modify|Transform|Free Transform. Pass the cursor over the path until you see the rotate cursor; rotate until you get a pleasing angle (see Figure 4.35).

Figure 4.35
The sport calendar title rotated.

2. In the Fill panel, select Linear for the Fill; in the Preset Gradient color set, choose white and black, and click the Edit button. Click once between the white and the black color icons. A new icon is added; click it and type in the Hex #66FFFF and then press Enter/Return. Click the black color icon, type in the Hex #6699FF, and press Enter/Return. No alteration was made to the gradient position. If you'd like to alter the placement of the colors, select the text and drag the gradient handles until you like the color placement.

3. Select the Text tool and click in the document. In the Text dialog box, type in the numbers "2001", highlight them, and choose a font; the one used here is BibleScrT with a size of 47, Bold and Italic, a color of white, and Smooth Anti-Alias edge. Click OK. Position the number according to Figure 4.34.

4. Open the tabs you made in Chapter 3. If you didn't make them, the file tabs.png file is in the sports folder; open it, drag it onto the sports calendar, and position it below the title.

5. To make the large blue shape, open a new document (File|New) with a size of 200 pixels wide by 150 pixels high. Select the Rounded Rectangle tool and draw a rectangle to cover the canvas of the new document. Open the Object panel (Window|Object) and set the Roundness to 20. Select the Subselection tool and select the rectangle. When the dialog box opens asking about ungrouping, click OK. Figure 4.36 shows the placement of the points. The points you will alter are in the lower-left corner and the upper-right corner.

Figure 4.36
The points on the new shape.

Figure 4.37
The new position of the four corner points of two corners.

6. In Figure 4.36, you can see two points in the lower-left corner. With the Subselection tool, select the corner point that is on the left edge and click and drag it in toward the center (see Figure 4.37). In the top-right corner, select the point that is on the right edge and click and drag it down a bit and then into the center. Select the second point in the

lower-left corner and click and drag it out toward the edge of the canvas to elongate the point. Repeat for the top-right point. Figure 4.37 shows all four moved points.

7. In the Fill panel, select Linear as the Fill; select blue, red, yellow as the Preset Gradient color set (any three-color gradient will do); and then click the Edit button. Click the first color well on the left and select white as the color. Select the center color well, type in the Hex #66CCFF, and press Enter/Return. Click the last color well on the right and select black for the color. Figure 4.38 shows the gradient position. Drag the gradient handles to match.

Figure 4.38
The gradient position of the new shape.

8. Select the Rectangle tool and draw a rectangle in the center of the shape you are still working on. In the Info panel, set the Width to 80 and the Height to 75. Center the rectangle to a position where it looks good to you. Shift+select the large shape and the rectangle and then choose Modify|Combine|Punch.

9. To add depth to the shape, open the Effect panel and choose Bevel And Emboss|Inner Bevel, with a Bevel Edge of Smooth, a Width of 10, a Softness of 3, and the Button preset of Raised. Notice how the punched area gets the same effect applied to it. Figure 4.39 shows the completed shape. Drag the shape onto your sports calendar document and place it according to the finished project (refer to Figure 4.34).

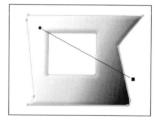

Figure 4.39
The large shape for the sports calendar.

10. Open the spiderweb.png file (made in Chapter 3) and drag it onto the shape you just drew and added to the main canvas. Drag it over the center opening and choose Modify|Arrange|Send To Back. The football and other little pieces of clipart are all in the sports folder; open each one and drag it into position.

11. Note the little rectangle behind the large shape. To draw it, select the Rectangle tool and draw a rectangle on the canvas. In the Info panel, set the size to a Width of 67 and a Height of 61. In the Stroke panel, use Pencil, 1-Pixel Soft, with a Tip size of 2 and a color of white. In the Fill panel, choose Linear, and set the color the same as in Step 7. Figure 4.40 shows the position of the gradient handles. Place the rectangle over the large shape according to the finished project and choose Modify| Arrange|Send To Back.

Figure 4.40
The gradient position of the small rectangle.

12. Select the Rectangle tool and draw a rectangle for the calendar top. In the Info panel, set the Width to 116 and the Height to 17. In the Fill panel, choose Solid, click the color well and type in Hex #34679A, and then press Return/Enter. Select the Text tool and click in the rectangle

you just drew. In the Text dialog box, type the word "September", choose a font, and select Smooth Anti-Alias from the Edge option. The font used in this example is Arial, with a size of 67 and a color of yellow (Hex #FFFF00—if you type in the number, you will need to press the Enter/Return key). When your selections are made, click OK. Drag the text to the center of the blue rectangle and position it according to the finished project.

13. The calendar is provided in the sports folder. For this example, a screen shot was taken of the Windows calendar, the calendar part was cropped using the Crop tool, and the Info panel was used to resize to a Width of 116 and a Height of 19. Position the calendar below the month bar. If you would like the calendar to change when a tab is clicked, you can use the sample calendars supplied in the Chapter 4 sports folder. See Chapter 7 for instructions on how to make disjointed rollovers (click one area and have an image appear somewhere else).

Editing Paths with Vector Mode Editing Tools

The Vector mode editing tools perform some unique functions, as you will see in the following exercises and projects. You can push and pull points visually without editing separate points, and you can change the look of a path by "scrubbing" it. Figure 4.41 shows the Vector mode editing tools. From left to right, they are as follows: Freeform tool, Reshape Area tool, Path Scrubber tool-additive, and Path Scrubber tool-subtractive. The next icon, which normally doesn't appear with the first four but has been shown here for demonstration purposes, can be found by clicking on the little arrow on the Brush tool icon; it is called the Redraw Path tool. The last icon is the Knife tool (it changes to the Eraser tool in Bitmap mode), which is shown here for demonstration purposes as well.

Figure 4.41

Vector mode editing tool icons.

Freeform Tool

The Freeform tool enables you to push or pull points to adjust the shape of a path. The biggest difference between using this tool and using the Subselection tool to move points is that the Freeform tool automatically adds points as you push or pull a new shape. When you select the Freeform tool and move the cursor toward the path, the cursor gets a little *s* next to it. The *s* indicates that the Freeform tool is in use and that the pull pointer is in position to pull the selected path. To use the Freeform tool, follow these steps:

1. Open a new document (File|New) with a size of 300 pixels by 300 pixels and a white canvas.

2. Select the Rectangle tool and draw a rectangle. A rectangle was intentionally used in this exercise to demonstrate a point, which you will see in a moment. Select the Freeform tool and move the cursor toward the bottom of the rectangle to push in on it. Notice that no little *s* appears next to the cursor. Try to click and drag up on the rectangle's edge. You will get an error message saying the tool can only be used on paths. Considering that a rectangle in Fireworks is a path, you may wonder about this error message. What happens is that the Rectangle tool automatically groups the four points of a rectangle; most functions in Fireworks won't work on grouped objects, and grouped objects won't be recognized as a path. To overcome this minor obstacle, just select the Subselection tool and try to move a point. A dialog box asks whether you want to ungroup; click OK. Or, you could choose Modify|Ungroup (whichever is easier for you) and then select the Freeform tool again. Now as you approach the rectangle's edge, you will see the little *s*.

3. With the Freeform tool selected, click anywhere on the bottom line and push it up; then try clicking and dragging another part of the bottom line down to get a feel for how the tool works. Figure 4.42 shows several practice push-up, drag-down, and up-and-over movements.

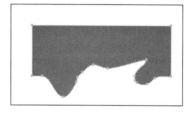

Figure 4.42
A rectangle altered using the Freeform tool.

4. As you work with the Freeform tool, you may notice a little *o* near the cursor. Place your cursor inside the shape and click. You will see a large circle; push it toward an edge and see what it does. It's an unusual tool and may take some getting used to, but it is an easy way to form a curved shape or to even out one that is jagged. You can also use the circle to push from outside the shape; when you see the little *o*, just click and drag to push in.

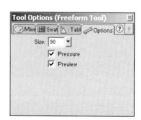

Figure 4.43
The Freeform Tool Options panel.

5. To change the size of this circle, double-click the Freeform tool to access the Freeform Tool Options panel, shown in Figure 4.43. When you have the size adjusted properly, push or pull your shape. It may take a few tries to get the size of the tool correct.

Redraw Path Tool

The Redraw Path tool is in the same area with the Paint Brush tool. If you have read the Fireworks 4 manual or the help files, disregard them, because they both show the Freeform tool icon but call it the Redraw Path tool. (The correct icon image is shown on page 114 of the manual, but the wrong image and cursor are displayed on page 118.)

The Redraw Path tool will really take some getting used to. Often, the results it will produce are unpredictable until you have practiced with it a while. After you learn how to use the tool properly, however, it can be useful for touching up a small area. To use the Redraw Path tool, follow these steps:

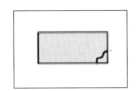

Figure 4.44

A new path drawn with the Redraw Path tool.

1. Draw a path, or use a rectangle shape and ungroup it (Modify| Ungroup). Be sure you have a stroke applied (Window|Stroke) or you won't see the path you are redrawing.

2. Select the Redraw Path tool from the Paint Brush flyout.

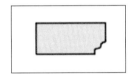

Figure 4.45

A path drawn with the Redraw Path tool.

3. Select the path to alter, place the cursor (a circle) over the path's line, and click and drag to reshape it. Put the cursor a bit past the right-bottom point, to the left, and then curve up to the right side to cut out a corner (see Figure 4.44). Figure 4.45 shows the results when you release the mouse.

When you draw the new path, be sure you start on the path line and end on another path line. Notice in Figure 4.46 how the new line went beyond the path. The cutout area was the result of that redraw.

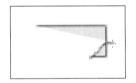

Figure 4.46

A line drawn with the Redraw Path tool that extended the path's edge.

Reshape Area Tool

The Reshape Area tool works much like the Freeform tool. What separates the Reshape Area tool from the Freeform tool is its ability to warp an entire image. By setting the size of the circle in the Tool Options to be larger than the path to alter, you can get some pretty interesting warped effects. Figure 4.47 shows the Reshape Area tool pushing a path.

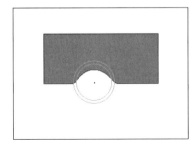

Figure 4.47

The Reshape Area tool pushing a path.

Another difference with the Reshape Area tool compared to the Freeform tool, is the added control. The Strength setting is an additional option in the Reshape Area Tool Options panel (see Figure 4.48). You may have noticed in Figure 4.47 that an additional circle appears in the Reshape Area tool cursor. The Strength setting determines how strong the pull is for the path that is between these two circles. The Pressure settings are for use with a pressure-sensitive tablet.

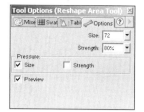

Figure 4.48

The Reshape Area Tool Options panel.

To use the Reshape Area tool, follow these steps:

1. Draw a path and then select it.

2. Double-click the Reshape Area tool icon to access the Reshape Area Tool Options panel. Set the Size and the Strength you want for the cursor.

3. Push on a path to reshape it. Although this tool is very easy to use, it will take you a little time playing with it to get a feel for the strength you like and the size you need.

Making the IDea Bookstore Header

The IDea Bookstore needed a new navigation design on its Web page, and needed it within two days. Because of the time constraint, any shortcuts that didn't require a lot of vector drawing were welcome. The first version of the IDea Bookstore heading, shown in Figure 4.49, was totally unacceptable and quite ugly, but it was a start. Figure 4.50 shows the finished version after following the steps in this project. (The menus are added in Chapter 7.)

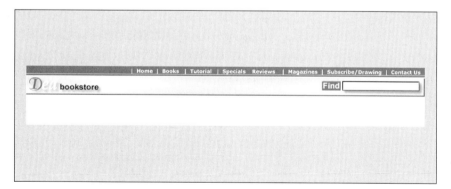

Figure 4.49

The first version of the IDea Bookstore header.

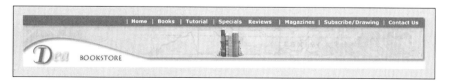

Figure 4.50

The finished version of the IDea Bookstore header.

The second and third versions were worse than the first version; a bulge was pulled down under where the name is. But the bulge was inspirational in that it inspired thinking in the opposite direction. Instead of pulling the bulge down, how about pushing it up? That did the trick. To redesign this header, follow these steps:

1. In the Chapter 4 resource folder on this book's CD-ROM, open the bookstore2.png file. A few things have been done for you. (If you prefer to do every step, open the bookstore1.png instead.) If you see green boxes (slices) and they are distracting to you, click the right Hide/Show Slices icon in the bottom of the toolbar in the View section. (The label names of the icons can be confusing because the tool tip names are the same for the two icons in the View section. The black and white icon on the left is the view without slices; the green and red icon on the right is the view showing the slices.) The following steps were done to the bookstore.png file for you:

   - The yellow area of the heading was originally too small, and thus was enlarged by selecting it and using the Info panel to change the Height to 60 pixels.

   - The burgundy bar was changed to a Height of 20 pixels in the Info panel. In the Effect panel, Shadow And Glow|Drop Shadow was selected, using the default settings.

   - All the text in the burgundy bar was Shift+selected and, using the up arrow key, nudged until it was centered.

   - A new fill was added to the gold bitmap area by opening the Fill panel and choosing Pattern, Other and selecting the fillgold.png file (located in the Chapter 4 resources folder).

   - The Find button and box were deleted. An HTML form box was added in Dreamweaver for the header used on the Web site.

2. Select the bookstore name and drag it off to the left, so that it is out of the way for now. The gold section is now ready to get a new shape. The gold rectangle is already ungrouped and is a path in both bookstore1.png and bookstore2.png. Double-click the Reshape tool, and set the Size to 150 and the Strength to 90. If this size doesn't work for you, change it. Remember, Edit|Undo is a wonderful command.

3. Click and hold down the mouse in the canvas area and slowly move it up toward the right corner to push a curve (see Figure 4.51).

Figure 4.51
The curve being formed in the
IDea Bookstore header.

4. Push until you get the shape you want.

5. Open the Effect panel, choose Shadow And Glow|Drop Shadow, and accept the defaults. You can move the bookstore name in the cutout opening of the curve.

6. If you'd like to change the color of the IDea part of the logo, choose Modify|Ungroup, select the *e*, and choose a gold color from the Fill panel. While you have the *e* selected, open the Effect panel, double-click Drop Shadow, and change the shadow color to black. Repeat for the letter *a* and change the shadow color for the *I* and the *D*. Select the word *Bookstore* and change its shadow to black also.

7. Open the books.png file from the Chapter 4 resources folder and drag it into place on the header.

Path Scrubber Tool

The Path Scrubber tool alters the stroke of a path after it's been drawn. The state of a path can be altered by the settings in the Path Scrubber Tool Options panel. The best way to explain this tool is to demonstrate its use. To use the Path Scrubber tool, follow these steps:

1. Open a new document (File|New) with a size of 200 pixels by 200 pixels. Click Custom and choose black for the background.

2. Select the Line tool and draw a line on the canvas. Open the Stroke panel and choose Air Brush, Basic, a color of white, and a large tip size of 60 for easy viewing.

3. Double-click the Path Scrubber tool-subtractive to open the Path Scrubber Tool Options panel (see Figure 4.52). Leave the Pressure and the Speed checked and set the Rate at 50. Place your cursor outside of the end of the stroke; see Figure 4.53 before you click. The image on the left is the placement of the cursor; click once and the result is the image on the right.

Figure 4.52
The Path Scrubber Tool Options panel.

Figure 4.53
Cursor placement to subtract from the path.

4. Repeat Step 3, except change the Rate to 100 and then view the difference. This will help you determine how to set the Rate and where to place the cursor to achieve the desired result. Select the Path Scrubber tool-additive and click alongside the path; the stroke begins to fill back out.

PROJECT Making a Custom Flair

A finished flair called flair.png is in the Chapter 4 resources folder. Many different ways exist to make a flair; the technique used in this project produced a nice flair rather quickly. You will start with a larger-sized flair so that you can see what you are doing. After you get it to look the way you like, you can always resize it. The flair you will make in this project is shown in Figure 4.54.

Figure 4.54
The flair that will be made in this project.

To make a flair, follow these steps:

1. Open a new document (File|New) with a size of 100 pixels by 100 pixels. Click Custom and choose black for the background.

Note: If you get a warning that the Path Scrubber tool can only be used on a path with pressure sensitivity, check to be sure the path you are working on is still selected. If you want to use strokes such as the Pencil, double-click the tip image, select the Sensitivity tab, enter a pressure value, and click Apply.

2. Select the Line tool and draw a line at an angle on the canvas. In the Stroke panel, choose Watercolor, Thin, a color of white, and a tip size of 10.

3. Double-click the Path Scrubber tool–subtractive to access the Path Scrubber Tool Options panel. Set the Rate at 25. Click once on each end point of the path. Change the Rate setting to 5, press Enter/Return, and click once on each side of the ends to taper further. Figure 4.55 shows the placement of the cursor.

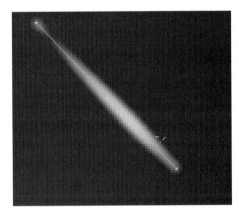

Figure 4.55
Placement of the cursor to subtract a bit more from the path's stroke.

4. With your path selected, press the Q key on the keyboard to access transform functions. Move your cursor until you see the Rotate tool, and then click and rotate to a position you like. Choose Edit|Duplicate, press the Q key again, and rotate the second path at an angle to the first path to resemble a flair. You could just stop now, but the flair could use a little more glare in the center.

5. Select the Ellipse tool and draw a small circle. In the Info panel, set the size to a Width of 15 and a Height of 15. Use the keyboard arrow keys to nudge the circle over the intersection of the two paths. In the Stroke panel, choose Air Brush, Basic, a tip size of 2, and a color of white. In the Fill panel, choose Solid and a color of white. In the Layers panel, set the Opacity to 50. If you want to see what the circle looks like so far, click anywhere on the blank canvas. You will see that the circle is too defined. (You can see definite edges instead of a gradual fading into the background. To look like a glow from the center of a flair, you want the circle to be softer.)

6. With the Pointer tool, select the circle again and choose Xtras|Gaussian Blur. A dialog box opens that says the object needs to be converted to a bitmap; click OK. In the Gaussian Blur dialog box, type in "2" for the Blur Radius and click OK. If you like the way the blur makes the center look, you are done. If not, select Edit|Undo and reapply a stronger blur or a weaker blur. You could also undo a few more times and alter the circle's size and the opacity level, depending on how pronounced you'd like the center glow.

Knife Tool

The Knife tool is in the same location as the Eraser tool. In Bitmap mode, it is the Eraser tool; in Vector mode, it is the Knife tool. The Knife tool works only on paths, not on bitmaps. You can use the Knife tool to cut an open path in pieces or a closed path apart.

As with the majority of the other Vector mode editing tools, you can double-click the Knife tool icon to access its Tool Options panel. But you won't get what you expect. Macromedia didn't change the tool options for the Knife tool, so what opens is the Eraser Tool Options panel; there are no options for the Knife tool. To use the Knife tool, follow these steps:

1. Open a new document (File|New) with a size of 300 pixels by 300 pixels and a white canvas.

2. Select the Rectangle tool and draw a rectangle; fill it with any color you'd like.

3. Select the Pen tool and click several points to form a jagged line of sorts. In the Stroke panel, choose a tip size of 4 or greater so that you can see the line easier.

4. Select the Knife tool and click and drag it through the rectangle. Start at the top and drag all the way through. The slice won't be apparent when you are done. Select the Pointer tool and click anywhere other than the rectangle to deselect the rectangle. Then, click one side of the rectangle and drag. This will separate the piece you just cut.

5. Repeat Step 4 on the line you drew.

PROJECT Converting a Company Logo into a Vector Image

To draw a vector version of a graphic, such as a logo, you can either scan the image into Fireworks or import it from a saved file. By using the techniques in this project, you can produce a vector version of the image that can be resized and easily changed for future uses:

1. Open the starting file for this project, which is tracelogo.png in the Chapter 4 resources folder. Click the red circle with the white *X* on the bottom of the document window to leave Bitmap mode. In the Layers panel (Window|Layers), click the yellow folder icon on the bottom to add a new layer.

2. To aid in the tracing of the raster (bitmap image) shape, you need to set up guides. The tracelogo.png file has the guides in place for you, as shown in Figure 4.56.

Figure 4.56
The position of the guides for tracing the IDea logo.

3. Select the Zoom tool to enlarge the area of the *I* and the *D*, which will be traced first. Select the Rectangle tool and draw a rectangle over the base of the *I*. From the Fill panel, select Gray for the color so that you can easily see what you are drawing (see Figure 4.57).

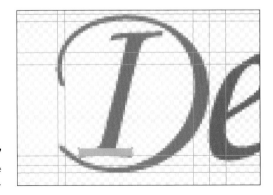

Figure 4.57
A rectangle drawn over the base of the *I*.

4. Choose Modify|Transform|Skew and transform the rectangle to fit the base of the *I*. When it is positioned, choose Edit|Duplicate and drag the copy to the top of the *I*.

5. Select the Rectangle tool and draw a rectangle over the body of the *I*. Choose Modify|Transform|Skew and position the rectangle over the *I*, as shown in Figure 4.58. If the depth of the rectangles isn't right (too thin or too thick), then choose Modify|Scale to make those adjustments.

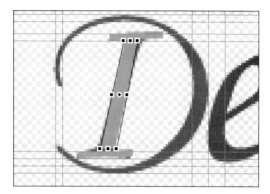

Figure 4.58
Rectangles drawn over the *I* to form the letter.

6. Select the Subselection tool, Shift+select the three rectangles, and choose Modify|Join.

7. Select the Ellipse tool. Using the guides, draw a circle around the outside of the *D* and a second circle on the inside of the *D*. In the Stroke panel, set the Stroke to Pencil and 1-Pixel Soft. In the Fill panel, select None for the Fill. With the Subselection tool, Shift+select both circles and choose Modify|Join (see Figure 4.59).

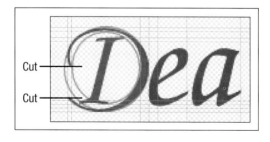

Figure 4.59
Two ellipses drawn around the *D* and joined.

8. Select the Knife tool and make a cut through both circles just below the end of the *D*'s top and just above the end of the *D*'s bottom curve (see Figure 4.59). Select the Pointer tool and click anywhere on a blank canvas area. Then, select the portion between the ends of the *D*. Delete each circle's segment.

Note: The tip of the top of the *D* and the end of the *D* need the points from each circle to be on top of each other to close the path. This may alter the shape of your letter, so you may want to do this portion first and then adjust the rest of the shape. If you have a difficult time seeing just the circle lines, you can turn off the visual of the bitmap layer temporarily by clicking the eye icon in the Layers panel next to the bitmap layer. Click it again to return the visibility.

9. Each point can still be manipulated. With the Subselection tool, select and move points to conform to the letter *D*. You will need to pull a Bézier control handle to get a curve that fits. For instance, the point in the center circle just below the top of the *D* needs to be moved up and the control handle needs to be pulled up to fit the curve. The top point of the outer circle needs its handles pulled out to expand a bit. The adjustments that need to be made are going to depend on the circles you drew and how close you got them to the *D*. Some areas may need an extra point to get the curve just right. To add a point, select the Pen tool and click the path where you need it.

10. When you are finished with the letter shape, you can select the underlying bitmap image in the Layers panel and click the trash can icon to delete it.

11. To fill the letter, open the Fill panel and choose the color you want. In the Stroke panel, change the stroke to the color of the letter. If the letter won't fill, then the path isn't totally closed. To close the path, select the Pointer tool, draw a selection around the two points at the end of the *D*, and choose Modify|Join; repeat for the other tip of the *D*. It will now fill.

12. By using these techniques, you can convert any letter or bitmap image into a vector shape. It does take some time, but it's worth it in the end. You will have a scalable vector logo to use in print as well as on the Web. Repeat Step 7 to complete the *e* and the *a* if you'd like further practice.

Moving On

You should now be extremely comfortable working with the various vector tools. You now have an arsenal of different shapes and freeform tool techniques with which to draw your custom-made objects and line drawings.

In Chapter 5, you will master the bitmap tools and learn to apply masks. You will learn how to color-correct images and make composite images.

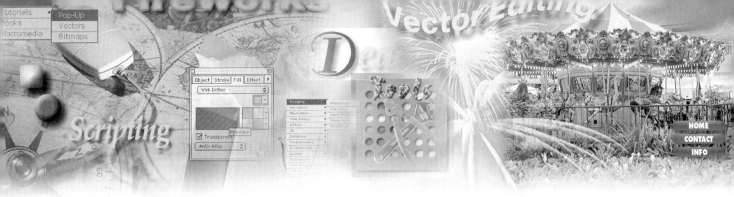

Chapter 5

Working with Bitmap Images

This chapter describes using the selection and image editing tools of Fireworks 4 to manipulate photographs (bitmapped images). You'll discover how to apply transparency expertly, achieve seamless compositions, and produce images without halos or jagged edges. Learn how to use levels to make tonal adjustments, and how to use the Rubber Stamp tool to repair flawed images.

Bitmap Mode

Once they are scanned and digitized, photographs are composed of pixels, the smallest component of a bitmapped image (also known as a *raster* image or, in Fireworks, an *image object*). Pixels are little squares of color resembling a mosaic composition, with a bunch of tiny squares making up the image. Editing pixels involves adding, removing, or coloring individual pixels.

The pixels are what distinguish a bitmapped image from a vector image, which consists of paths. A *path* is a line with at least two points. Because vector objects (called *objects* in Fireworks) are made up of a series of lines, they are fully scalable. Conversely, because each image contains a fixed number of pixels, pixel images lose detail as they are scaled up. When you scale a bitmapped image up in Fireworks, Fireworks has to guess which pixels need to be resampled to "fake" the detail in the increased space. This stretching of pixels results in what is known as a *pixilated image.* You can identify pixilated images by the obvious squares that can be seen or by the blurring of detail. The more an image is stretched, the worse it looks. On the other hand, if you have a bitmapped image that is larger than needed, you can scale it down, which resamples the pixels into a smaller area, producing a sharper image with more detail.

Resolution is a word that comes up often when working with bitmap images. Pixel-based images, which bitmaps are, are resolution dependant. The size of the pixels and the height and the width of a bitmap image are fixed. The resolution is what determines how many pixels exist per inch; this is known as dots per inch—dpi. The degree of resolution of an image is determined when a scan is taken, or, if you use a digital camera, before you shoot the image. The higher the resolution, the more pixels exist per inch—and, consequently, the bigger the image can be without degradation. Because Fireworks specializes in producing graphics for the Web, the resolution of 72 dpi is sufficient. (Print resolutions are usually about 300 dpi.) Fireworks is not suitable for printing using a four-color process, because it is an RGB-only environment. This means that only the red, green, and blue channels are used (like a monitor), whereas printing uses CMYK—cyan, magenta, yellow, and black.

Fireworks has a separate environment called Bitmap mode for working with bitmap images. Bitmap mode has tools available that are used for editing just bitmapped images, such as the selection tools and the blur tools from the Xtras menu. Although you have to be in Bitmap mode to edit bitmapped images, you usually do not have to make a conscious effort to open Bitmap mode. As soon as you click a bitmap tool, such as the Magic Wand or a Marquee tool, you are automatically in Bitmap mode. Plenty of visual clues alert you that you are using Bitmap mode. The most obvious is the blue-striped border around your image; others include a red circle with a white x at the bottom of your document window, and the document's title bar, which says Bitmap Mode (see Figure 5.1). If you want to manually activate Bitmap mode, simply select one of the Marquee tools.

Figure 5.1
Bitmap Mode is displayed on the document's title bar.

Obtaining the Images Needed

You'll need to have a source for images when you want to produce composite images, which are great for Web page graphics and specialized Web page headers, or navigation interfaces. You can scan images from your own photo collection, use a digital camera to acquire photos (see the Resources Appendix C for the ones that have been tested), or purchase images from a professional photo reseller. For this book, Comstock Images (**www.comstock.com**) has graciously provided a CD-ROM with over 12,000 comping images, which you can locate with a keyword browser. All the images used in this chapter are provided by Comstock Images, Royalty Free Division. For faster access, a low-resolution copy of each image used for the projects in this chapter can be found in the Chapter 5 resource folder of this book's companion CD-ROM.

Editing Preferences

By choosing Edit|Preferences (Ctrl+U/Cmd+U) and selecting the Editing tab, you can customize the way you produce graphics. You can change cursors, alter the visual clues about Bitmap mode, and configure the way you view an image to the way you prefer to work. Figure 5.2 displays the options available.

Precise Cursors

The default cursor is a representation of the tool you have selected. For instance, the Pen tool shows a pen tip, and the Rubber Stamp tool shows a stamper. Tools such as the Brush tool and the Rubber Stamp tool change to a circle the size of the selected brush when clicked. This method is desirable when painting areas of an image or using the Rubber Stamp, but if you need to make a precise selection, you may want a crosshair cursor.

If you check the Precise Cursors option in the Editing tab (refer to Figure 5.2), the Rectangle, Lasso, Polygon, Ellipse, and Magic Wand selection tools will be

> **Note:** The Web object tools—Hotspot and Slice—use the Precise Cursor with or without the Precise Cursors option checked.

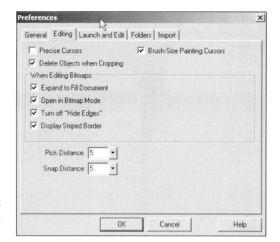

Figure 5.2
The Editing tab of the
Preferences dialog box.

changed to a precise cursor. The Pen, Pencil, and Brush drawing tools also are changed to the Precise Cursors. Other tools affected include the Eraser and the Paint Bucket tool.

Delete Objects When Cropping

When you crop an image, by default, the cropped area eliminates the extra pixels forever. If you prefer not to lose the pixels but to simply resize the image to the shape you have cropped, uncheck the Delete Objects When Cropping option in the Editing tab.

Expand to Fill Document

If you choose the Expand To Fill Document option in the Editing tab, the blue-striped border expands to surround the entire document. Everything within the document can now utilize pixel editing. If the Expand To Fill Document option is unchecked, the blue-striped border will surround only the image, limiting the editable portion to the one image's area. The option of not expanding to fill the document applies to documents that have a combination of images and vectors within them.

If you open a document that contains only one image object, it will automatically fill the document.

Open In Bitmap Mode

If you check the Open In Bitmap Mode option in the Editing tab, any image object you open will automatically open in Bitmap mode. If you prefer to automatically open in Vector mode, then uncheck this option. Of course, opting to automatically open in Vector mode would necessitate entering Bitmap mode before using the bitmap tools such as the Magic Wand tool, the selection tools, or the Rubber Stamp tool.

Turn Off Hide Edges

If you check the "Turn Off Hide Edges" option, you can hide the selection edges (also known as "marching ants"), the dotted line that moves around the selection. Hide Edges also hides the blue lines designating a selected object path and the blue-striped line surrounding an image object. These visual clues are valuable because they indicate what is selected, but sometimes they obstruct your view of an area that you need to work on, particularly if it's a small area. If you uncheck this option, the edges stay hidden until you go back and check it. Don't let the hidden feature fool you, though—the selection is still there; you just can't see it. If you forget to deselect when you complete a task and are baffled when you can't edit another area, be sure your selection is deselected first.

Display Striped Border

If the striped border, which is added to an image object by default to indicate you are in Bitmap mode, bothers you, you can uncheck this option in the Editing tab to make it go away. If you want to remove the border temporarily, choose View|Hide Edges.

Distance Settings

The Editing tab has two distance options: Pick Distance, which determines how far from an object you need to be before it is selected, and Snap Distance, which determines how close an object must be to the grid or guidelines before it snaps to either of them. Both the Pick Distance and Snap Distance options have a range of 1 to 10 pixels.

> **Note:** When you check the Turn Off Hide Edges option in the Editing tab of the Preferences menu, it is not the same as selecting View|Hide Edges. When you use View|Hide Edges, the edges are hidden only until you make a new selection.

Working with Selection Tools

The selection tools are only available when editing bitmap images. The bitmap selection tools include the Rectangular Marquee, Oval Marquee, Polygon Lasso, Lasso, and Magic Wand. The selection tools are used to isolate problem areas, to select an area to apply effects to, to color-correct, or to select any other area that needs special attention. They are also used to select specific areas to copy or to cut from an image. Each selection tool has a specific function and works in a specific way. You will learn how to use each selection tool to its full advantage. The ability to make a specific selection will enable you to alter an area of an image without the fear of going over the lines and harming other areas not intended for editing. When you make a selection, that area is the only area that will be affected by anything you do or apply.

Rectangle and Oval Marquee Tools

The Rectangle and Oval Marquee tools make selections according to their respective shapes. Click the tool of your choice and drag over an area of the image. To move a selection made with a Marquee tool, hold down the Alt/Option key and drag the selection to another location in your document. To draw a constrained shape, a perfect circle, or a square, hold down the Shift key and draw.

> **Note:** You can also set constraints on both the Rectangle and Oval Marquee tools by double-clicking the marquee icon. Figure 5.3 shows the Marquee Options panel with the submenus showing on both options.

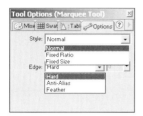

Figure 5.3
Marquee Options panel.

After you make a selection, it will be surrounded by a moving dotted line, sometimes referred to as "marching ants." This area will be isolated from the rest of the image. Within the selection area, you will be able to colorize; add effects, fills, textures, and gradients; and perform a number of other alterations.

Changing the Shape of a Selection

If you've made your selection using a rectangle or a circle, but want to add to your selection details that are outside of this shape, you can easily do so. To add to the selection, put your cursor just inside the selected area, hold down the Shift key, and drag with the Rectangle, Oval, or Lasso tool to enclose the new area, ending inside the current selection. To add a totally new selection, simply press the Shift key and make the selection. Subtracting from a selection works the same way, except you press the Alt/Option key to subtract.

Modifying a Selection

When you need to modify a selection, you have a number of options to choose from. To make a modification, choose Modify|Marquee and choose any of the options, such as Expand, Contract, Smooth, Border, Feather or Inverse The Selection, or Select Similar. The other options are to Save Selection and Restore Selection. These are used in the Selective JPEG function of optimizing images (see Chapter 6).

Figure 5.4
The Magic Wand tool's
Options tab.

Magic Wand

The Magic Wand tool works differently than all the other selection tools. The Magic Wand tool makes selections based on color. You determine the range of color in the selection by setting the tolerance. To set the tolerance of the Magic Wand tool (double-click the Magic Wand tool icon), you use the Magic Wand tool's Options tab, shown in Figure 5.4. The higher you set the Tolerance, the more colors will be added to the selection; 0 is one pixel, one color.

If your selection is pretty close to the shape you want and just needs a bit of cleaning up (a few stray pixels here and there), you can smooth out the selection by choosing Modify|Marquee|Smooth and then choosing the number of pixels you'd like to smooth. You can also expand or contract the selection by choosing Modify|Marquee|Expand or Contract.

Polygon Lasso

The Polygon Lasso tool is used for making precise selections of irregular-shaped areas. To use the Polygon Lasso tool, select it and click where you want to begin the selection. Keep adding points by clicking around the area you are selecting until the selection is complete. Double-click at the starting point to close the selection. You will see blue lines as you click another point; if the line isn't conforming to your shape, then add another point (click) a bit closer to the last point.

Using the Polygon Lasso tool has a few drawbacks. First, it is difficult to edit selections made with the Polygon Lasso tool. You can add to the selection by holding down the Shift key and clicking the area you want to add, but doing it this way is a bit flaky; sometimes the Polygon Lasso tool will conform to the area you are clicking, and sometimes it shoots out on its own. If you need to add to a Polygon Lasso selection, holding down the Shift key and adding with the Lasso tool is more accurate. To subtract from the selection, hold down the Alt/Option key and select the area to delete. The second drawback is that if you use the Polygon Lasso tool to make a selection that you want to cut from a photograph, you permanently lose the surrounding pixels.

The solution to these two problems is to use the Pen tool to make the selection. To edit this type of selection, you simply move the points; to cut the selection out, you use a mask. These topics are discussed in much more detail later in the "Masking Images" section of this chapter.

Applying Feathering to a Marquee Edge

Feathering the edges of a selection aids in inserting a portion of one image into another image, avoiding sharp, distinctive edges. The feathered edge is the transition from being opaque to being transparent. These are the steps to take to apply feathering to any marquee edge:

1. Make a selection with a Marquee selection tool.

2. In the Marquee tool's Options panel (accessed by double-clicking any Marquee tool), under the Edge choices, select Feather, and enter the number of pixels wide you'd like to have feathered. The larger the number, the larger the area affected.

To add a feathered edge to a photo, follow these steps:

1. Open any photo.

2. Select the Oval Marquee tool and draw an ellipse over the part of the photo you'd like cut out.

3. Double-click the Oval Marquee tool and in the Marquee tool's Options panel, select Feather and 30 pixels (less if your image is small).

4. You can now copy (Ctrl+C/Cmd+C) and paste (Ctrl+V/Cmd+V) into a new document.

Inverting Selections

Often, you will want to invert a selection. For example, if a background is easier to select than the object you want selected, you would simply select the background and choose Modify|Marquee|Select Inverse. If you are working on part of an image that is selected and then want to work on the rest of the image, you could invert the selection.

In the preceding feathering example of the oval picture, you could add another step:

5. Choose Modify|Marquee|Select Inverse and press the Delete key to clear the background of the image.

PROJECT Using the Polygon Tool to Select

In this project, you will get hands-on practice using the Polygon Lasso tool to precisely select a large portion of an image. Getting this selection just right has some challenging aspects. The selection needs to be accurate and not loose, because it is going to be used in a later project in which the background is going to be severely blurred. If the selection isn't accurate, the edges will be noticeable. Follow these steps:

1. Open the file called popout.png in the Chapter 5 resources folder on this book's CD-ROM. You will be selecting the foreground elements of the computer and the two people. Figure 5.5 shows the image you are drawing the selection around.

Figure 5.5
The photo before the selection is made.

2. Double-click the Polygon Lasso tool. In the Polygon Lasso tool's Options panel, select Feather and 3 pixels wide. Start by clicking on top of the computer on the far left side. Get as close to the edge as possible. Go up the teacher's finger and around the girl. Take special care around the headset; finish going around the teacher, down her back along a straight line to the bottom of the document, across to the left side, and up to the starting point. Double-click the starting point to close the path.

3. If you see areas you need to add to the selection, then hold down the Shift key, select the Lasso tool (not the Polygon Lasso tool), and add the areas.

4. In areas where you may have gotten too much of the background, hold down the Alt/Option key and with the Lasso tool, draw around the area to deselect. This image will be used in another project to alter the background, but because it's a marquee selection you won't be able to save it. Figure 5.6 shows the photo with the foreground selected.

Figure 5.6
After the polygon selection is made.

Repairing Images

Old family photos are a wonderful source of interesting imagery. More and more of these types of photos are finding their way onto the Web, especially with the 1950s style being so popular. Old photos are great candidates for repair, but almost any image you use will probably need something fixed on it. Special care needs to be taken when repairing an image with texture, patterns, or shadows. That pretty much covers all images, because most images have at least one of these qualities.

You will use two repair techniques. One technique uses the Rubber Stamp tool, and the other uses the Blur filter. The Blur filter is included because of its unique use in image retouching. The Rubber Stamp tool is a must-learn, because it is the tool you will use most often to repair images.

Using the Rubber Stamp

The Rubber Stamp tool works as you would expect a rubber stamp to work. Press it in the ink (over a part of the image) and then press the stamp's impression in another area. The Rubber Stamp tool excels at covering blemishes and removing small items from a photo. It gets really challenging when you try to repair a highly textured or patterned area. To learn how to stamp, where to stamp, and how to get the stamping samples, follow these steps:

1. Open the stamping.gif file from the Chapter 5 resources folder on this book's CD-ROM. You are going to be removing only the horizontal line from this image, leaving the vertical lines intact.

2. Select the Rubber Stamp tool from the toolbar. The first thing that you will do is to remove the horizontal line from the stamping.gif image. This image presents a few problems. It has a distinct pattern, so the stamping needs to be done carefully, and you will be removing a line near the vertical line, which must be done without affecting the vertical line.

Note: The Aligned option means that the sampling spot is aligned with the Rubber Stamp tool; as the Rubber Stamp tool moves, so does the sampling point.

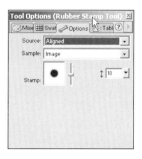

Figure 5.7
The Rubber Stamp tool's Options tab.

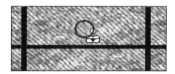

Figure 5.8
The placement of the Rubber Stamp's sampling point.

Note: Double-clicking the Zoom tool returns your document size to 100 percent.

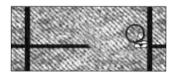

Figure 5.9
The Rubber Stamp tool in action.

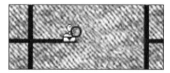

Figure 5.10
New sample size and location.

Figure 5.11
No noticeable pattern effect.

3. You need to set the size of the area you are sampling from. To do this, double-click the Rubber Stamp tool, which opens the Options tab (see Figure 5.7). Leave Source set to Aligned (the options are Aligned or Fixed) and set the Stamp size to 18.

4. You need to set a sampling point, which is the area you are copying pixels from. To set the first point, click just above the horizontal line; see Figure 5.8 (a stroke has been added to the sampling point for easier viewing; normally, it is not this thick). Then, click the Rubber Stamp tool just below and a bit to the right of the sampling point. (You will see why in a moment.) You can see the placement of the sampling point and the Rubber Stamp tool in Figure 5.8.

5. Click the Zoom tool (magnifying glass) in the toolbar, and then click your image to zoom in closer. Click the Rubber Stamp tool one time just over the horizontal line, move it a bit to the right, and click again. You will notice that as you move to the right, the sampling point moves with you; this is the result of the Aligned Source setting. Repeat this action until you reach the vertical line. Figure 5.9 shows why you placed the Rubber Stamp tool a bit to the right of the sampling point. To remove the horizontal line all the way up to the vertical line, place the Rubber Stamp against the line. If the sampling point were directly above the Rubber Stamp tool, you would be copying part of the vertical line also.

6. Look at Figure 5.9 again. Do you notice anything wrong? You can see a distinct pattern in the area just removed. Try a different sampling position and size for the left side, and move the Rubber Stamp tool a bit to the left of the sampling point to avoid sampling from the left vertical line. Double-click the Rubber Stamp tool and change the Stamp size to 8 pixels.

7. To sample an area, hold down the Alt/Option key and click to set the sample area; set it as close to the horizontal line as you can get it, without touching the horizontal line (see Figure 5.10).

8. Click the horizontal line to remove it, clicking only once at a time. If you click and drag, definite blurring will occur. In Figure 5.11, you can see that the pattern effect isn't noticeable. The closer you can get to the area being repaired, the less noticeable the repair is. Sampling points could also be taken from the bottom of the line, as well as the top, to maintain pattern integrity.

9. You have one more feature to try out. Double-click the Rubber Stamp tool to bring up the Rubber Stamp tool's Options tab. Change the Source from Aligned to Fixed, which sets a sampling point that doesn't move. To copy the horse soldier in the top-right corner to the top-left corner of stamping.gif, change the sampling point size to 75 pixels. Click in the center of the horse and the circle will surround it perfectly (see Figure 5.12).

10. Move the Rubber Stamp tool to the location you want the image stamped to and click. That's all there is to it.

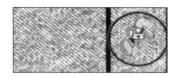

Figure 5.12
Fixed sampling point set.

You don't even have to sample from the current document. If you have another document open, you can set your sampling points from it and stamp onto the current document. Getting really good at using the Rubber Stamp tool takes some practice, patience, and a bit of trial and error. If you have an image of someone's face with wrinkles or skin discolorations that you want to remove or repair, be sure to sample from all around the flawed area to maintain skin texture.

> **Note:** On my version of Fireworks 4 on a PC, it was difficult to reset the sampling point using the Alt key. Sometimes it worked, and sometimes not. If this happens, click the pointer tool, and then select the Rubber Stamp and simply click to reset your sampling point.

Applying Blurring

Blurring an image or parts of an image can produce some pretty great effects, as you'll see in the following projects. Using the Blur filter can hide defects or make an image seem to pop off of the page. To use the Blur filter in Fireworks, follow these steps:

1. Select the image or part of an image you'd like to blur.

2. Choose Xtras|Blur and then select from one of three choices: Blur, which has no options, Blur More, which has no options, or Gaussian Blur, for which you set the pixel amount of the blur.

3. With Blur and Blur More, all you do is select and it is applied. With the Gaussian Blur, you click OK after you set the pixel amount.

> **Note:** You will be able to see a preview of the Gaussian amount currently set, but if you change the number, it may not automatically change the preview. If this is the case, you need to click OK and choose Edit|Undo if you don't like the effect.

PROJECT Removing Wrinkles

You will be amazed at how easy it is to take 10 or 20 years off of someone's face. This can be done without ever changing a single pixel on the original image. To remove the wrinkles from a photo of a person's face, follow these steps:

1. Open the beforewrinkles.png file from the Chapter 5 resources folder on this book's CD-ROM. Figure 5.13 shows the woman who would like 20 years taken off her face without plastic surgery.

Figure 5.13
Lady with wrinkled face.

2. Zoom in a bit to get a better look at the wrinkles. Double-click the Lasso selection tool and, in the tool's Options tab, select Feather and a value of 1. Draw a selection around the wrinkles near the left eye. Don't get too close to the eye.

3. Hold down the Shift key and, with the Lasso tool, continue to select any area on the woman's face that is showing age; for example, between the eyes, near the right eye, large areas on both sides of the mouth, a bit above the upper lip, and the neck area (see Figure 5.14).

Figure 5.14
The wrinkles selected on the woman's face.

4. With the selections made, choose Edit|Copy or press Ctrl+C/Cmd+C. Add a new layer by clicking the yellow folder at the bottom of the Layers panel.

5. Be sure the second layer is selected and choose Edit|Paste (or press Ctrl+V/Cmd+V, which is a bit easier). The reason you pasted the selections is so that any changes made to the selections will not affect the original image. Click the eye icon next to the Background layer to turn it off. This looks quite odd, but this is all that will be affected by the next change. Click the eye icon back on.

6. With the second layer still selected, choose Xtras|Blur|Gaussian Blur, enter "4.5", and click OK.

7. The results are much better, but you can try to remove even more wrinkles. Make new selections around the eyes and any other wrinkled areas that didn't quite get removed. Copy, add a new layer, and paste.

8. Choose Xtras|Blur|Gaussian Blur and enter a value of 4.

9. You can see that the adjustment made is a bit too much, because some of the texture of the skin has been lost, and it's obvious that a touch-up has been made. To fix that, simply lower the opacity of the last layer with the most recent changes. In the Layers panel, change 100 to 50 percent (far top-left corner).

10. One more alteration was made; this woman's teeth are far too yellow. With the Lasso selection tool (Feather of 1 still selected), go around the teeth, top and bottom. Choose Xtras|Adjust Colors|Hue and Saturation and set the Lightness to 30. Be sure the Hue and Saturation are both at 0 or you will really get some funny-looking teeth. Click OK.

11. Deselect the teeth (Ctrl+D/Cmd+D) and you are done; the results are shown in Figure 5.15 and in this book's Color Section.

Figure 5.15
A much younger looking woman.

PROJECT Making an Image Pop Out

This project uses the same image you practiced on using the Polygon Lasso tool; Steps 1 through 4 are the same as in the previous exercise using this tool, and Step 5 adds a blur to the background:

1. Open the file called popout.png in the Chapter 5 resources folder on this book's CD-ROM. You will be selecting the foreground elements of the computer and the two people.

2. Double-click the Polygon Lasso tool. In the Polygon Lasso tool's Options tab, select Feather and use 3 pixels wide. Start by clicking on top of the computer on the far-left side. Get as close to the edge as possible. Go up the teacher's finger and around the girl. Take special care around the headset; finish going around the teacher, down her back and then along a straight line to the bottom of the document, across to the left side, and up to the starting point. Double-click the starting point to close the path.

3. If you see areas you need to add to the selection, then hold down the Shift key, select the Lasso tool (not the Polygon Lasso tool), and add the areas.

4. In areas where you may have gotten too much of the background, hold down the Alt/Option key and, with the Lasso tool, draw around the area to deselect (see Figure 5.6 to see the photo with the fore-ground selected).

5. Select Modify|Marquee|Select Inverse.

6. Select Xtras|Blur|Gaussian Blur and a Blur setting of 8; use a higher number if you want the background blurred even more. Click OK. The foreground is now the only focus of the image, as shown in Figure 5.16.

Figure 5.16
The foreground of the image now pops out.

Adjusting Tone and Color

Traditionally, tonal and color adjustments have been destructive in the sense that once you made a change, pixels were lost permanently. The only way to make adjustments if you went too far (removed or adjusted more than you wanted to) or changed your mind was to start over with a saved version of the image. Fireworks has now made tonal and color correction a Live Effect, meaning they are totally editable. The best way to adjust the tonal range—the shadows, midtones, and highlights—is to use the Levels dialog box, in which you can get visual clues to the problem areas. Changing a color or adding color can be done quickly and easily using the Hue and Saturation filter.

Using Levels to Adjust Tonal Range

The Levels dialog box puts a lot of control at your fingertips; Figure 5.17 shows the controls available from within the Levels dialog box. You will be using most of these controls in the following exercises and projects.

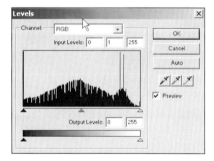

Figure 5.17
The Levels dialog box.

Reading the Histogram

The Levels dialog box is accessed by selecting an image and choosing Xtras|Adjust Color|Levels. At the top of the dialog box is a box containing the letters RGB; if you click the arrow next to it, you can select individual channels, Red, Green, or Blue.

The center image of the dialog box, which resembles a mountain, is the histogram. The spikes and peaks show you where the detail in your image is. On the left are the shadows, in the middle are the midtones, and to the right are the highlights. Ideally, a balanced histogram is desired. Too many shadows will hide detail, too many highlights will cause the image to appear washed out, and too many midtones will cause the image to appear dull and lifeless.

The histogram in Figure 5.17 has a good balance of shadows, midtones, and highlights. A histogram that is lacking severely in one or more of the areas is a great candidate for tonal adjustments. As you do some of the projects in this section, you can compare the before and after histograms to get a feel for how they look when an image has the proper tonal balance.

The sliders just below the histogram add shadows if you drag the left slider to the right, and add highlights if you move the right slider to the left. The middle slider adjusts the midtones. A quick way to adjust tonal balance is to move the shadow and highlight sliders to the base of the "mountain." You can do this in RGB, but then all the channels are affected at once. The result is much better if you make the adjustments in each channel.

PROJECT Correcting the Tonal Range of an Image

To correct the tonal range of an image, follow these steps:

1. Open the weddingbefore.png file from the Chapter 5 resource folder on the book's CD-ROM, shown in Figure 5.18. It's pretty washed-out looking.

Figure 5.18
The photo before tonal adjustments are made.

2. Choose Xtras|Color Adjust|Levels. Figure 5.19 shows the Levels dialog box with the histogram for this image. This image has quite a few spikes and peaks all over it. As a test and to demonstrate a point, leave the Channel set at RGB for now, move the left (black) slider directly below the histogram just to the edge of the "mountain" where the shadow detail starts, and move the right slider to the right edge where the highlight detail begins. See Figure 5.20 for the settings.

Figure 5.19
(Left) The Levels dialog box showing the histogram of the before image.

Figure 5.20
(Right) The changed histogram in the RGB channel.

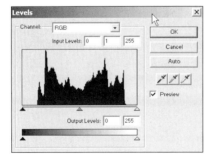
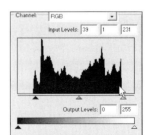

3. As you can see, the image is now a bit better, but it could be much better. Click Cancel and choose Xtras|Adjust Colors|Levels to bring up the Levels dialog box again. This time, make the tonal adjustments in each color channel.

4. Select the Red channel, move the left slider to the beginning of the shadow detail, and move the right slider to the beginning of the highlight detail. Do this for the Green and the Blue channels as well. Figure 5.21 shows each channel after it has been adjusted.

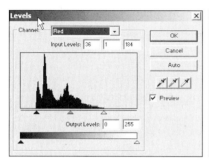 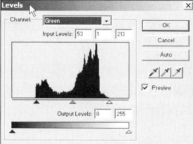 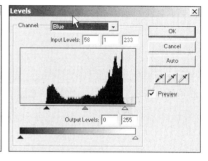

Figure 5.21
The histogram of each separate RGB channel.

5. Select the RGB channel to note the changed histogram. It now has many fewer spikes and peaks and it appears more rounded. Click OK to accept the changes. The result is shown in Figure 5.22; a much better representation is included in this book's Color Section.

Figure 5.22
Image with tonal corrections made.

Setting the Highlights and Shadows with the Eyedropper

To the right of the histogram in the Levels dialog box are three Eyedropper tools. The first one is used to select a shadow point; the second is used to select a neutral gray area (the midpoint); and the third is used to select a highlight point.

To use the Eyedropper tools, you click the one you want and take a sampling from the image. When you choose an area to sample the highlights (the lightest area you can find), everything brighter than the highlight you sampled will be white. With the shadow point, everything darker than the point you select will become black, making the image too dark if your sample isn't dark enough. It's quite difficult at times to determine where the lightest or darkest area is. Fireworks doesn't provide color information from the Levels dialog box, so follow these steps as a workaround:

1. Open the Info panel (Alt+Shift+F12/Option+Shift+12), click the right-pointing arrow, and select RGB.

2. Click the Eyedropper tool and try to locate the darkest point in your image. As you pass the Eyedropper over the image, look in the lower-left corner of the Info palette and you will see the RGB numbers for the area. Locate the closest number to 0; a range of 5 to 10 is fine. Remember the area.

3. Repeat for the highlight area, except that the numbers should be in the range of 240 to 250. Take note of the location again.

4. To adjust the levels: Proceed by choosing Xtras|Adjust Colors|Levels.

5. Click the Select Shadow Color Eyedropper tool and sample from the area you located in Step 2.

6. Click the Select Highlight Color Eyedropper tool and click the lightest area you located in Step 3.

7. Making changes using these two eyedropper tools often is enough to remove any color cast and fix the tonal adjustments. If the image is still a bit too dark or light, adjust the sliders at the very bottom of the Levels dialog box. The slider on the left, which appears black, will lighten when moved to the right. The slider on the right, which appears white, will darken when moved to the left.

8. When you are satisfied with the results, click OK.

Adjusting Color Casts

If an image has a green cast (photos taken under florescent lighting often do), then select the Green channel from the Levels dialog box and move the middle slider a bit to the right. This adds a little magenta, which neutralizes the green cast.

If you have a blue cast, then select the Blue channel and move the middle slider to the right, adding yellow.

Note: To instantly change your cursor to a precise cursor, press Caps Lock. The precise cursor remains only if you hold the Caps key or the left mouse button while you use the precise cursor.

Note: When you add a color on the opposite side of the color spectrum, it neutralizes a color cast. The opposite of green is magenta, the opposite of blue is yellow, and the opposite of red is cyan.

PROJECT Correcting the Tonal Range Using the Eyedroppers

To evaluate the difference between tonal corrections made by adjusting the levels in individual channels and tonal corrections made by adjusting the tonal value using the Eyedropper tools, follow these steps:

1. In the Chapter 5 resource folder on the CD-ROM, open weddingbefore.png and select it.

2. Open the Info panel (Alt+Shift+F12/Option+Shift+12), click the right-pointing arrow, and select RGB.

3. Click the Eyedropper tool and try to locate the darkest point in your image. As you pass the Eyedropper over the image, look in the lower-left corner of the Info palette and you will see the RGB numbers for the area. Locate the closest number to 0; a range of 5 to 10 is fine. It's really tough to find the darkest spot in this image (the sleeve just below the hand is the best I could find). Remember the area.

4. Repeat for the highlight area, except that the numbers should be in the range of 240 to 250. The lightest area I could locate was the highlight at the top of the veil; again, in this image, it is difficult to find a bright enough spot. Take note of the location again.

5. Choose Xtras|Adjust Colors|Levels.

6. Click the Shadow Eyedropper tool and click the darkest spot you could find in the image.

7. Click the Highlight Eyedropper tool and click the lightest spot you could find using the Info panel.

You can see right away that this adjustment isn't nearly as nice as the one done within the color channels. The highlights and the shadows are too muted to get a good sampling for the adjustment. You have much more control over the range of tone within the channels.

PROJECT Adjusting the Levels for a Snow Scene

This project will convert a muted, lifeless photo of snow-covered pine trees into a scene that is sharp and interesting:

1. In the Chapter 5 folder on the CD-ROM, open snow.png.

2. The highlight area and shadow area have been marked for you in Figure 5.23. With the image selected, choose Xtras|Adjust Color|Levels.

3. Click the Shadow Eyedropper tool and sample in the dark area circled in Figure 5.23.

Figure 5.23
Snow scene with the highlight and shadow areas marked.

4. Click the Highlight Eyedropper tool and sample in the light area circled in Figure 5.23.

5. Click OK when you are finished. This image will be used again in the "Adjusting Hue and Saturation" section later in this chapter. Choose File|Save As, and name your image. Figure 5.24 shows how much sharper this image is now.

Figure 5.24
Snow scene with the levels adjusted.

Using Auto Levels

Auto Levels applies Fireworks' best guess as to which tonal areas need correction and adds the maximum tonal changes. Often, it works great. For instance, the preceding project with the wedding couple under water looks great with Auto Level applied, but try it on the globe.png file (in the Chapter 5 folder on the CD-ROM) and see what happens. Select the file and choose Xtras|Adjust Color|Auto Levels. It looks pretty neat, but the purple, yellow, and dark blue instead of the orange glow and black silhouettes may not be what you are looking for. It's always a good idea to know how to fix an image yourself so when an automatic tool, such as Auto Levels, doesn't do the job, you can.

Adjusting Brightness and Contrast

The Brightness and Contrast filter deserves a mention here because far too many people grab it to lighten or darken an image. Although this filter is made for adjusting brightness and contrast, it's just not the "best" tool for the job. The best tools to use are the Curve and Levels filters. If you are intimidated with levels and curves, though, or need a quick fix, use the Brightness and Contrast filter. This filter, however, makes too drastic a change to the entire image, and you have extremely low control. If you want to control your results, practice with levels and curves. They really are not too hard to understand once you start practicing using them. If you do choose the Brightness and Contrast filter, the best way to use it is to select your image, choose Xtras|Adjust Color|Brightness/Contrast, and click OK.

Understanding Curves

The Curve filter is similar to the Levels filter except that it offers more precise control. Curves enable you to adjust not only the highlights, midtones, and shadows, but also any color along the tonal range, without affecting other colors. The only thing lacking in the Curves dialog box is a histogram, which shows you what areas of shadow, highlight, or midtones need to be adjusted.

The Curves dialog box, shown in Figure 5.25, may look pretty intimidating at first glance. Actually, it is quite intimidating. You have more control over adjusting color if you are familiar with how to lock down color sections and adjust just certain areas of the curve (where you see the diagonal line), and know how to locate specific color problems. These kinds of adjustments are beyond the scope of this book, however. What needs to be done to correct the majority of photos can be done in the Levels panel.

> **Note:** Changes made using levels and/or curves are global changes, which affect the entire image or selection you are working on. While in the Levels or Curve filter dialog box, you cannot pick and choose where to apply the changes.

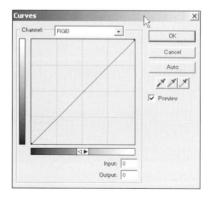

Figure 5.25
The Curves dialog box.

The Input box displays the changes made on the horizontal axis, which affects the brightness. The Output box displays the changes made on the vertical axis, which is representative of the new brightness value.

Adjusting Hue and Saturation

The Hue and Saturation filter changes the color hue of a selected image or a selection. This filter works great to add subtle color or to totally change the color of an image or object. This is the filter to use when you want to change the overall color of an image. You've seen Web sites that use the same image header throughout the site, except that different sections utilize different colors; this is the tool to use to achieve that effect.

To apply the Hue and Saturation filter, make a selection and choose Xtras|Adjust Color|Hue And Saturation. Move the sliders for the Hue, Saturation, and Color until you get the desired results. Select the Colorize option to change the color.

PROJECT Adding Color to a Bland Image

In this project, you will use the same photo of the snow-covered trees for which you adjusted the tonal value. To add a bit of interest to the photo while keeping it realistic, you will add some color to the pine trees:

1. Open your saved version of the snow scene with the adjusted levels that you did in the previous project. Select the Crop tool and crop around the large trees; also leave the one stand of smaller trees in the background. This little section will be needed later.

2. Select the Polygon selection tool and make a loose selection around the main body of large trees and the little trees. You don't need to be exact around the branches, just close. But, do take extra care not to get the sky in the selection.

3. Choose Xtras|Adjust Colors|Hue And Saturation. The Hue/Saturation dialog box opens, shown in Figure 5.26.

Figure 5.26
The Hue/Saturation dialog box.

4. Don't check the Colorize box. To get a deep green, which looks realistic, use a Hue of –72, Saturation of –40, and Lightness of 7. You can experiment with the Colorize option if you'd like. The colors are not as deep as you get with the box unchecked. Click OK when you find the color that appeals to you.

5. The trees are now green. If your selection was too loose, you will see a green shadow in the sky area. If this is the case, then simply select

Edit|Undo and use the Alt/Option key to subtract from your selection. In either case, *do not* turn off the selection yet. If you already have, choose Edit|Undo to get back to the selection.

6. Another problem needs to be corrected, however. The snowcaps are also tinted green. You need to make a small alteration to the selection. Select the Lasso selection tool, hold down the Alt/Option key, and subtract from the tree edges to alter the selection edge, making it not touch any of the branches that have sky between them. You are going to lighten the snowcaps, so the selection can be brought in from the edges of the trees some. Also remove any of the dark shadows under the trees from your selection if the shadow is in the selection now. The selection boundaries are shown in Figure 5.27.

Figure 5.27
The selection around the trees.

7. Choose Xtras|Adjust Colors|Levels. Remember that the highlight sample you take with the Eyedropper tool makes any highlight colors lighter than the sample white. With this in mind, select a medium shade of green from one of the snowcaps on the branches. If the image goes too white, then cancel and come back to this point, and then select a bit lighter green.

8. The shadows within the tree were also tinted with a dark green; to correct that, select the Shadow Eyedropper tool and sample the shadow outside of your selection area. There you have it, a tonal-corrected and colorized stand of pine trees (see Figure 5.28).

Figure 5.28

A stand of pine trees with color added.

Masking Images

Fireworks 4 enables you to combine an image to a path or use an image as a mask object. A mask object is what you apply the mask to; it resides above the image to be masked. (A mask isn't applied directly to the image.) A mask object contains a fill, which affects the pixels of the image or object that is being masked. The effect the mask has on the object being masked depends on the black and white values of the mask; where the mask is white, it will be transparent; where the mask has black, the image shows through. The varying degrees of gray determine the amount of transparency. Live Effects and styles can be added to a path object and used as a mask object.

Using a Bitmap Mask

You can draw a bitmap mask by using the bitmap tools, such as the Paint Brush, Pen, Rectangle, Oval, or Polygon. For example, if you have an image that you want to fade into another image, you would use the Rectangle drawing tool to draw over the image. Or, you can use an existing image. To demonstrate using an existing image, follow these steps:

1. Open the weddingafter.png file from the Chapter 5 resource folder on this book's CD-ROM.

2. Open the bear.gif file from the Chapter 5 resource folder (see Figure 5.29).

3. Drag the bear image on top of the wedding water photo.

4. You need to select both the bear and the wedding photo. Because you can't see them both visually, you will need to select them by Shift+selecting them from the Layers panel.

5. Choose Modify|Mask|Group As Mask (see Figure 5.30).

Figure 5.29
A bear to be used as a mask.

Figure 5.30
A photo inside the shape
of a bear.

Using a Vector Path as a Mask

You can use any vector path (shapes made using vector tools such as the Pen) as a mask to cut out the image below it. The image will be masked to the vector path. To mask to a vector path, follow these steps:

1. Select the vector path/shape you want to use and Shift+select the bitmap image.

2. Choose Modify|Mask|Group As Mask.

Adding Transparency to a Mask

Adding transparency to a mask is the most frequently used technique for seamlessly blending images together or for removing parts of an image. Transparency is achieved by using a black-and-white gradient fill in the masking object or image. Wherever there is black, the underlying image will be visible; wherever there is white, the underlying image will be invisible. The shades of gray render the transparency according to the lightness or darkness of the gray. To add transparency to a mask, follow these steps:

1. Open any image.

2. Click the yellow folder icon on the bottom of the Layers panel to add a new layer.

Note: Fireworks 4 help added the version 3 instructions for using a vector as a mask, which specify to copy or cut the path and then to paste it as a mask. This is no longer necessary; simply use Group As Mask, just like you would for a bitmap mask group. The old method will still work, but the new one is a bit easier.

Note: If you want to preserve the transparency mask or alpha channel from Fireworks to be used in other applications, use the PNG32 format for export and set the Matte color to Transparent in the Optimize panel.

To open a PNG file that contains an Alpha channel in Photoshop, use the Magic Wand tool to select the dark area containing the transparency, and then delete the selected area to return to the correct display of the image.

3. Select the Rectangle drawing tool and drag a rectangle (on the second layer) over about half of your image.

4. Open the Fill panel (Shift+F7), select Linear from the Fill category, and choose Black, White from the Preset gradient color sets.

5. Shift+select the rectangle and the image and choose Modify|Mask|Group as Mask. Notice that where there is black in the rectangle, you can see the image, and where there is white, it fades into the image below.

Editing a Masked Group

To alter where the transparency is located, or the amount of transparency in certain parts of the mask, select the object with the gradient and then choose Edit|Select All. In the Layers panel, click on the gradient mask icon (there is a little pen icon on it). The gradient handles will now be available, and you will see a round handle and a square one. By clicking and dragging the round handle, you move the position of the black fill or the area that is not transparent (unless your gradient is filled with the colors reversed). Clicking and dragging the square handle does the opposite. These handles can be moved to any position on or off the document window.

To edit the gradients color position, choose Edit|Select All and click the gradient icon in the Layers panel. To move the position of the gradient, drag the handles until the gradient is positioned where you'd like it to be. For complete instructions on using gradient fills, refer to Chapter 2.

To modify the underlying image of the mask group, select the mask icon in the Layers panel and make your changes.

PROJECT Avoiding Halos on Image Cutouts

A technique you will most likely repeat again and again is cutting out an image from another image. One of the biggest problems designers face when using this technique is a "halo" around the image they cut out. This halo effect occurs because part of the background is *anti-aliased* with the edges of the image. For example, if the background is black and you are transferring the cutout to a white background, some varying shade of black will be mixed in with the image edges where it was anti-aliased. Numerous workarounds exist to avoid this effect, but all you need is one that works. This project will remove a yellow bag from a hot-pink background.

Cutting Out Using a Selection Tool

The selection tools can be used to remove images, but making precise selections is difficult if the selection is complicated. The other drawback is that after you deselect the selection, you can only get it back by using the Edit|Undo command. If you save the file, the selection isn't retrievable. Follow these steps:

1. Open bag.png from the Chapter 5 resource file on the book's CD-ROM.

2. Double-click the Polygon Lasso tool. In the tool's Options tab, choose Feather using 3 pixels wide.

3. Make a selection of the edges of the bag and tissue paper. If your selection is overinclusive or underinclusive, then use the Shift key to add to the selection or the Alt/Option key to subtract (see Figure 5.31).

Figure 5.31
The selection outline of the bag and tissue paper.

4. Copy by pressing Ctrl+C/Cmd+C or by choosing Edit|Copy.

5. Open a new document. What is really nice is that the new document size is automatically the right size to fit what you have copied to the clipboard. Make the background transparent and click OK.

6. Paste the contents of the clipboard into the new document by pressing Ctrl+V/Cmd+V or by choosing Edit|Paste.

7. To test your edges, choose Modify|Canvas Color and choose Custom; try white and then black. If your selection was good, the bag should look great, with no jaggies or halos.

8. Because this particular image is a photo, it is best suited to the JPEG format; select JPEG in the Optimize panel with a quality of 80. If the background you are placing this image on is anything other than white, select the background color from the Matte settings (or type in the Hex number) and export (see Chapter 6).

Cutting Out Using a Mask

You may find this technique the better choice for cutting out objects, because you have much better control over the selection area. By using a mask, you can edit the boundaries of your selection at any time by selecting the various points with the Subselection tool and repositioning them. You will primarily use a vector path as a mask using the Pen tool, but sometimes a soft-edged Paint Brush tool might be better suited to paint the edges of the selection. To cut out an image using a mask, follow these steps:

1. Open the bag.png file from Chapter 5 resources folder on the book's CD-ROM.

2. Make your selection using the Pen tool. Click points around the bag and tissue.

3. To fine-tune your selection, zoom in and choose the Subselection tool (the white arrow) and click a point that needs adjusting. Click and drag the point to the desired location.

4. Open the Fill panel (Shift+F7), select a solid fill of black, and set the Edge to Feather; 2 or 3 pixels will do. Click the Stroke tab and select None for the stroke. The feather will give a smooth edge to your selection.

5. Shift+select the path and the image (bag).

6. Choose Modify|Mask|Group As Mask.

7. To test your edges, choose Modify|Canvas Color and check white, for a white background; repeat and choose Custom using black for the background.

8. Save a copy of this file before you export. (You'll need it again.)

Note: After you test your image, if you think the edges are too blurry, then go back and change the Feather setting of the path to a lower number.

PROJECT Producing a Composite Image

A composite image is an image containing pieces of other images. Putting all the pieces together can be challenging. You want each item to blend seamlessly and appear to belong in the composition. Composite images often combine elements together to convey an idea, thought, or concept. In this project, you will combine two image objects, which you will first remove from their original backgrounds onto a new background:

1. Open the mousemap.png file from the Chapter 5 resource folder and minimize it for now. Also open one of your saved bag cutouts.

2. Open bag.gif.

3. Use the Polygon Lasso tool to make a selection of the tissue paper.

4. Choose Xtras|Adjust Colors|Hue And Saturation. Check the Colorize option and use the following settings: Hue 31, Saturation 47, and Lightness 24 (for this example, you may use any color you'd like); click OK. Drag the bag onto the map background and position it in the lower-right corner.

5. Open the compass.png file from the Chapter 5 resource file, double-click the Pen tool, and set the Edge of the fill (in the Fill panel) to Feather with a value of 6 pixels.

6. Using the Pen tool, click around the compass, starting from the right-top corner; go around the compass, across the bottom, and up the side to connect the path.

7. Open the Fill panel (Shift+F7) and select Linear in the Fill category. Also in the Fill panel, click the preset gradient color drop-down menu and choose black and white.

8. You need to alter the angle and positioning of the fill. Select the gradient object to see the gradient handles (or click the mask icon in the Layers panel), and move the circle to the position shown in Figure 5.32.

9. Select the gradient and the bitmap image by Shift+clicking. Choose Modify|Mask|Group As Mask.

10. If you have a problem similar to Figure 5.33, an obvious line, then select Edit|All. Click the gradient icon in the Layers panel and from the Stroke panel, select the Airbrush, Basic with a 6-pixel stroke. Set the color to white (which will make the stroke transparent).

11. Drag the compass onto the map and position it in the left corner. The angle with the transparency isn't quite right, so it needs to be adjusted.

12. Select the compass and choose Modify|Transform|Free Transform. Hover the mouse over the compass edge until you see the Curved rotate tool. Move and rotate until you get a position you like.

13. Unselect by clicking outside of the image, and your composition is ready for export.

Figure 5.32
Adjusting the gradient fill.

Figure 5.33
An obvious line around the compass.

 A Shopping Spree

A composite image can convey ideas or concepts you want your user to respond to. The image in Figure 5.34 could imply that you need to make a shopping list, using your mouse to locate a place to shop anywhere in a global market via the Internet.

To make this composite image consisting of two background images and three other elements, follow these steps:

1. Open the pencil.png file in the Chapter 5 resource folder on the book's CD-ROM.

2. Open the rose.png file in the Chapter 5 resource folder. Add a new layer by clicking the yellow folder icon at the bottom of the Layers panel.

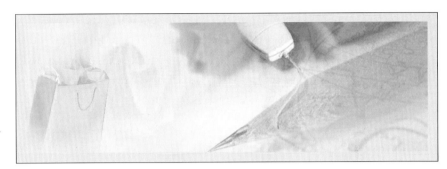

Figure 5.34
A composite image conveying
Internet shopping.

3. Select the Rectangle drawing tool and draw a rectangle to cover the
   entire rose.

4. From the Fill panel (Shift+F7), choose Linear and black and white for
   the fill. Shift+select the rose and the gradient-filled rectangle, and
   choose Modify|Mask|Group As Mask.

5. The gradient position needs to be altered. If you select the image and
   can't see the gradient handles, then select the mask icon on the gradient layer in the Layers panel. The gradient position used is shown in
   Figure 5.35.

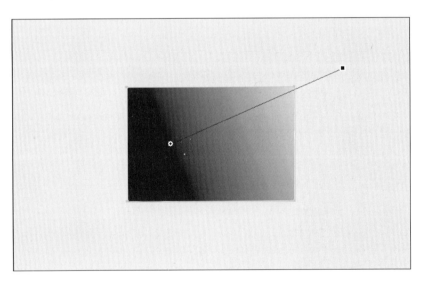

Figure 5.35
The gradient position used for
the rose.

6. Drag the rose to the right corner of the pencil background and click
   and drag the outside point; stretch it to the top of the image and to the
   right a little bit.

7. To help the rose blend into the background better, lower the opacity to
   70 percent (Fill panel in the left-hand corner).

8. The next element is the bag.png that you worked with earlier. Open it, draw a selection with the Pen tool around the bag and the tissue, and add a mask (full instructions for the masked bag are in the "Cutting Out Using a Mask" section earlier in this chapter). If you have saved a version of the bag with a mask already, you can skip this step.

9. From the Fill panel (Shift+F7), choose Linear and the preset gradient of black and white. Select the gradient and drag the handles so that the black is at the top of the bag and the white fades into the bottom of the bag. See Figure 5.36 to see the gradient placement.

10. Shift+select the bag and its mask and choose Modify|Mask|Group As Mask. Drag the bag onto the composite image and position it. Drag one of the corners in to make the bag a bit smaller.

11. Open the mousemap.png file from the Chapter 5 resource folder on the book's CD-ROM. Using the Pen tool, make a selection around the mouse and part of the cord. From the Fill panel, choose Solid and fill with black.

12. Select the selection and the background image and choose Modify|Mask|Group As Mask. Save this file as "mouse.png".

13. Open the mousemap.png file again and add a new layer by clicking the yellow folder icon in the Layers panel. This time, select the Rectangle drawing tool and draw a rectangle over the entire image. From the Fill panel, select Linear and the black and white preset gradient. Adjust the gradient with the handles so that the black is in the upper-right corner and the white is in the lower-right corner.

14. Shift+select the background and the rectangle and choose Modify|Mask|Mask As Group.

15. Drag the mousemap onto the composite image. Move it to fit in the lower-right corner. Set the Transparency of this layer to 30 percent in the Layers panel. If it isn't blending properly, click the mask icon to edit it (see Figure 5.37 to see the mask icon in the Layers panel) and adjust the transparency to fade into the background.

16. The last element is the mouse.png you saved, which you should open now. Drag the mouse onto the composite and position it on top of the very faded mouse in the background.

17. Select the Crop tool and crop the document to the desired size.

You can open the pencilshavings.png file and examine the Layers panel. By clicking the mask icon, you can see all the gradient placements used.

Figure 5.36
The gradient placement on the shopping bag.

Figure 5.37
The mask icon in the Layers panel for the masked group.

Moving On

You should now be extremely comfortable making selections and making masks. You are now able to cut out any image and blend it seamlessly into any other image you'd like. You also learned how to make tonal corrections to the shadows, midtones, and highlights in your images, as well as how to make color changes.

In Chapter 6, you will learn how to slice your designs and optimize them to get the smallest size possible for use in Web pages.

Chapter 6

Divide and Conquer

This chapter explores how to intricately slice (divide) complicated designs and add hotspots to an image to produce an image map. You will discover ways to conquer those pesky overlapping slices as well as learn how to use a new feature of Fireworks 4 that enables you to optimize parts of your document with different settings—even within the same slice! Finally, exporting and time-saving commands are explained.

Working in the Web Layer

When working with hotspots and slices in this chapter, remember that the Web layer is the special layer that contains all the hotspot coordinates and slices that you've made in your document. Everything on this layer is shared across all layers, meaning that if a slice or hotspot includes elements that are actually on different layers, the slice or hotspot is active on each layer of the element. For example, a button with text may be on two layers—the object or button shape on one layer, and the text on another. If you make the button, including the text, a hotspot or a slice and add a rollover behavior to it (explained in detail in Chapter 7), the action would be triggered anywhere on the button—not just on the text or just on the button shape, but anywhere on the whole slice or hotspot area.

> **Note:** Image maps produce a map code like this: <map> in your HTML document. It's important to understand that the map coordinates are not attached to a particular image, but rather are embedded in the source code.

Hotspot Overview

Hotspots are areas on an image that enable browser interactivity. To generate a hotspot, you use the Hotspot tool to mark a region of your image, which then allows you to add behaviors to that region. If you have an image that you want to use as a navigation bar, or you want a portion of the image to be "hot"—a link taking the user somewhere or activating an event—you'll need a hotspot. For instance, you can use a hotspot to activate a pop-up window. By adding hotspots, and then linking them and/or adding behaviors, you have converted your image into an image map. To add a hotspot, follow these steps:

Figure 6.1
Setting the hotspot attributes.

> **Hotspot Shapes**
>
> Hotspot shapes can be moved and resized with the Transform tool or with the numeric positioning in the Info panel.

1. To make a simple image map of a navigation bar, draw a rectangle about 600 pixels wide by 20 pixels high and type a few names you want to link, such as Home, Products Service, and E-Mail.

2. Select the Rectangle Hotspot tool from the toolbar and draw over each link name. You will see a blue semitransparent box over each word.

3. Select one hotspot at a time and set its attributes in the Object panel (Windows|Object); see Figure 6.1.

Hotspot Tools

You can define three different shapes for hotspot areas by using the various hotspot tools: the Rectangle Hotspot tool, the Circle Hotspot tool, and the Polygon Hotspot tool. To access the hotspot tools, hold your cursor over the hotspot tools icon (see Figure 6.2) in the toolbar. If you click and hold the little arrow in the corner of the icon, a pop-up menu will appear with the rectangle, circle, and polygon shapes, from which you can choose the one you want to draw with. Your newly drawn hotspot will be ready to receive an event or a URL.

Figure 6.2
The hotspot tools icon.

> **Note:** If you are working on a vector or text-type image map, the hotspot tools will be available to you. If you are defining a hotspot on a bitmap image, the choices may be grayed out; to activate them, click the Web layer and they will be available.

Using the Rectangle Hotspot Tool

The Rectangle Hotspot tool works just like the Rectangle tool. You simply click the Rectangle Hotspot tool from the toolbar and draw a selection. To add a rectangular hotspot, follow these steps:

1. Select the Rectangular Hotspot tool and draw over a rectangular shape. Your hotspot will be added.

2. To add a link, open the Object panel (Window|Object), type in a URL and Alt text, and select the shape of your hotspot from the Shape box.

Using the Circle Hotspot Tool

The Circle Hotspot tool works just like the Ellipse tool. Select the Circle Hotspot tool from the toolbar and draw a circular selection. To add a circular hotspot, follow these steps:

1. Select the Circle Hotspot tool and draw a circular shape. Your hotspot will be added.

2. To add a link, open the Object panel (Window|Object), type in a URL and Alt text, and select the shape of your hotspot from the Shape box.

Using the Polygon Hotspot Tool

The Polygon Hotspot tool works a little differently from the Rectangle and Circle Hotspot tools. Instead of just dragging out a shape, with the Polygon Hotspot tool, you click a starting point and then click points around a shape to connect the lines. It's a bit like connecting a dot-to-dot drawing, except the dots and the lines that you place are automatically drawn. To make a polygonal hotspot selection, follow these steps:

1. Click the Polygon Hotspot tool.

2. Choose a starting point on your object and click. Continue clicking around the shape.

3. Click the starting point to close the selection. The area near Cyprus, which is shaded and surrounded by points, is the polygonal hotspot area in Figure 6.3.

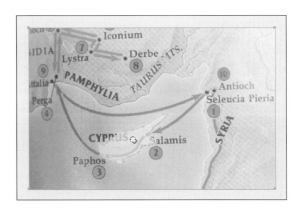

Figure 6.3
A polygonal hotspot defined.

PROJECT Making an Image Map

You can find the file reviewsheader.png in the Chapter 6 resources folder on the book's CD-ROM. This is one of the headers from the IDea bookstore, which was produced in Chapter 4. The source file is made available for you to practice with only. It is copyrighted material. To make the links hot or active, you have to have slices or defined hotspots. This particular header doesn't require slicing (it weighs in at only 17KB), so adding hotspots is the best choice. To add hotspots, follow these steps:

1. Open the reviewsheader.png file.

2. Click the Rectangle Hotspot tool in the toolbar (translucent blue rectangle) and draw separate rectangles over Home, Reviews, Contact Us, and the *Reviews by Joyce* title. The title *Reviews by Joyce* is going to be a hotspot because the users of this site are used to it being a link from a previous version. Figure 6.4 shows the hotspots used in the Reviews header.

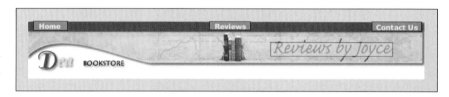

Figure 6.4

Setting the hotspots on an image map.

3. Click the Home hotspot and open the Object Inspector if it isn't open (Alt+F2/Option+F2).

4. In the URL section, type "http://je-ideadesign.com". If this were on your own site, you could use a relative path leading to your home page. When you link to sites outside of the one you are developing for, the entire URL needs to be present, including the **http://**.

Figure 6.5

Adding the URL and alternate tags.

5. Type the alternate text (what a user sees when hovering the mouse over the hotspot area) in the <Alt> area, shown in Figure 6.5.

6. Export any way you wish. This example was exported as a Dreamweaver Library item and was extremely easy to insert into existing Dreamweaver Web pages. You can learn more about integrating with Dreamweaver in Chapter 9. If you were going to use this in another editor, you could use the HTML And Images export option.

Note: If a menu contains a link to a JavaScript menu or JavaScript placed in the head, a Library item won't work.

Slicing

Slicing an image is one of the most important things you will do in Fireworks. The decisions of whether to slice your document, where to slice your document, and how to slice your document all contribute to how, and sometimes whether, users will view your Web pages. Slicing, when needed, allows for better and specialized optimization to decrease the file size. Using slicing techniques is vital to the final display of your project if you have an image that fits the profile of images needing slicing (see the next section).

To Slice or Not to Slice

Before beginning to slice your image, you need to understand why it needs to be sliced, or whether it needs to be sliced. Many people mistakenly believe that slicing always increases the loading speed. This usually isn't so; in most cases, the page actually takes longer to load, because every slice is being requested from the server, resulting in more hits to the server. Slicing does make the page "appear" to load faster, because the user can see parts of the image before the whole thing loads. This is an important perception—it beats staring at a blank page.

Many reasons exist to slice an image:

- If an image is over 20KB, it needs to be sliced to form the perception that it's loading faster.

- If you need to export some slices as JPEGs and some as GIFs, or GIF animations within the same document, then slicing is best way to go; that way, some of the slices can use a different format to suit your needs.

- If you want to attach behaviors such as rollovers to an area, it has to be a slice object.

- If you place the same slice on every page using the repeating element, slices help the loading of your Web pages when you have a logo or other repeating elements in the Web site.

> **Note:** When you have a logo or element that is repeated often within your site, be sure that the element or slice is linked to the same image file. That way, after the server retrieves it one time, it is in the browser's cache. If you use the same image and put it in different folders, then the server will have to fetch it each time.

Another wonderful advantage of slices is that if you need to update one section or slice, you don't have to redo the whole image. For instance, suppose you have a complicated navigation bar that you have optimized, sliced, exported, and incorporated into every page on a large site. You then discover that one of the major links is spelled wrong. You can fix a copy of the one image (or two, if it's a rollover), optimize it, export it, and upload it to replace the image with the error.

Slicing Tools

The slicing tools are the Rectangle Slice and Polygon Slice tools. The Rectangle Slice tool works the same way as the other Rectangle tools in Fireworks; click and drag over the area you want to define. The Polygon Slice tool also works the same way as the other Polygon tools in Fireworks; click a starting point and click to add points to define a shape.

What is often confusing is that you are allowed to define a polygonal shape with the Polygon Slice tool, but the polygonal shape cannot be exported as a polygon shape. All slices are rectangular, without exception. What will happen is, the polygonal shape will be cut into a series of rectangles that will fit together with the polygon shape enclosed. The polygon will have extra areas around it defined as rectangular slices. The benefit of using the Polygon Slice tool may seem dubious because it's cut into rectangles anyway, but it can be much easier to cut the shape if you define it the way it is and have Fireworks cut it up appropriately. On the other hand, if your shape is large and contains other slices within it, you could end up with a lot more slices than necessary. Thus, defining your own slices would be better than allowing Fireworks to generate them for you.

Using the Guides

Before you actually begin to slice an image, you need to set up a few aids for yourself. Using guides is an efficient way of defining your slices. Guides not only provide a visual aid, but they also aid your selection if you have the Snap To Guides option checked, allowing selections within a set amount of pixels (determined by you) to automatically snap to the guide. To set up guides, follow these steps:

> **Note:** You can set your own preferences regarding how the Snap To Guides function responds. Choose Edit| Preferences and click the Editing tab. In the Snap Distance dialog box, enter the number of pixels from the guide your object needs to be before it snaps to the guide.

1. Open a new document, choose File|New, and set to any size. To enable the guides, the rulers have to be visible. From the menu bar, choose View|Rulers.

2. Choose View|Guides|Snap To Guides.

3. To place guides, click a horizontal or vertical ruler and drag a guide into your document.

The guide will not be visible until you begin to pull it onto your document, at which point you will see a green line, which is the default color. Figure 6.6 shows the placement of the guide. A guide was placed between each link name, and below the link bar. To really see what is happening, open the guides.png file located in the Chapter 6 resource folder on the book's CD-ROM.

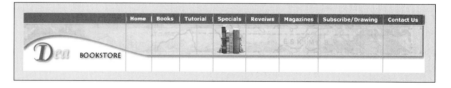

Figure 6.6
Guides placed on an image.

Defining the Slices

You could just export your whole image right now (guides.png), and Fireworks would automatically slice it for you. Wherever you see a guide, it would become a slice. To do this, you would choose File|Export and then choose HTML And Images and under the Slices option, choose Slice Along Guides. But this technique usually produces far too many images; besides, it would defeat the purpose of slicing this image. Without the slices being defined, you still couldn't add behaviors. To slice the guides.png image, follow these steps:

1. To begin slicing, select the Rectangle Slice tool (to the right of the Hotspot tool) from the toolbar.

2. Following the guides already placed in guides.png, place your cursor in the upper-left corner and drag to the right corner and down to the guide below the menu.

3. Repeat Step 2 for the rest of the slices (see Figure 6.7). The slicing lines are not that thick; they were increased for your viewing purposes. On your practice file, these lines are red.

4. After you complete the slicing, save your file to use later.

> **Note:** A green overlay will appear when a slice is drawn. You can toggle this view on and off by using the icons in the toolbar located at the bottom section, labeled View.

Every time you define a slice Fireworks automatically places red lines where additional slices could be placed to totally slice the whole page. As you make additional slices, the red lines change. You could stop slicing after a few slices and allow Fireworks to use its own guides (the red lines) to slice the rest of the image, or you could continue to slice the entire image or you could export just the slices you made. Figure 6.7 shows a heavy black border around the slices made in this image. The thick border is not what you will see, it was enhanced for viewing.

> **Note:** The best way to learn what gets sliced and what doesn't is to make yourself a practice folder to export into. Try making a few slices and export (File|Export) using the HTML And Image settings, or just the Images selection. Then try it using the Export Using Guides option.

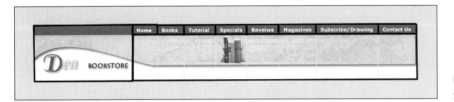

Figure 6.7
Slices used in slicing a header.

Naming Slices

The naming of slices is done in the Optimize panel (Window|Optimize). Auto-naming of slices is the default setting. Auto-naming uses the root name of your document plus the row number and column number. With auto-naming, the bookstore header file names would look like this: bookstore_r2_c4.gif. To name your own slices, follow these steps:

1. After you make a slice, open the Object panel if it isn't already open (Alt+F2/Option+F2).

2. Figure 6.8 shows some of the options available for your slice. For now, uncheck the auto-naming option and type in your own name. Don't type in the file extension, just the name (no spaces or invalid characters).

Figure 6.8
Assigning custom names to slices.

3. If you'd like to customize the auto-naming feature, select File|HTML Setup and click the Document Specific tab. Figure 6.9 shows the options with the current default settings. You can set up a default any way you'd like. For instance, you could put the word *slice* where the columns currently are. The down arrows give you some options to choose from. When you are done, click the Set Defaults button to save.

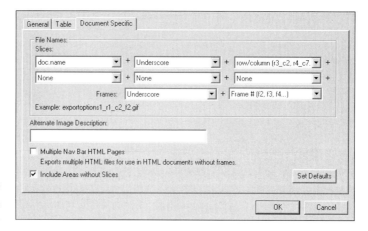

Figure 6.9
The Document Specific setup dialog box.

Adding URLs and Alt Tags

Many designers believe that every image with a link should contain an Alt tag. You should include alternate text on logo images with or without a link, so that while the image is loading, the user can see what is coming, or if they have images turned off, they can read a description of what is there. What you put in the alternate text area is what the user sees before the image loads when the mouse is placed over the image. This may also expedite browsing, because the user may find a link they want via the Alt tag and click it before the page is finished loading. To add alternative text or URLs to your images, follow these steps:

1. Click the object you want to add a URL or alternate text to. If the Object panel isn't open, select Window|Object.

2. In the URL box, type in the link.

3. Type in a Target if you have one. The target choices are:

   • *_blank*—blank loads the linked document in a new, unnamed browser window.

   • *_parent*—parent loads the lined document in the parent frameset or window of the frame that contains the link. If the frame containing the link is not nested, then the linked document loads into the full browser window.

- *_self*—self loads the linked document in the same frame or window as the link. This target is implied, so you usually don't need to specify it.

- *_top*—top loads the linked document in the full browser window, thereby removing all frames.

4. Add the alternate text in the Alt box.

Now your slice is ready to interact.

Object Slicing

Object slicing is great if you have individual objects on your page, such as buttons or a logo. In the previous exercise, the menu bar was all one piece. Using object slicing is a quick and easy way to add a slice, especially if you are not slicing the whole page but just certain parts of it. To slice an object, follow these steps:

1. Select the object you want to make a slice of.

2. On a PC, right-click (on a Mac, Ctrl+click) and choose Insert Slice. It doesn't get any easier than that.

Not only is object slicing easy, but you have choices, as well. This tool does have some drawbacks, however, especially if you are slicing buttons and the area behind them. Using the Add Slice feature will most likely produce extra slices unless your buttons are literally touching each other. The area between the buttons will be made into additional slices.

Text Slices

The purpose of text slices is to have a slice area in which you can enter HTML text. You can type in this text either from within Fireworks or in your HTML editor. To define a text slice, follow these steps:

1. Select the slice you want to be reserved for text.

2. In the Object panel, click the down arrow next to the image and choose Text. If you want to add text from within Fireworks, do it in the white box under the Text selection you just made in the Object panel. You can also add the text later in an HTML editor. That's all there is to it; the slice color will turn a darker green and a label of Text Slice will replace the Slice label.

Slicing Challenges

You likely will encounter two potentially frustrating challenges when working with slices: overlapping slices and the generation of sliver slices. When you define your slices, occasionally they will overlap. Or, if the slice isn't quite big

Note: Alternative text entered in the Alternate Image Description box via the Document Specific tab found in the Export panel under Options (File|Export|Options|Document Specific) applies to the entire image, not just a slice. Use this option when there are no slices. To add alternate text to slices, enter it in the Object panel for the individual slices (applies to hotspots as well).

Note: Fireworks 4 provides other ways to do the same thing. For example, with the object selected, you could choose Insert|Slice. Or you could use a keyboard command of Alt+Shift+U/Option+Shift+U.

Note: Text boxes have no border, cell padding, or cell spacing, which will place your text right up against the edge of the area. If there is a bordering image or background, it will be quite unsightly. The problem can be solved by inserting blank text images before and after the text box, or by inserting slices before and after the text box. The extra text boxes or slices can then be filled with the background color or background image in your image editing program.

enough to reach the neighboring slice, an extra image will be generated to fill the gap. These extra images are quite often only 1 or 2 pixels big. You would think that the snap-to guidelines would eliminate both of these problems. Unfortunately, they don't eliminate either problem; even with the distance snap set to 3 or 4 pixels away, the slices still don't snap perfectly.

Sliver Images

Often, your final sliced document will export with extra, unwanted images containing slices that may be 2 or 3 pixels wide. It doesn't hurt to use these slices, because they won't have an adverse effect on the final design. However, they will add an extra hit to the server, and all the extra slivers make editing more difficult. You will have to decide how precisely you want to slice. To identify and eliminate unwanted images, follow these steps:

1. After you have your page sliced up, export to your practice folder (more on exporting later in this chapter). Then choose File|Open and locate the files you just saved. The Open dialog box in Fireworks 4 is nice because you can see a preview of each slice quite easily as you click on each image.

2. Choose File|Open, click each slice's name, and track down any slivers. If you named your slices with unique names, then locating the slivers will be easy—they will have names such as rootnamef4_r3_c4.gif.

3. In your document, drag the slice borders a bit, usually 1 or 2 pixels, to eliminate the slivers.

4. Export again (it's easier to identify the new slices if you delete the old ones before exporting into the same folder). Don't worry about any optimization settings. At this point, you are simply setting up all the slices and eliminating the slivers.

5. Check the images again to see whether you got them all. If not, keep going.

Eliminating slivers is a trial-and-error process; you will need to decide whether it's worth it.

Overlapping

Overlapping slices are almost as difficult to identify as those pesky sliver slices. Overlapping slices offer a slight visual clue, however. The red slice lines are a tad thicker where they overlap. Even so, it is still difficult to locate the offending slices that are intruding on their neighbors' space. To locate and eliminate overlapping slices, follow these steps:

1. Identify where the overlap is occurring.

2. With the Pointer tool, click the edge of the slice and adjust the size.

Altering Slices Generated by the Button Editor

In the sample image, you will see two buttons made with the Button Editor. The lines indicate where the slices are. An extra slice is present between the two buttons. The steps required to eliminate this extra slice are much different than the steps required to eliminate regular slices. If you alter the size of the slice as you would alter normal slices, the whole button will be resized.

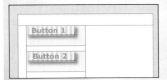

Buttons made with the Button Editor.

1. To alter the slice size, click the first button and open the Info panel (Window|Info) if it isn't open yet.
2. Write down the X and Y coordinates. If you happen to have a shorter slice that you want to alter and match to another, then write down the height and width, as well.
3. Repeat Steps 1 and 2 for the next button.
4. In the sample presented here, the X,Y coordinates of button 1 are 14 and 19, respectively. The X,Y coordinates for button 2 are 16 and 62. Because you are trying to increase the height only of button 1 to encompass the space between the two buttons, you need to calculate the Y coordinate needed to fill the space. To determine it, subtract the Y coordinate of button 1 from the Y coordinate of button 2. The difference is 43.
5. To make the change, double-click button 1 to open the Button Editor.
6. If you are asked whether you are editing the current instance or all instances, choose current.
7. In the Button Editor, click the Active Area tab. Be sure the Set Active Area Automatically option is checked.
8. Enter "43" in the height area in the Info panel and press Return or Enter, and the change will be made.

Slices readjusted.

Here is where your math skills come in handy. If you want to adjust both buttons to encompass half the space each, do the math and follow the same procedures.

Even after you adjust the slice, it's difficult to eliminate all the overlaps. An easy way to check for overlapping slices is presented in the slicing project following this project, using a command that is included on this book's CD-ROM.

PROJECT Slicing Up a Whole Web Page

For this project, you need to open the gamecontrol1.png file, located in the Chapter 6 resource folder on the book's CD-ROM. Although this is an early version of the final product, not a completed interface, it will work just fine for this project.

Slicing Buttons without the Canvas

To export just a button or row of buttons, you will need to trim the excess working area before exporting. From the menu bar, choose Modify|Trim Canvas.

Follow these steps:

1. You need to have your rulers visible (View|Rulers) and set guides. The gamecontrol1.png file already has the guide set (the green lines are guides, the red lines are the slice marks). A horizontal guide is placed on top of the first button, and under each button after that. The vertical lines were pulled to the right edge of the button controls, to the left edge of the button controls, and to the right edge of the frame around the car.

2. Every rectangle you see outlined by green lines could become a slice, but that would be way too many images. To begin adding slices, click the Rectangle Slice tool and place the cursor in the top-left corner of the document. Drag to the first guide and to the right edge of the document. Nothing in this whole area requires a behavior, so the one slice is fine. Red lines will automatically be placed; just ignore them.

3. Place your cursor in the top-left corner of the first guide (bottom of your first slice) and drag to the third guide over to the left edge of the button panel.

4. Place your cursor in the top-left corner just below the last slice and drag to the bottom of the document over to the first vertical guide.

5. Place your cursor in the top-left corner of the first vertical guide next to the car and drag to the last horizontal guide (not to the bottom) and over to the button bar's left edge.

6. Place your cursor in the top-left corner, just below the slice you just made, and drag to the bottom of the document and over to the last guide.

7. Now add a slice for the remainder of the right side of the button bar. Place your cursor in the top-left corner of the last vertical guide and drag to the bottom of the document and over to the right edge of the document.

8. The only slices left are the buttons. Carefully place your cursor in the top-left corner of each button and drag to the lower-right corner. Repeat for each button.

9. Click each slice one at a time and give each a unique name. Open the Object Inspector (Alt+F2/Option+F2), uncheck Auto-naming, and type a name. While you are here, add a URL to the slices that need it and add alternative text to the slices that will be links.

10. Because this document has so many gradients, it needs to be optimized (more details on optimization are provided later in this chapter) as a JPEG; this document was saved at an 80% Quality setting.

11. If you followed along on the unsliced version of gamecontrol1.png, save now (File|Save As). A sliced version is also available in the resources folder; it is called gamecontrol.png.

Removing the Sliver Slices

You will most likely have some sliver slices (thin 1- or 2-pixel images) that you don't need; to remove them, follow these steps:

1. Make a practice folder and choose File|Export. Choose the HTML And Images option and check the Include Areas Without Slices option.

2. Select File|Open and navigate to your practice folder. Locate any auto-named images. To aid in locating the culprits, notice the preview; you can see not only the image, but the height and width, as well. Click Cancel; you were using the Open dialog box only as a preview.

3. When you think you've tracked down any sliver slice, locate it in your image (you have to be in the slice view), and use the Pointer tool to drag the slice boundaries just a tiny bit.

4. Delete the files in your practice folder so that you can tell which ones are new, and Export again.

5. From the File menu, open and click any remaining slivers, and repeat Steps 2 through 4 until you eliminate them all.

Overlapping

Slices that overlap happen quite frequently. To identify and eliminate them, follow these steps:

1. To help correct the problem of overlapping slices, the Commands|Brian Baker folder on the book's CD-ROM includes a command called SliceOverlapDetector. Copy it and place it in your Fireworks 4| Configuration|Commands folder (you learn how to make your own commands later in this chapter).

2. From the menu bar, choose Command|SliceOverlapDectector. A dialog box will open telling you that any overlapping slices will be shown when the dialog box is closed. Click OK.

3. Now you can see an outline around those pesky offenders. Using the Pointer tool, adjust slightly.

4. Run the command again to check whether you still have any overlaps, and, if so, repeat until they are all fixed.

5. Save.

Exporting It All

Now you have one final step:

1. Choose File|Export and choose the appropriate settings (see "Exporting," later in this chapter).

Other than a few other alterations, this Web page is complete and ready to be used—that is, if you were its owner (Jeffrey Roberts does maintain copyright on this one; refer to Chapter 3).

Converting an Image Slice into a Great-Looking Text Box

Text boxes pose a problem if your background isn't a solid color or if the text box area is a different color than the background. The problem is that the text butts right up against the edge of the text box. To see how to make a text box that blends seamlessly into a background with a gradient, open the gamecontrol1.png file that you saved in the previous project, and follow these steps:

1. If you are using the gamecontrol1.png file, select the slice that is between the car and the button bar. Export this slice and save it in your practice folder; note its name, because you will use it later.

2. With the slice selected that you want to make into a text box, open the Object panel (Alt+F2/Option+F2) and, under the Type option, choose Text.

3. When this text box is exported, it will load as a white box (which, of course, won't do), plus any text entered in it will be right up against the edge. To fix this problem, select the Slice tool, place it in the top-right corner, and drag to the bottom of the text box. Don't worry about the exact size.

4. With your new slice selected, open the Info panel (Alt+Shift+F12/ Option+Shift+F12) and enter "20" for the Width and "160" for the Height. Press Enter or Return.

5. Repeat Steps 3 and 4 on the right side of the text box, and leave these slices as images.

6. Choose File|Export and export HTML and images into your practice folder. Don't worry about the other options just yet. (But, if you are impatient, you can jump ahead to the "Exporting" section of this chapter.)

7. This step is in preparation for finishing this effect in Dreamweaver. Open the image of the text box before it was altered that you saved in your practice folder in Step 1.

8. Open a new file, select the Rectangle tool, and draw a rectangle; its size doesn't matter. In the Info panel, set the Width to 20 and the Height to 160 and then press Enter or Return.

9. Drag the rectangle you just drew on top of the background text image. Align it to the left side. Pull out a vertical guide to the right edge. Move this rectangle to the other side and pull out a vertical guide to the left. You have just marked the text area.

10. Delete the rectangle you used as a guide. Select the Crop tool from the toolbar and crop the center portion of the background. Press Enter or Return.

11. Before you save, double-check the size by choosing Modify|Image Size. It should be 141 pixels wide and 160 pixels high. If it is just a tad off, adjust here. Save this cropped version of the background in your practice folder; choose File|Export, and in the Save As type box, choose Images Only.

Finish in Dreamweaver 4

A demonstration version of Dreamweaver 4 is included on the book's CD-ROM. To edit and set up the text box using the Web pages background in Dreamweaver 4, follow these steps:

1. The rest of this process is a bit tricky and is being completed in Dreamweaver. If you are using another application, go to the menu bar and choose File|HTML Setup. In the General tab, select the editor you use. The instructions may vary slightly for each one.

2. Open your HTML editor; in this case, Dreamweaver 4 is being used. Locate the HTML file you just saved and open it. You will notice the white box. In Figure 6.10, you can see the two image slices highlighted.

Figure 6.10

Text box appearance in
Dreamweaver 4.

3. Select the first slice to the left of the text box. In the Property Inspector (see Figure 6.11), locate the file name, copy it, and delete the image.

4. You will notice the Property Inspector changes. With your cursor in the cell where the image used to be, paste the file name into the Bg box, as shown in Figure 6.12.

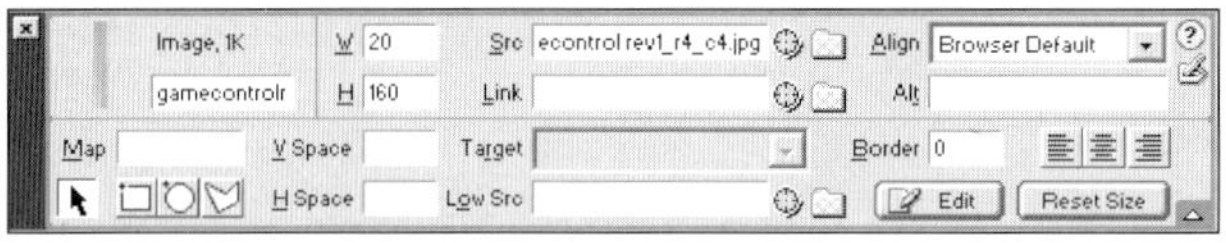

Figure 6.11

Dreamweaver's Property
Inspector.

Figure 6.12

Dreamweaver's Property Inspector
with a background added.

5. Repeat Steps 3 and 4 for the other image (right side) slice.

6. Open a new file in Fireworks and choose the Rectangle tool from the toolbar. Draw a rectangle. From the Info panel, enter a Width of 20 and a Height of 160. Press Enter or Return.

7. Back in Dreamweaver, place your cursor inside the text box. From the Property Inspector, either type, paste, or locate the file name you just saved. You can locate it by clicking the yellow folder icon and selecting the appropriate file.

8. Insert your cursor in the text area, click the Text tool (A), and type some text. Figure 6.13 shows the completed text box.

Figure 6.13
The invisible text box.

Optimization

The technology for high-speed Internet connections is improving every day, but the majority of users in the world—the Internet is global—still use modem connections. And even though users in most U.S. urban areas enjoy all kinds of options for high-speed connections, most rural areas don't yet have those options, nor do a lot of other countries. When you get used to using high-speed connections, it can be really easy to forget that many users don't have such access. Maybe sometime in the near future file size won't be a concern, but for now it still is. You will want to keep in mind that the larger the file or combination of files on a Web page, the longer it will take to load.

Optimization, or getting your image to the smallest possible size while retaining an acceptable quality, is one of the most important factors in how fast your Web page loads. You now not only can export with GIF, JPEG, or PNG images in the same document, but you can actually apply different settings to specific areas of a JPEG image. The file types currently available for the Web include the PNG format, but this format is not yet supported by all browsers, so you may want to hold on using that one just yet.

Selective JPEG Compression

In this section, you will discover the many ways to cut down on file size and make tradeoff decisions based on the quality versus the file size. By now, you have used the Optimize panel many times, so in this section, you will concentrate primarily on the newest feature of selective quality optimization.

You can optimize the background of a JPEG image at a lower quality setting to emphasize the foreground image. Or, you can use a lower setting for most of a document and select the areas that have "blockies," the areas that appear a bit block-like and blurry when a JPEG image has been compressed too much,

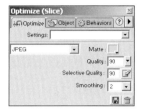

Figure 6.14

The Optimize panel for JPEG.

Figure 6.15

The Optimize panel for GIF/PNG.

Note: If you have more than one area to use selective compression on, they must all be selected now or you will have to start over and make your selections again, including all the areas that need the selective JPEG compression applied. These selections are going to become a JPG mask, and there can be only one per document.

Figure 6.16

The JPEG selective settings.

and optimize at a different setting. To use selective JPEG compression, follow these steps:

1. Click the first slice you want to optimize. The new Optimize panel for JPEG is shown in Figure 6.14, and the GIF/PNG Optimize panel is shown in Figure 6.15.

2. As a quick review, the Optimize panel is where you choose the file format: JPEG, GIF, GIF Animations, or PNG. You also choose the quality settings for JPEG or the number of colors for GIF, and whether you want transparency or not. For this exercise, you need to choose JPEG.

3. Click the background layer to make it active and be sure it isn't locked.

4. Click the Lasso selection tool and draw around the area you would like compressed at a higher quality setting. If there is more than one area, then press Shift and make your next selection.

5. Select Modify|Selective JPEG|Save Selection As JPEG Mask.

6. You can set the selective settings from the menu bar by choosing Modify|Selective JPEG|Settings, but the quicker way is to do it right in the Optimize panel. The Selective Quality option will be grayed out; click the icon and check Enable Selective Quality, and type in the quality number you want. You can change the overlay color if you'd like. The settings are shown in Figure 6.16.

7. Time to preview and see whether your setting works. From the menu bar, choose File|Preview In Browser and select your browser.

8. If you are happy, great. If you need to try another quality setting, simply change the number in the Selective Quality box in the Optimize panel.

9. To edit the JPEG mask, you can delete and start over by choosing Modify|Selective JPEG|Remove JPEG Mask. If you simply want to add to or subtract from the current mask, go to Modify|Selective JPEG| Restore JPEG Mask As Selection. With the selection active, you can use the Shift key and draw another area or add on. If you want to delete a portion, then hold down the Alt/Option key and draw around the area to remove.

10. Save the mask by choosing Modify|Selective JPEG|Save Selection As JPEG Mask.

Much of the optimization process is trial and error; choose your settings, preview, and repeat until you get an acceptable image. With certain types of files, especially flat-colored areas, you will be able to use some of the preset settings.

PROJECT Repairing a Web Page Title

The title on the Game Control Web page used an 80 percent Quality setting, which doesn't look very good. Open the gamecontrol1.png file (gamecontrol.png is the completed one) from the Chapter 6 resources folder of this book's CD-ROM. The before and after images for this project can be found in the Color Section. Locate the web racin' title and note the blurriness and artifacts. Next to the blurry image is the fixed one, which looks much better. To see how this image was repaired, follow these steps:

1. With the gamecontrol1.png file open, open the Layers panel (F2), scroll to the bottom, and select the bitmap layer.

2. From the toolbar, select the Lasso tool. Draw around the entire title.

3. On the menu bar, select Modify|Selective JPEG|Save Selection As JPEG Mask.

4. Open the Optimize panel (Window|Optimize). The Selective Quality setting will be grayed out. Click the icon, check Enable Selective Quality, and type in the Quality number 100. You can try different settings, but for this part, anything below 100 isn't worth the lower quality for 1 or 2KB.

5. While you are fixing this page, select the line's slice below the text box area. See the Color Section for an example of this also.

6. In the Optimize panel, change the Quality setting of just this slice to 100.

Setting Transparency

Transparency is available for GIF files and PNG files. The choices for transparency are Index Transparency and Alpha Transparency. The difference is often confusing. To see the difference first hand, follow these steps:

1. Select the Rectangle drawing tool and draw a square filled with white.

2. Draw another square in the center of the white one and fill it with black.

3. Draw a third square filled with white and place it over the black square; it should look like Figure 6.17.

> **Note:** When choosing Alpha Transparency, the view may not always show properly. Try clicking No Transparency first and then reselecting Alpha Transparency. Index Transparency has a default color of white, but it changes according to the color of your canvas. This feature comes in really handy when you're trying to eliminate halos around your image; see Chapter 5 for more information on avoiding halos.

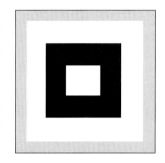 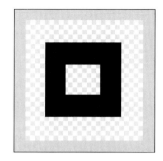

Figure 6.17
(Left) Black and white squares ready for transparency to be added.

Figure 6.18
(Right) The white background and the white in the foreground image disappear.

4. From the Optimize panel, be sure Matte is set to none and choose Index Transparency, the result of which is shown in Figure 6.18. The Index Transparency setting is the background color. This option will remove not only the background but also any other areas that contain this color. Notice that the white box in the center is also gone.

5. Because the removal of color from other areas usually isn't acceptable, another option exists: Alpha Transparency, which removes only the background color, as shown in Figure 6.19.

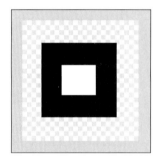

Figure 6.19
Alpha Transparency applied.

Exporting

Before you begin exporting, it's important to have your site structure set up. If you set up your folders locally in the same way that they will be uploaded, it will save you many headaches. If you are using Dreamweaver and save your site files in one folder and then move the file to another folder, all of the links to your images will be broken, so it's better to save in the same folder that the file will ultimately be in.

When you choose to export images as well as the HTML of a Fireworks document, the images and the HTML file (containing a table that places all the image slices back together) are generated. This HTML file and the images must be saved in the same folder as the file you will insert the Fireworks code into, or else all of your image links will be broken. For example, a simple site structure might be a site folder called Bookstore with a subfolder named images and another subfolder called assets. If your site's HTML/HTM files are kept in the

Bookstore folder, you would want to export your Fireworks document containing the HTML document into the Bookstore folder and designate that the images be exported to the images folder.

Export Options

You have the option of using the Export Wizard, but the regular Export option, which offers plenty of choices, will be used in this exercise. Take a look at the export options that are available by following these steps:

1. Choose File|Export. The Export panel opens, as shown in Figure 6.20. This figure shows both of the pop-up menus open (for illustration purposes only; normally, only one pop-up can be viewed at a time).

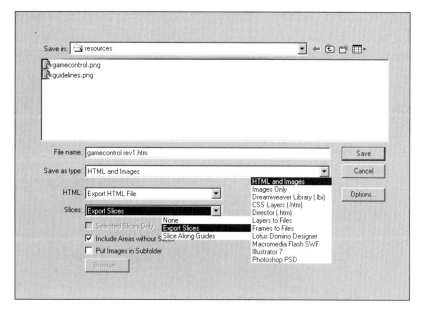

Figure 6.20
The options available in the Export panel.

2. The first task is to name your file and select the folder to save it in; remember to save in the same folder as the Web page that will contain the Fireworks code.

3. Select the type of file you are exporting. For the entire document with HTML code and image slices, choose HTML And Images.

4. Under Slices, you can choose to export no slices, export the slices you defined, or have Fireworks slice along the guidelines you placed.

5. The other three export options are Selected Slices Only, Include Areas Without Slices, and Put Images In Subfolder. When you choose the Put Images In Subfolder option, you can specify which folder to export your images into. Upon export, your HTML file will be placed where you have selected and the images will be placed in a separate folder, if you so choose.

Options Button—General Tab

Within the Export panel is an Options button with more options. Click it to open the HTML Setup dialog box. The General tab is where you choose the application you will be using the code in, the extension of your choice, whether or not to add comments, and whether or not you want everything in lowercase.

Table Tab

The Table tab (see Figure 6.21) has some really important options. The Space With options include 1-Pixel Transparent Spacer, which is probably the most often-used choice because it generates a transparent image as a space holder. This is particularly important for Netscape browsers, because a blank cell in a table without a spacer can cause the table to break down. The transparent images help keep a table's integrity. When you export, the folder you exported to will have one file called spacer.gif. This is a 1 pixel by 1 pixel transparent file that is used as a spacer to keep a table's structural integrity. This spacer is known by several names and is frequently called a *shim* or a *transparency.gif*.

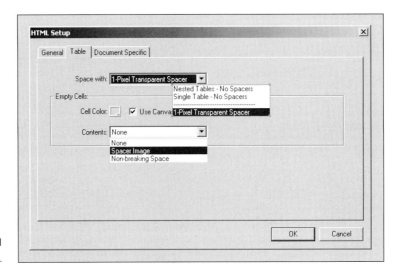

Figure 6.21
Table options tab.

You can also choose to export using a nested table, which places one table into another table. This sort of table layout does not require spacers. Or, you can choose to export just a table with no spacers at all. It will probably be fine in Internet Explorer, but Netscape Navigator often will not hold the table's integrity if empty cells exist. To help prevent the presence of an empty cell, you could also choose Non-breaking Space instead of Spacer Image for the Contents option.

If your table has an image in every cell, then Single Table–No Spacers will work just fine.

Document Specific Tab

This tab was discussed earlier in the chapter. It is where you set the default of auto-naming your slices.

Commands

Commands are similar to actions in other applications. You can make your own commands or use one of the many offered on the Internet (see Appendix C for specific links). You also can find a selection of commands on the book's CD-ROM in the Commands folder. To make your own commands, follow these steps:

1. Perform the steps involved in a task that you may want to repeat.

2. Choose Window|History or Shift+F10 to open the History panel.

3. Click the right-pointing arrow, choose Save As Command, and name the command (see Figure 6.22).

Figure 6.22
Save As Command.

You can automate many tasks using commands, such as changing document sizes, colors, and resolutions or applying special effects. You can even record making a rollover and then apply the same settings to other buttons. In the next project, you save a command for making a navigation bar that can be used over and over.

PROJECT Making a Command for a Navigation Bar

Navigation bars quite frequently consist of rectangular buttons used as links to the Web site's content. You need to make the navigation bar only one time. If you record your actions and save them as a command, you can make future navigation bars instantly. This type of nav bar would be suitable for non-rollover navigation.

To make a navigation bar command, follow these steps:

1. Decide what size layout you are designing for. The current trend is toward 800×600, so try that for now. From the menu bar, choose File|New and make it 790 pixels wide by 40 pixels high.

2. For this command to work properly, set the color now (there was some trouble setting the color later on). To set the color, click on the color well in the color section of the toolbar and type "#66A385" for the color.

3. Select the Rectangle tool from the toolbar and drag a rectangle over the entire length of the document.

4. To make the rectangle exactly 30 pixels high, open the Info panel (Window|Info) and type "30" in the Height box and "790" in the Width box (if any other number is there). Press Enter or Return to accept the changes.

5. With the rectangle selected, go to the Effect panel (Alt+F7/Option+F7), click the right-pointing arrow, choose Shadow And Glow|Drop Shadow, and accept the defaults by pressing Enter or Return.

Note: Actions (or steps) that you take while making a command may appear below a line in the History panel. If the step you took shows below the line, you will need to find a workaround or try a different technique. Actions below the line may not play back properly (they usually won't). But just because an action or step doesn't work on one project, doesn't mean it won't work on another. For instance, moving an object in position worked in one project and didn't in another.

Note: When you pull the guides out, be sure your cursor is in the canvas area before you release the mouse, or the guide won't be placed.

6. You now need to align the buttons. The normal procedure for aligning items is to use Distribute Widths from the Modify menu. But using this command places the step below the line in the History panel (see the note in the Commands introduction). The workaround is to manually place the objects using guides with the Snap To Guides option selected. Pull a vertical guide out to each of the following positions: one line past the 0 mark; two lines past the 100 mark; three lines past the 200 mark; one line before the 350 mark; one line after the 450 mark; two lines past the 550 mark; and three lines past the 650 mark. Pull one horizontal line down from the top just a tiny bit.

7. Click the Rectangle tool and place your cursor in the top-left corner of the first guide. When you are right over it, the cross turns pink. Drag a small rectangle.

8. In the Info panel, type "100" for the Width and "23" for the Height and press Enter or Return.

9. In the Styles panel (Shift+F11), click Style number 16 to apply to the button.

10. Repeat Step 9 for six more buttons.

11. Remove the guides by dragging them off the document.

12. In the History panel (Shift+F10), select all the steps (actions) up to this point by Shift+clicking. Click the right-pointing arrow and select Save As Command. Name your new command (here it is saved as Navbar) and click Save.

This command will now show up in the Commands menu. You don't even have to close Fireworks and reopen it to activate the command. To apply the command, simply open a new document, 790 pixels by 40 pixels. From the Commands menu, click Navbar (or whatever you named your command) and you have an instant navigation bar. Figure 6.23 shows the completed navigation bar.

Figure 6.23
The completed navigation bar.

This bar is completely editable; you can change color, style, effects . . . everything. You can use the one provided for you in the Commands|Joyce folder on the book's CD-ROM. In Fireworks 4, copy and paste navbar.jsf into the Fireworks4|Configuration|Commands folder. If you made your own command, it is automatically there. Editable gold text is included in the Navbar2 command if you'd like to try it out.

Don't be fooled by how easy this command seemed to be. The instructions were written after much trial and error; it was far from easy. Many of the original actions I tried—such as the alignment command from the Modify menu, removing guides, and copying and pasting—showed below the line in the History panel. I had to try different techniques until I found what would record properly.

Many commands, however, are quite easy to produce, such as the golden text included in the commands folder on the book's CD-ROM and the Copyright command, which is the next project.

PROJECT Making a Command for a Copyright Notice

The command we'll compose in this project provides a really fast way to add a copyright notice to your documents. Thus, you no longer have to remember the copyright symbol numbers to put in the text box every time you need to insert the copyright symbol. To save this command, follow these steps:

1. Open a new document, 200 pixels by 20 pixels.

2. Select the Text tool from the menu bar and type your copyright notice. To get the copyright symbol, hold down the Alt/Option key and type "0169" using the numeric keypad. (All special characters above 128 on a PC need to be keyed in via the numeric keypad.)

3. An alternative to inserting the symbol by using the numeric keypad is to copy and paste the copyright notice from another document right into the text area. Then you can highlight the notice and select the Font you want to use; Verdana is used here with a point size of 10.

4. From the History panel, click the right arrow and select Save As Command. Name the command and click OK.

Moving On

You should now be ready to tackle any slicing challenge that comes your way. You have learned how to slice, how to eliminate sliver images, and how to fix overlapping slices. You also learned how to use the new Selective JPEG feature and how to choose the best export options. Using the Save As Command feature, you can now automate parts of your workflow.

In Chapter 7, you will discover how to produce the very popular pop-up menus, one of Fireworks 4's hottest new features, as well as other rollover techniques to spice up your Web pages.

Chapter 7

Navigation Magic

This chapter provides you with several Web page navigation solutions. These solutions include the extremely popular new pop-up menus, as well as navigation bars, disjointed rollovers, and simple rollovers—all of which can now be made interactive even if you don't know any JavaScript code. But, for those who want to tinker with the code, the pop-up menus and other features can be customized with a few code tweaks.

Navigation Solutions

Enabling users to easily navigate your Web site is of utmost importance when designing the site. Users get very frustrated when they arrive at a page and can't figure out how to get to where they want to go. Fireworks 4 offers several different navigation solutions, from which you can choose the best technique for your Web site.

Pop-up menus are all the rage these days and can be made quite easily with Fireworks 4's newest feature—the Set Pop-Up Menu Wizard. However, the pop-up menus don't come without a few problems. The "Pop-Up Menus" section of this chapter will dig into the problems and offer solutions.

A navigation bar, which is a group of buttons that appear on every page of a Web site, is another navigation option. A navigation bar is a great way to add consistency to your site, and it offers the added benefit of being easy to edit. (You won't have to redesign the whole site when a change needs to be made to the navigation bar only.)

Simple rollovers, which have an Up state and an Over state only, are probably the most widely used type of JavaScript button on the Internet. Fireworks 4 makes it easier than ever to produce simple rollover buttons.

Another navigation solution is the popular disjointed rollover. A disjointed rollover occurs when you click a button and an image or text appears in another location of the page. Recall the web racin' game interface you made in Chapter 4. In this chapter, you're going to apply a disjointed rollover to that interface, so that when a particular button is clicked, the image in the picture frame will change.

Using the Button Editor

The Button Editor is one of the easiest editors to use. Don't let its simplicity fool you, though, because it really streamlines your workflow by enabling you to apply up to four different states for the same button in one location. It will probably be the easiest, fastest, and most efficient way of making multiple-state buttons that you'll ever find.

The majority of Web navigation buttons on the Internet use JavaScript to make them interactive, such as rollovers. By using the Button Editor, you can make interactive JavaScript buttons without having any knowledge of JavaScript code. Fireworks generates the necessary JavaScript code for you automatically. You can change the states for a button simply by changing the appearance of each state. Any button produced with the Button Editor is automatically made into a symbol. If you want more than one button, you simply drag another instance onto the canvas.

The following are the four different states of a button:

- *Up*—The default appearance of the button as first seen by the user.

- *Over*—The way the button looks when the user passes the mouse pointer over it. The Over state alerts users that this button is "hot," meaning that it leads to another page when clicked.

- *Down*—The appearance of the button after it has been clicked, which often appears as if the button has been pressed down. In Fireworks, you can set the Down state to be active on the page that is being clicked to, to designate the button as the current page.

- *Over While Down*—The appearance of the Down state button when the mouse pointer moves over it.

Another important feature of the Button Editor is that when you alter the text on the Up state button, the text is automatically updated for the other states as well, eliminating the need to change the text on all four buttons.

Making a Button Symbol

You can make a button directly in the Button Editor or convert an existing button into a button symbol and edit it in the Button Editor. A button symbol encapsulates up to four different button states and moves as a unit. Instead of spending lots of time reproducing similar buttons, you simply have to place a symbol onto your canvas and edit the text and link. To use the Button Editor, follow these steps:

1. To make a button from scratch, open a new document, File|New. Then choose Insert|New Button, which opens the Button Editor. If you want to convert a button graphic into a button symbol, choose Insert|Convert To Symbol, select Button as the animation type, and click OK. If you double-click the button, the Button Editor will open.

2. The Button Editor has several different tabs. When you click each one, Fireworks gives you a description of what the corresponding state does. The Up state tab should be the active one. Select a drawing tool and draw your button.

3. Select the Text tool and type the text you want on the button. Remember that the text is fully editable and can easily be changed later. Use the center text alignment from the Text Editor so that the text maintains its centered position.

4. Click the Over tab and click the Copy Up Graphic button (see Figure 7.1) to put a copy of the Up state in the Over state's editing box. Now you can change the fill of the Over state, or add a stroke or a Live Effect to it. Be sure the button (or text if you have any) is selected so that the effects are added.

Note: The Info panel (Alt+Shift+F12/Option+Shift+F12), which is housed with the Stroke and Fill panels by default, can be used while you are in the Button Editor. To get an exact-sized button, type the dimensions in the Height and Width boxes in the Info panel.

Note: If you plan to use the button in a navigation bar, don't put the text on the button. (You will learn the reason for this later in the chapter, in the section "Navigation Bars.")

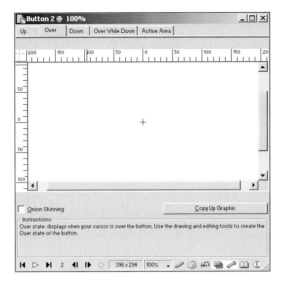

Figure 7.1

The Copy Up Graphic button in the Button Editor.

Note: For any of the button states, you can import a button, draw a unique button, or drag a button from another document, instead of using the Copy Up/Down Graphic button.

5. Click the Down tab, click the Copy Over Graphic button, and make any changes to the appearance. If you want to see all the buttons at one time, click the Onion Skinning checkbox (see Figure 7.1). To have the Down state active on the page that clicking the button brought you to, check the Show Down State Upon Load option box, located above the Onion Skinning option. For the Down state, you will probably want to remove the Over state. For example, if you were to add a glow in the Over state and then click the Copy Over Graphic button while in the Down state, you would want to set the stroke to None in the Down state.

6. If you want to use an Over While Down state, which isn't as widely used as the other three states, click its tab, click the Copy Down Graphic button, and make any changes you desire.

7. Click the Active Area button; you will see a slice added to your document automatically. The Active Area is set to Automatic by default and generates a slice large enough to cover all the button states. (There is one slice for all four button states; you can change the size by dragging the slice points.)

8. If you want to add links to your buttons, click the Link Wizard button. See the "Link Wizard" sidebar for more information about this button.

9. Close the Button Editor. An instance of the button is automatically placed in your document, indicated by the little arrow in the corner. Figure 7.2, showing the Preview tab, also shows the instance of the symbol in your document. You can't see the arrow in Figure 7.2 because it is in preview mode.

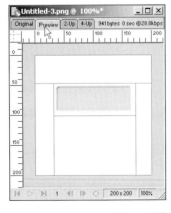

Figure 7.2

Preview the button states.

Link Wizard

This image shows the first tab of the Link Wizard, which is the Export Settings tab; you can select a preset, or click the Edit button to have access to the full range of optimization options.

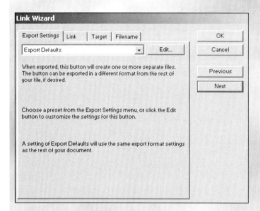

The Link Wizard's Export Settings tab.

The second tab is the Link tab. In this tab, you add the URL you want to link to, the alternate text, and any text you'd like to appear in the status bar of the browser.

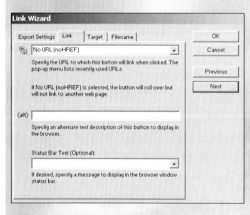

The Link Wizard's Link tab.

The other two tabs in the Link Wizard are the Target tab, which is where you set a target window or frame for the link to open in, and the Filename tab, which is where you name the button either manually or by using Fireworks' auto-naming feature.

10. After you close the Button Editor, the symbol is automatically added to the Library panel. To add more buttons to your document, drag them from the Library panel by clicking and dragging either the button symbol or the name of the symbol onto your document. Figure 7.3 shows the symbol in the Library panel.

11. You can easily preview your new button by clicking on the Preview tab in your document window, passing your mouse over the button, and clicking on the button to see the different states.

Figure 7.3
The button symbol added to the Library panel.

Editing Button Symbols

Editing the buttons you have made is quite simple. The following is a list of the different portions of your buttons and the steps for editing each portion:

- *Text*—Select the text you want to edit, open the Object panel (Alt+F2/Option+F2), and type in the new text. This works only if the button symbol has text on it.

- *Button characteristics*—Double-click to open the Button Editor, click the tab for the state or states you'd like to alter, and make your changes. Close the Button Editor when you are done.

- *Imported symbols*—When you edit an instance of a button, it breaks the link with the original object, allowing you to make changes in the new document without affecting any documents containing the original symbol. To update an imported button, click the right-pointing arrow in the Library panel and choose Update from the pop-up menu.

- *Active area*—If you want to change the active area of the button slice, you must do so from within the Button Editor. For specific details on how to calculate the size of the slice you need, refer to Chapter 6.

Using the Library Panel

Libraries are really timesavers, because they enable you to use symbols over and over again. Because buttons are used frequently, managing them through the Library panel is convenient. All you have to do is drag and drop a symbol from the Library panel into your document.

Two types of libraries exist: the type that a document contains by default, and the type that you can generate and save. The default library is generated as soon as you convert an object into a symbol, which includes the symbols that the Button Editor adds. This library is saved along with the document; when you open it again, the library is available. For instance, if you have a set of buttons that you'd like to have available for other projects, you can save the library for use in any document. The next section explains how to do this.

Exporting Libraries

If you have a series of symbols that make up a navigation system, you may want to save the set as a library. To save a library of symbols in your current document to use again or to share with someone else, follow these steps:

1. Open the Library panel by choosing Window|Library.

2. Click the right-pointing arrow and choose Export Symbols from the pop-up menu to open the Export Symbols dialog box (see Figure 7.4).

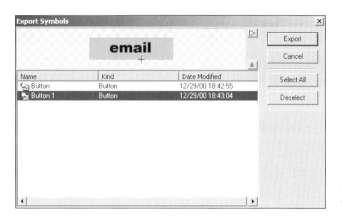

Figure 7.4
The Export Symbols dialog box.

3. Select the symbols you want to export (only those in the current document will be available). If you want to export them all, choose Select All; if you want several in a row, Shift+click to select the group; if you want to pick and choose, press Ctrl/Option and click the desired symbols. When you are done, click Export.

4. Name your library, choose where you want to save it, and then click Save. A library can be saved anywhere you like. Just remember that when you import a library, you have to be able to find where you saved it.

> **Note:** For libraries that you think you may use often, save them or move them to the Fireworks Library folder, which is in Macromedia\Fireworks 4\Configurations\Libraries. By placing your files there, you can easily access them by choosing Insert|Libraries.

Importing Libraries

To use a library that you have saved in your current document, you need to import it. To import a saved library, follow these steps:

1. Open the Library panel (if it isn't already open) by choosing Window|Library.

2. From the pop-up menu, choose Import Symbols.

3. Locate your saved library, select it, and click Open.

4. The Import Symbols dialog box opens with the list of symbols in the library you selected to save. Choose the symbol (or symbols) that you want and click Import.

Navigation Bars

A navigation bar, also called a *nav bar,* contains a series of buttons that usually appears on every page of a Web site. In this section, you will see how to make an entire navigational system into a symbol, as well as how to make a button set to reuse as a nav bar. The project at the end of this section is a custom application that combines techniques from both of the two nav bar methods—using the best techniques from each—to produce one super navigation bar symbol.

Making a Navigation Bar into a Symbol

You can make a nav bar into a symbol and reuse it as a complete unit, rollover states and all. This technique has a few caveats, and it isn't necessarily the best choice. Follow these steps to make a symbol out of a navigation bar:

1. Open a new document (File|New); a size of 200 pixels wide by 400 pixels high is being used in this exercise.

2. Open the Library panel and import the samplesymbols.png file from the Chapter 7 resources folder on this book's CD-ROM. Alternatively, you can choose Insert|New Button and make a button symbol (refer to the instructions in "Making a Button Symbol," earlier in this chapter). A symbol is added to the Library panel. Leave this file open.

3. Choose Insert|New Symbol. When the dialog box opens, choose Graphic and click OK.

4. In the Symbol Editor, draw or drag an interface into it. You can open the navback.png file from the Chapter 7 resources folder and drag it into the Symbol Editor (see Figure 7.5).

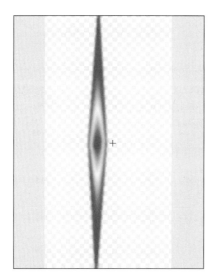

Figure 7.5
The navigation bar background in the Symbol Editor.

5. In the Layers panel, click the right-pointing arrow and choose Share This Layer. If you don't do this step, you will get a white box around your buttons in the different states.

6. To get your buttons into the Symbol Editor, drag an instance of Button from the Library panel (if you imported it in Step 2; if you did not, you can do so now).

7. The next step is to add text to the buttons. If you are using the sample supplied, you can skip this step through Step 9. If you are not using the sample, all of your buttons currently have the same text on them. To change that, double-click near the instance arrow (the little arrow in the corner of the instance in your document). A dialog box will ask whether you want to edit all the instances or just the current one; select Current. You are still in the Symbol Editor.

8. With the button in the Up state, select the Text tool and click the button. The Text Editor will open. Change the text and click OK. You only have to do this to the Up state. A dialog box asks you whether you want to update the other states. Click OK and close the Symbol Editor.

9. Repeat Steps 7 and 8 for the rest of your buttons.

10. You will now have a symbol instance of an entire nav bar in your document window. To align the buttons, put one near the top and one near the bottom, Shift+click to select each button, and choose Modify| Align|Distribute To Heights. Figure 7.6 shows the final image in the Symbol Editor.

11. To reuse this nav bar, you must export the symbols from the Library panel. Click the right-pointing arrow and choose Export Symbols to open the Export Symbols dialog box. Select as many symbols as you want to export or Select All, and click the Export button. In the Save As dialog box, locate the folder where you store library symbols (see "Exporting Libraries") and place the symbols there. Figure 7.7 shows the completed nav bar as a symbol in the document window.

> **Note:** Editing this type of a navigation bar is not very easy. This is one entire symbol; you do not have access to the individual buttons. To edit the symbol, you have to double-click it and edit from within the Symbol Editor. Another thing to note is that editing the button symbol does not change all the instances at once, only one at a time. The reason for this is that as soon as you edit the text, each button becomes a new symbol.

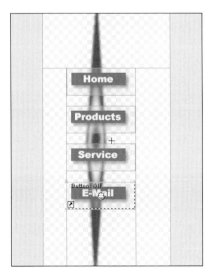

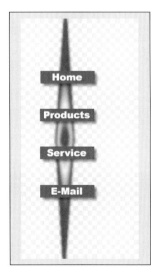

Figure 7.6
(Left) The final navigation bar in the Symbol Editor.

Figure 7.7
(Right) The finished navigation bar in the document window.

Note: This navigation bar is in the Chapter 7 resources folder on this book's CD-ROM and is called navbarsample.png. The symbols are saved as Sample Symbols.png, so you can experiment with them if you'd like.

Figure 7.8

A series of buttons aligned.

Figure 7.9

A series of vertical buttons with text and a drop shadow.

Using Editable Button Symbols for Navigation

In this exercise, you will make buttons with four states and combine a series of buttons with different text to use as one navigation bar. This example will make a new symbol out of each button. These are the buttons you used in the previous exercise named samplesymbols.png (Chapter 7 resources folder on this book's CD-ROM). To make this type of nav bar of just buttons, follow these steps:

1. Open a new document that is large enough to hold several buttons.

2. Choose Insert|New Button and make a button with three or four states. Add any text you'd like (in this sample "Home" was used) to the Up state and then copy and paste the text into the other states. Close the Button Editor when you are done.

3. Either drag additional instances of the button symbol just made from the Library panel onto your document or copy and paste the instance of the button symbol already in the document as many times as you need. Position the first one where you want it to be and the last one where you want it to be. Don't worry about the middle ones. To align them all, Shift+click all the buttons and then choose Modify|Align| Distribute Heights (if the buttons are vertical). You can see the vertical alignment in Figure 7.8.

4. To edit the text on each button, select the button and change the text in the Object panel (Window|Object).

5. If you want to add a drop shadow to the buttons, double-click each one to open the Button Editor. You will automatically be in the Up state in the Button Editor. While still in the Button Editor, open the Effect panel (Window|Effect) and from the pop-up menu, choose Shadow And Glow|Drop Shadow and accept the defaults (see Figure 7.9). Close the Button Editor when you are done making changes to each button.

6. In the Library panel, click the right-pointing arrow and choose Export from the pop-up menu. Name your nav bar with a unique name and save it.

PROJECT Making an Editable Symbol with Text

In this project, you'll make a nav bar that is a symbol and that is editable, as well. This technique is the only way to change the properties of the original symbol and have all the buttons change, even with text already on them. To make this very useful nav bar, follow these steps:

1. Open a new document that is 110 pixels wide by 200 pixels high.

2. To make a button for your navigation bar, choose Insert|New Button.

3. In the Button Editor, draw a rectangle (don't worry about the size). With the rectangle selected, open the Info panel (Window|Info), set the Width at 101 and the Height at 33, and then press Enter or Return.

4. From the Stroke panel (Window|Stroke), select Pencil, 1-Pixel Soft, and a color of Hex #D8150D.

5. From the Fill panel (Window|Fill), choose Solid and a color of #009966.

6. From the Effect panel (Window|Effect), click the down-pointing arrow and choose Bevel And Emboss|Outer Bevel, Flat, a Width of 3, and a Softness of 3. Figure 7.10 shows the Up state of the button.

Figure 7.10
The Up state of the racin' button.

7. Click the Over tab and click the Copy Up Graphic button. With the button still selected, go to the Fill panel and choose Solid and a color of Hex #FFFF00 (yellow).

8. Click the Down tab, click the Show Down State Upon Load option, and click the Copy Over Graphic button. From the Fill panel, change the color back to green, Hex #009966. From the Effect panel, click the down-pointing arrow and choose Bevel And Emboss|Inset Emboss, a Width of 3, and a Softness of 3.

Note: You may have noticed that no text has been added to this button. The reason for this becomes apparent later on in the project, but for now, just know that it is important not to add text.

9. Click the Over While Down tab and click the Copy Down Graphic button. In the Fill panel, change the color to a deep green, Hex #336600, and close the Button Editor.

10. An instance of the button has been added to your document; just delete it. Notice that a symbol has been placed in the Library panel. Select your new document to make it active and choose Insert|New Button. The Button Editor opens in the Up state. From the Library panel, drag an instance of the button into the Button Editor—not the document.

11. Open the Layers panel (Window|Layers) and click the yellow folder to add a new layer. With the new layer selected (be sure it is on top of the first layer), select the Text tool and type the word "setup". This example uses the Font FlashDbol, 28-point, red Hex #990000, and Smooth Anti-Aliasing. Of course, you can use any font that looks good on the button.

12. If you copy the text from the Up state and paste it into each of the other states, it will be positioned in the same place. When you paste into each state, be sure the text is all going into Layer 2, not Layer 1. Close the Button Editor. As Figure 7.11 shows, the button is on Layer 1 and the text is on Layer 2.

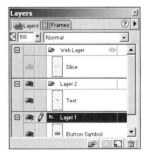

Figure 7.11
The Layers panel with two layers.

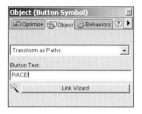

Figure 7.12

The Object panel with the button name changed.

13. Drag five more instances of this button on the document. Click the second button. In the Object panel (see Figure 7.12), change the text to "connect", press Enter or Return, and choose Current when the dialog box opens asking you to update Current or All. Repeat this process for the rest of the buttons. The words used in this interface are as follows: *setup, connect, track, level, laps,* and *RACE!*

14. Save this library of symbols as racinbuttonsymbol.png. A copy is in the Chapter 7 resources folder on this book's CD-ROM. Figure 7.13 shows all the completed buttons. Figure 7.14 shows all the buttons added to the Library, including the first blank one and six with text added.

Figure 7.13

(Left) Six buttons added for the racin' navigation bar.

Figure 7.14

(Right) Button symbols added to the Library.

Note: The buttons shown in Figure 7.13 can be used right now as is. They are fully editable by editing the blank button symbol. If you change the color of the original button symbol, all the other buttons with text change as well. That technique works here because the text is now on a layer, which is not shared. To test it out, double-click the blank button in the Library. In the Button Editor, select the button. From the Fill panel, change the color to blue and close the Editor. All the buttons in your nav bar are now blue.

PROJECT Designing the King of Navigation Bars

Now, you will combine the preceding projects to create a navigational background, which in turn will be turned into a symbol. To build this highly functional nav bar, follow these steps:

1. Open the racingnavback.png file from the Chapter 7 resources folder on the book's CD-ROM. This is the background of an interface produced in Chapter 3.

2. Open a new document that is 160 pixels wide by 410 pixels high.

3. Select the new document you opened to make it active, choose Insert|New Symbol, select Graphic, and click OK. You will now be working in the Symbol Editor—no matter what panels, layers, and so forth you use, *do not* close the Symbol Editor until the instructions say to. The steps will not work if you perform them outside of the Symbol Editor.

4. Drag the racin' navigation bar into the Symbol Editor and choose Modify|Trim Canvas to delete excess canvas (see Figure 7.15).

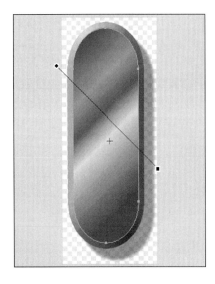

Figure 7.15
The navigational background in the Symbol Editor.

5. Open the Layers panel, select the interface, and choose Share This Layer from the pop-up menu.

6. From the Library panel, import the racinbuttonsymbols.png file you saved or open it from the Chapter 7 resources folder on this book's CD-ROM. Drag buttons 1 through 6 onto the interface background in the Symbol Editor.

7. Place the first button near the top and the last button at the bottom. Shift+click to select all the buttons, choose Modify|Align|Distribute Heights, and then choose Modify|Align|Center Vertical.

8. Open the Frames panel (Window|Frames), click the right-pointing arrow, and choose Add Frames. Add one frame for every state you have for the button. This example includes four states, so add three more frames and choose the After Current Frame option.

9. Close the Symbol Editor. You now have a navigation bar that is easy to use and can be updated easily. Don't forget to export the symbols in the Library for use again. Figure 7.16 shows the finished navigation bar.

Figure 7.16
The finished and fully editable navigation bar.

Rollovers

JavaScript rollovers all work the same way: When a cursor passes over the trigger image, a behavior or action is initiated. A number of behaviors or actions can be assigned to this trigger image, such as replacing the current image with another one or displaying a graphic or text in another location of the Web page. The trigger image is always a hotspot or a slice. Hotspots can be

Note: Both images must be the same size in a simple rollover. For instance, if you add a stroke to the Over state to add a glow, the image will be a bit larger. The first image will need its canvas expanded a bit to match the size of the second image. Things will go smoother if you have your images prepared and sized before you start implementing the rollovers.

used only to trigger events such as "Set Text of Status Bar", and cannot perform actions. They can, however, be used to trigger an event in another slice object. Because of their limited functionality, hotspots are not used in this book's examples. Slices, on the other hand, can trigger events and perform actions, and thus are used in the examples.

Making Simple Rollovers

A simple rollover occurs when a mouse passes over the trigger image and another one is displayed. These two images reside in the same space in different frames. When a mouse cursor passes over the trigger image (the slice containing rollover behaviors), an image from Frame 2 is swapped, giving the appearance that the original image is changing. A simple rollover contains one slice or hotspot and two frames.

To make a simple two-state rollover, follow these steps:

1. Select, draw, or import the image you want as the trigger image.

2. Place the image or button where you want it, and either choose Insert|Slice (or, on a PC, right-click and choose Insert Slice) or draw the slice by using the Slice tool.

3. In the Frames panel, add one more frame by clicking the New/Duplicate Frame icon.

4. Select Frame 2 and open or draw the second image. Place it over the first (trigger) image in your document. Note that this image is on a different frame. If you click Frame 1, you will see the first image; if you click Frame 2, you will see the Over state or swapped image.

5. From the document, select the slice you added.

6. Open the Behaviors panel (Window|Behaviors), click the + sign, and choose Simple Rollover (see Figure 7.17).

Figure 7.17
The Add Actions pop-up menu.

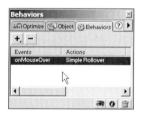

Figure 7.18
The Behaviors panel with a simple rollover added.

The onMouseOver Simple Rollover behavior has been added to the Behaviors panel, as shown in Figure 7.18.

Behaviors

The Behaviors panel is used to add multiple behaviors to a slice object. Using the Behaviors panel is not the only way behaviors can be added in Fireworks. For instance, when you made the nav bar, the Set Nav Bar Image was added automatically when you used the Button Editor. Another way behaviors can be added is by using the drag-and-drop feature presented later in this chapter.

Behaviors in Fireworks 4 are also compatible with Dreamweaver 4 behaviors, enabling you to edit the behaviors in Dreamweaver 4. The one exception is the new pop-up menus; they work in Dreamweaver 4 but can only be edited in Fireworks 4.

Making Simple Rollovers Using the Drag-and-Drop Method

Up until Fireworks 4, the Behaviors panel was the only way to make rollovers (as described in the "Making Simple Rollovers" section). Now you have another option—using drag-and-drop—which you'll see in a moment. To make a simple rollover using the drag-and-drop method, follow these steps:

1. Repeat Steps 1 through 5 in the "Making Simple Rollovers" section.

2. You will now have a button in Frame 1 and in Frame 2. With Frame 1 selected, click on the slice for the trigger image. You will see a little white circle in the middle of the slice; this is the drag-and-drop behavior handle. As you pass your mouse over the handle, the cursor changes into a hand. When you click and drag, this handle changes to a fist. Drag the fist to the edge of the button. A Swap Image dialog will come up. Select which frame to swap the image from   you can even swap an image from a file folder (just be sure the two images are the same size).

Making Disjointed Rollovers

A disjointed rollover occurs when a mouse pointer moves over or clicks the event or trigger image and another image is displayed in a different part of the Web page. You'll see disjointed rollovers used quite often on buttons, where the trigger area is a button and the target area displays a text description. In this exercise, you will use a new feature to Fireworks 4, the drag-and-drop method of adding a behavior, which is a fantastic timesaver. To produce a disjointed rollover, follow these steps:

1. Open the disjointedelements.png file from the Chapter 7 resources folder on this book's CD-ROM (see Figure 7.19).

Figure 7.19
The images used in this exercise.

2. Select the object that will be your trigger. In this exercise, you will be using a button called logos. You could also use a button symbol with different states; they work just as well, and you can still attach behaviors to the button.

3. Select the button and choose Insert|Slice. In the Object panel, name your button "logobutton".

4. In the Frames panel, click the right-pointing arrow and choose Duplicate Frame from the pop-up menu.

5. Open transportation.png from the Chapter 7 resources folder (this will be the swap image). Drag the logo on top of the frame. If the logo is above or covering the frame, choose Modify|Arrange|Send To Back. Make any adjustments to the placement. Select the transportation logo and choose Insert|Slice. If you click Frame 1, you will see the empty frame; if you click Frame 2, you will see the logo added. Figure 7.20 shows the change. Figure 7.21 shows the Layers panel at this point.

Figure 7.20
(Left) Frame 2 showing the new content.

Figure 7.21
(Right) The Layers panel with the objects and slices added.

Note: This button is called logos, but there is only one logo (Specialized Transportation). What you can do with this image is to make a simple animation (see Chapter 8) using several logos. You can then use the GIF animation as a target rollover image.

6. The next stage is to set up a swap image behavior for a disjointed rollover. Select the slice (also known as the *Web object*) over the button (trigger area). In the center of the button is a white circle; the pointer turns into a hand when it gets near this circle. Figure 7.22 shows this behavior handle. Click and drag the behavior handle (the cursor changes into a fist) to the slice covering the image you want to change, in this case the logo.

7. A Swap Image dialog box opens, which should say Frame 2 already because you have placed the image there. If you want to select another image, click the More Options button, and click OK.

8. Choose File|Preview In Browser or click the Preview tab in the document window to see your new disjointed rollover.

Figure 7.22
The drag-and-drop behavior handle.

PROJECT Adding a Disjointed Rollover to the Racin' Interface

In Chapter 4, you made a game interface called web racin'. It's a perfect candidate for a disjointed rollover. To add a disjointed rollover to this interface, follow these steps:

1. Open the gamecontrol.png file from the Chapter 4 resources folder on this book's CD-ROM.

2. In this project, the first button, setup, will be used. Select the button and choose Insert|Slice. In the Object panel, name your button "setup".

3. In the Frames panel, click the right-pointing arrow and choose Duplicate Frame from the pop-up menu. Open the redcar.png file from the Chapter 7 resources folder on this book's CD-ROM. Drag the car into the center of the frame in the game interface. When you have the car positioned, choose Insert|Slice. In the Object panel, name the slice "redcar". (The red car is borrowed from the Hemera Photo Objects 50,000 Premium Image Collection.)

4. The next step is to set up a swap image behavior that shows the car in the frame section of the document when a mouse cursor passes over the setup button. Select the slice (over the setup button). Click the drag-and-drop behavior handle and drag it to the red car. The Swap Image dialog will come up. Usually it lists Frame 2 in the Swap Image From box; if this is correct, click OK; if not, change the frame number or locate the file to swap.

5. That's a nice effect, having the car appear as you move your mouse over the button. You could even assign a link to the button in the Object panel (Window|Object), but if you want Over and Down states for the button, you need to use a button symbol. To use a button symbol you made in an earlier project, choose Edit|Undo Behavior and then delete the setup button.

6. Open the Library panel (F11). Click the right-pointing arrow and choose Import Symbols. Navigate to the Chapter 7 resources folder on this book's CD-ROM and locate the racinbuttonsymbols.png file. Select All and click OK.

7. Drag Button 1 into the place where the setup button used to be. Because it already has a slice attached, you simply have to click the drag-and-drop behavior handle and drag it to the racecar image.

8. If this were a real interface and you had swap images for every link, you would repeat Steps 2 through 4 (link only buttons) or Steps 2 through 7 (for the buttons with states) for the rest of the buttons. Figure 7.23 shows the disjointed rollover and the Over state.

Figure 7.23
The completed interface with a disjointed rollover.

Pop-Up Menus

The ability to design pop-up menus is the latest "must have" skill on a Web developer's list of abilities. Including pop-up menus on Web pages seems to be the latest rage, with a large number of people wanting to know how to make menus similar to Microsoft's pop-up menus. Pop-up menus aid tremendously in generating a clean look for a Web site. Instead of a lot of buttons or a huge list of links, a well-designed site usually has a menu containing the main categories of the site. When the mouse cursor passes over a category, a pop-up menu appears, which sometimes even includes a submenu. If you are developing a site with a large number of links, incorporating pop-up menus may be your solution.

The Set Pop-Up Menu Wizard is one of the newest additions to Fireworks 4. It certainly has gained the most attention in the user groups. This section shows you the basics of how to use the Set Pop-Up Menu Wizard in the way it is intended to be used. Later in this chapter, the "Advanced Editing of the Pop-Up Menus" section will show you how to do things the wizard wasn't intended to do. In this section, you will learn how to tweak the resulting menu to your liking (only for those who don't mind a bit of code) and get a look at some of the shortcomings of using an automatic tool.

Making an Instant Pop-Up Menu

This section explains how to make a pop-up menu, which is a relatively easy process. The only part that may prove to be a bit confusing at first is adding submenus. Thus, extra care is taken to give you the exact steps and illustrations for adding submenus. After you understand the indent and outdent concept, the rest is pretty easy. To make your pop-up menu, follow these steps:

1. Open a new document (File|New) with a size of 300 pixels wide by 300 pixels high.

2. Draw a rectangle and choose Insert|Slice. With the slice selected, choose Insert| Pop-Up Menu.

3. The Set Pop-Up Menu Wizard opens (see Figure 7.24). In the Text box, type the name of a menu entry, and if you want a link, type one in the Link box. Click the + sign next to Menu to add the menu item.

Long Links

If you have a really long link, you may discover that you can't type it in the Link box. If you are working with large links, before you begin your pop-up menus, open the URL panel (Window|URL). In the Current URL box (you don't even have to have a file open), type in a URL address and then click the + sign to add it to the URL Library. Now when you click the down arrow next to the Link box in the Set Pop-Up Menu Wizard, any links in the URL Library will be available.

Figure 7.24
The Set Pop-Up Menu Wizard.

4. Highlight the menu item in the Text box and type in the next entry. If you want a link, type it in and then click the + sign next to Menu.

5. The item you added in Step 4 has been added to the menu, but you want it to be a submenu item. Select the second entry and click the Indent icon (see Figure 7.25).

Figure 7.25
The Indent icon.

Note: Menu items are not indented. When you want an item indented, select the item, and then click the Indent icon which denotes an entry as a submenu. (Submenu items should be placed under the menu they are attached to.) When you want an item that appears indented to be a menu item (not a submenu), select the item, and then click the Outdent icon.

6. Continue adding menu and submenu entries. Click the Next button when you are finished.

7. Another Set Pop-Up Menu window opens in which you set the appearance of your menus. The choices are HTML menus or Image menus, which use a graphic as the menu:

- If you want an HTML-generated menu, click the HTML radio button. Select the Font, the point Size, the Up State text and Cell color, and the Over State text and Cell color (see Figure 7.26). Experiment a bit here until you get the look that you like. Click Finish when you are done.

Note: The fonts included in the Set Pop-Up Menu Wizard are the ones most likely to be on most computers. If you are using the Image option, only the graphic is exported, not the text; the browser renders the HTML text.

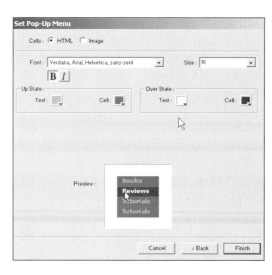

Figure 7.26
The Set Pop-Up Menu window showing the HTML option.

- Alternatively, you can use an image for the menu, by clicking the Image option. Now, you have additional choices (see Figure 7.27). Instead of just selecting the Text and Cell color options for the Up and Over States, you have a list of styles to choose from. The Image option uses a graphic that is a Style (more on using custom styles later in this chapter). See the upcoming section "Using Custom Styles for the Pop-Up Menu" for more information on this feature. Select a style and experiment.

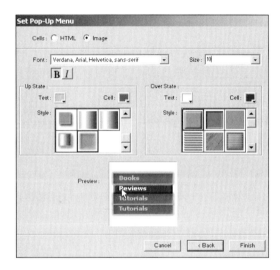

Figure 7.27
Set Pop-Up Menu window showing the Image option.

8. Click the Finish button. Unfortunately, you can't preview directly in Fireworks. To preview, choose File|Preview In Browser.

Exporting the Pop-Up Menu

After you complete the pop-up menu, you are ready to export it. For this exercise, choose File|Export|HTML And Images (Dreamweaver Library won't work; see Chapter 9 for a Macromedia workaround that allows you to use the pop-up menu as a Library item) and check the Put Images In Subfolder option. Browse to locate and add the image subfolder, and click Save when you are done.

Fireworks will generate all the JavaScript for the menu in a file called fw_menu.js, which is placed in the same folder as the HTML file. Be sure to upload the fw_menu.js file to your server or your menus won't work. Only one fw_menu.js file exists, no matter how many menus are included. If you have submenus, then an Arrow.gif image file is produced as well.

Using Custom Styles for the Pop-Up Menu

If you want to use an image menu design that isn't available in Fireworks, you can make your own design. You can make absolutely any design you want (graphic only, no text) for your image menu and save it as a style. If you want, you can make a whole set of custom styles and save the style(s) with a unique name (see Chapter 2 for details on making and saving styles).

Your custom styles can then be used for the pop-up menus. The styles for menus are not stored in the same location as the regular Style panel styles. When you make your own custom styles and save them, they can be found in Fireworks 4\Configuration\Styles. Copy the file you want and paste it into the Nav Menu folder, which is also in the Configuration folder. Every style file you have in the Nav Menu folder will automatically be available in the Set Pop-Up Menu Wizard.

PROJECT Making a Small Pop-Up Menu

In this project, you will make one pop-up menu using a custom style:

1. Open a new document (File|New), and then open the popupstarter.png file, which is in the Chapter 7 resources folder on this book's CD-ROM. Select one of the buttons and choose Edit|Copy and then Edit|Paste onto your canvas. Move the copy somewhere in the middle of your canvas to make adjustments to it. You are going to alter the look of the button and save it as a style to use for the menu.

2. Open the Fill panel (Window|Fill) and change the Texture to Sandpaper and 50 percent. Open the Effect panel (Window|Effect) and delete the glow. Save the style and put it in the Fireworks 4\Configuration\Nav Menu folder (see "Using Custom Styles for the Pop-Up Menu").

3. Select the Fireworks button and choose Insert|Slice. With the Fireworks button still selected, choose Insert|Pop-Up Menu.

4. The Set Pop-Up Menu Wizard opens. In the Text box, type "Books", and in the Link box, type "books.htm". Click the + sign next to Menu to add the menu item.

5. Highlight the word Books to change it, and type "Beginner" in the Link box; then highlight books.htm and type "booksbeg.htm". Click the + sign next to Menu.

6. Beginner has been added to the menu, but you want it to be a submenu of Books. Select Beginner and click the Indent icon.

7. Type "Intermediate" in the Text box and "booksint.htm" in the Link box and click the + sign. Repeat this step by typing "Advanced" in the Text box and "booksadv.htm" in the Link box and clicking the + sign. The Advanced submenu item may appear as a menu item (not in-dented); if it does, select it and click the Indent icon again.

8. To add the next menu item, type "Reviews" in the Text box and "reviews.htm" in the Link box and then click the + sign. This item should appear not indented. If it is indented, click the Outdent button to make it a menu item.

9. Type "By Joyce" in the Text box and "joyce.htm" in the Link box and click the + sign. With "By Joyce" selected, click the Indent icon.

10. Type "Off Site" in the Text box and "offsite.htm" in the Link box and click the + sign. It will probably still be indented; if it is not, select it and click the Indent icon.

11. For the last menu item, type "Tutorials" in the Text box and "tutorials.htm" in the Link box and click the + sign. It should be outdented.

12. For the last submenu, type "Beginner" in the Text box and "tutsbeg.htm" in the Link box, click the + sign, and click the Indent icon.

13. Type "Advanced" in the Text box and "tutsadv.htm" in the Link box and click the + sign; make sure it is indented. Figure 7.28 shows the completed menu list.

> **Note:** At the time this feature was tested, the Indent icon indented the first two entries, and the third entry automatically returned to Outdent. If you want more than two entries in a submenu, just select the entry and click the Indent icon again.

Figure 7.28
The completed menu list.

14. Click Next. The next window of the Set Pop-Up Menu Wizard opens. Select Image, locate the custom style you made and saved in Step 2, and select it. You can see a preview at the bottom of the dialog box. In this exercise, the default Font setting (Verdana, Arial, Helvetica, sans-serif) was used with a point size of 14. The Up State Text is color Hex #FFCC00, and Cell is color #0000FF. The Over State Text color is white (Hex #000000) and Cell is color #000084 (the default). Click the Finish button.

15. Export and save to a location where you can find this project for further editing.

Editing the Pop-Up Menu

The things that are editable using the Set Pop-Up Menu Wizard are the options within the wizard and the physical location of the menu in your document. To edit anything within the Set Pop-Up Menu Wizard, double-click the menu outline; when the wizard opens, make any changes you want.

To change the location of the menu, select the slice that the pop-up menu is attached to and drag the outline to a new position. Drag it to the center of the page. (This isn't where you will want it positioned, but it demonstrates that it can be moved anywhere.)

If you want to practice moving the menu, open the file you saved in the previous project. Click and drag the bottom of the menu outline to line up with the bottom and left side of the Fireworks button. You may need to preview a few times to get the position where you want it. Figure 7.29 shows the moved position of the menu.

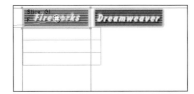

Figure 7.29

The pop-up menu lined up and in position.

Advanced Editing of the Pop-Up Menus

This section covers a few of the easier changes that can be made in the fw_menu.js file—the file where all the code for the menus is located.

Editing the Delay Time of the Menu Closing

To shorten the time it takes to close the menu when you move the mouse cursor off it, first open the fw_menu.js file from the pop-up menu you saved. If you need the fw_menu.js file, it can be found in the Chapter 7 popup folder on this book's CD-ROM. Open the fw_menu.js file in any text editor and go to line 454 (locating by line number is easy if you use an editor such as HomeSite; if you don't use such an editor, just scroll down until you find the code). The following is the code section that you are going to change:

```
function FW_startTimeout()
{
fwStart = new Date ();
fwDHFlag = true;
fwHideMenuTimer = setTimeout("fwDoHide()", 1000);
}
function fwDoHide()
{
if (!fwDHFlag) return;
var elapsed = new Date() - fwStart;
if (elapsed < 100) {
```

```
fwHideMenuTimer = setTimeout("fwDoHide()", 1100-elapsed);
return;
}
fwDHFlag = false;
hideActiveMenus();
window.ActiveMenuItem = 0;
}
```

You need to change only three lines. First, change 1000 to 10 in the following line:

```
fwHideMenuTimer = setTimeout("fwDoHide()", 1000);
```

Next, change 100 to 10 in the following line:

```
if (elapsed < 100) {
```

Finally, change 1100 to 11 in this line:

```
fwHideMenuTimer = setTimeout("fwDoHide()", 1100-elapsed);
```

By changing the elapsed time to a much lower number, the menu will disappear as soon as you move the mouse off of the trigger image.

Editing the Bevel Borders of the HTML Menu

To change the colors of the HTML style menus, locate the code that follows this paragraph in the fw_menu.js file. If you need the fw_menu.js file, it is located in the Chapter 7 popup folder of this book's CD-ROM. You can open the fw_menu.js file in any text editor, including Notepad. Locate each line and substitute the Hex number you want. Any changes made to the fw_menu.js file will affect all menus using this file.

The darker highlight color is

```
this.bgColor = "#555555";
```

The outside menu border color is

```
this.menuBorderBgColor = "#777777";
```

The lighter highlight color is

```
this.menuLiteBgColor = "#ffffff";
```

To change the bevel color (which is the lighter highlight color), open the fw_menu.js file and locate this line of code:

```
this.menuLiteBgColor = "#ffffff";
```

Change it to the following (or any color you want):

```
this.menuLiteBgColor = "#0000ff";
```

To edit just one menu, you can edit the code in the HTML file generated from the pop-up menu saved in an earlier project (the finishedpopup.htm file is in the Chapter 7 popup folder of this book's CD-ROM). Open the HTML file in any editor and locate this code (lines 32 through 40, near the bottom of the first script):

```
window.fw_menu_0 = new Menu("root",100,17,"Verdana, Arial,
Helvetica,
sans-serif",10,"#66cc00","#ffffff","#0000ff","#000084");
  fw_menu_0.addMenuItem(fw_menu_0_1,"location='books.htm'");
  fw_menu_0.addMenuItem(fw_menu_0_2,"location='reviews.htm'");
  fw_menu_0.addMenuItem(fw_menu_0_3,"location='tutorials.htm'");
   fw_menu_0.bgImageUp="images/fwmenu1_100x17_up.gif";
   fw_menu_0.bgImageOver="images/fwmenu1_100x17_over.gif";
   fw_menu_0.fontWeight="bold";
   fw_menu_0.hideOnMouseOut=true;
   fw_menu_0.childMenuIcon="images/arrows.gif";
```

The second-to-last Hex number is the border color, and the last Hex number is the cell color. The very last line of code shows you the folder that the arrow image was saved in.

Editing to No Borders

To eliminate the beveled border altogether, locate this code, which is on lines 25 and 26 of the fw_menu.js file:

```
this.menuBorder = 1;
this.menuItemBorder = 1;
```

Change it to the following:

```
this.menuBorder = 0;
this.menuItemBorder = 0;
```

Editing the Size of the Pop-Up Menu

The menu sizes are in the HTML code generated for your pop-up menu. The size measurements are on line 32 of the example. If you need the finished-popup.htm file, it is in the Chapter 7 popup folder of this book's CD-ROM:

```
window.fw_menu_0 = new Menu("root",100,17,"Verdana, Arial,
Helvetica,
sans-serif",10,"#66cc00","#ffffff","#0000ff","#000084");
```

The numbers 100 and 17 are the width and height dimensions. If you want two lines of text, you can add a <**br**> tag.

Editing the Dividing Lines in the Menu

The pop-up menu items are automatically divided by a line. If you don't want this line or if you'd like it to be more pronounced, you can edit the Fireworks-generated code to alter its appearance.

A programs such as HomeSite makes locating code with line numbers in it quite easy: The numbers are in red. Open the fw_menu.js file (located in the Chapter 7 popup folder of this book's CD-ROM) and look for the following code on lines 25 and 26:

```
this.menuBorder = 1;
this.menuItemBorder = 1;
```

Change the 1 to 0 to eliminate the line totally, or to a larger number if you want a larger dividing line:

```
this.menuBorder = 0;
this.menuItemBorder = 0;
```

PROJECT Adding a Pop-Up Menu to an Existing Navigation Header

The IDea Bookstore header that was made in Chapter 4 needs two pop-up menus added to the navigation bar. This is a real operating bookstore that grew so fast that it outgrew its old navigation bar quickly. The new pop-up menus were added to the navigation bar and the navigation bar was then added to the entire site within one day. To add the new pop-up menus to the navigation bar, follow these steps:

1. Open the bookstore.png file in the Chapter 7 resources folder of this book's CD-ROM. The header you will be working on is shown in Figure 7.30.

Home | Books | Tutorial | Specials | Reveiws | Magazines | Subscribe/Drawing | Contact Us

BOOKSTORE

Figure 7.30
The IDea Bookstore header.

2. Select the Books button, choose Insert|Slice, and then choose Insert|Pop-Up Menu.

3. The Set Pop-Up Menu Wizard opens. In the Text box, type "Imaging". You don't need to enter a URL in the Link box. Click the + sign to add the menu item. This is a menu item with a submenu, and only the submenu items will have links.

4. Type "Photoshop" in the Text box and "bitmaps.asp" in the Link box and click the + sign to add the menu item. Click the Indent button to place this item in a submenu.

5. Repeat Steps 3 and 4 until the whole menu is complete (if you want). This is a huge menu for a real bookstore. Figure 7.31 shows most of the menu and its links. To see it in its entirety, open the completed file bookstorefinished.png, select the Books slice, and double-click the blue outline to open the Set Pop-Up Menu Wizard.

Figure 7.31

The Set Pop-Up Menu Wizard with the menus added.

6. Click Next. the next window of the Set Pop-Up Menu Wizard opens. The Cells option is set to HTML and the Font is Verdana with a Size of 10. For the Up state, the Text color is #FFCC00 and the Cell color is #990000. For the Over state, the Text color is #990000 and the Cell color is #FFCC00 (the colors are simply reversed in the two states). Click Finish.

7. Click the blue outline and move it into position, as shown in Figure 7.32.

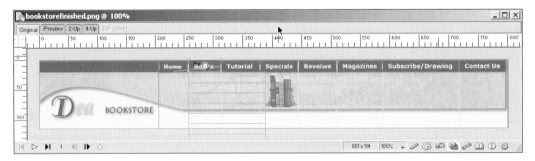

Figure 7.32

The position of the Books menu.

8. A second menu is needed for the Tutorial button. Select the Tutorial button, choose Insert|Slice, and then choose Insert|Pop-Up Menu.

9. Type "Photoshop" in the Text box and "http://books.je-ideadesign.com/viewlets/psresources.htm" in the Link box. Repeat this step for the rest of the menu items; the names for the menu items are shown in Figure 7.33. This menu has no submenus.

Figure 7.33
The menu items added to the Tutorial button.

10. Click Next. The next window of the Set Pop-Up Menu Wizard opens. The Cell setting is HTML and the Font is Verdana with a Size of 10. For the Up state, the Text color is #FFCC00 and the Cell color is #990000. For the Over state, the Text color is #990000 and the Cell color is #FFCC00. Click Finish.

11. Click the blue outline and move it into position.

12. Choose File|Export|HTML And Images and check the Put Images In Subfolder option. Browse to locate and add the image subfolder and click Save when you are done. The fw_menu.js file has now been generated.

13. To get rid of the white bevel, locate the following code, which is on lines 25 and 26 of the fw_menu.js file:

```
this.menuBorder = 1;
this.menuItemBorder = 1;
```

Change it to the following:

```
this.menuBorder = 0;
this.menuItemBorder = 0;
```

The Bookstore header with the Books pop-up menu is shown in Figure 7.34.

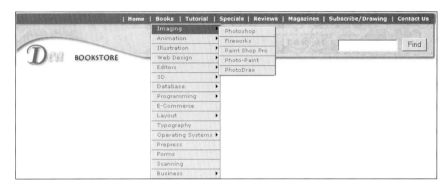

Figure 7.34
The finished Book
pop-up menu.

Limitations of the Pop-Up Menus

A few of the problems you may encounter using Fireworks 4 pop-up menus include the following:

- Pop-up menus do not span frames. If you have a menu in a top or side frame, the only part of the menu that will show up is whatever fits in the current frame. If you must use frames, this probably isn't the menu solution for you.

- Customization of any serious nature involves knowing how to hand code JavaScript.

- The absolute positioning of the pop-up menus causes several problems when placing the code into other editors. Editors that don't handle layers can't place the pop-up menus without hand coding.

- Pop-up menus cannot be used in a centered table in your layout. Other layout workarounds must be used, such as layers that have absolute positioning. How to position pop-up menus in Dreamweaver is covered in depth in Chapter 9.

Limitations aside, the pop-up menu feature of Fireworks 4 is a terrific time-saving addition.

Moving On

You should now be able to implement a variety of different navigational interfaces for your Web sites. You have learned how to add behaviors to images and buttons to produce simple rollovers, disjointed rollovers, and navigation bars. Add to this mix the new pop-up menu skills, and you are ready to tackle any navigational challenge.

In Chapter 8, you will learn how to make animated GIFs in Fireworks 4. You'll learn how to make an animated logo and a banner ad. You will get hands-on experience controlling the animation's timing, looping, and opacity, and even information on how to export it for use as an animated GIF or a SWF file for use in Flash.

Fireworks 4 Studio

This Studio showcases many of this book's projects made using the powerful features of Fireworks 4. Use this section for reference or inspiration, and when you see something you like, flip to that chapter and start producing it. The source files for all these images can be found on this book's CD-ROM, so you can use them in the learning process.

Blending modes in Fireworks 4 can produce interesting effects by blending the colors, values, and hues of the blending or top image with the base or bottom layer (see Chapter 1). In the top left image, the Multiply mode has been used to blend the colors from the mountain scene with the colors of the sand scene producing a darker image. The bottom left image shows the result of the Difference mode being applied to the mountain and sand scenes.

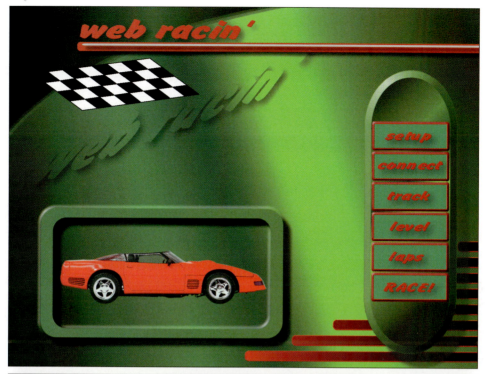

Vector tools (see Chapters 3 and 4) provide great flexibility, allowing you to draw images that can be resized without losing integrity or detail. Vector drawing tools and gradients were used extensively to design the interface in the top image. The bottom image also uses vector tools as well as a bitmap background, custom gradient for lighting effects, and clipart.

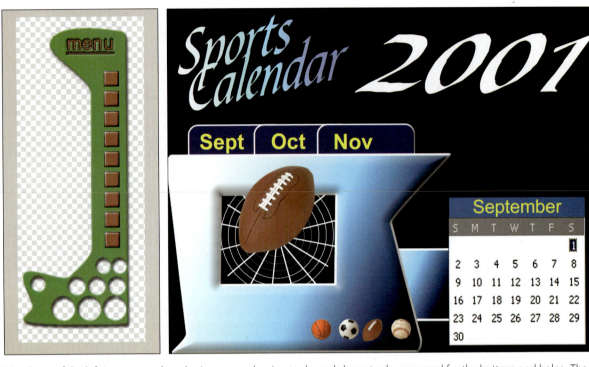

The shape of the left image was altered using vector drawing tools, and shape tools were used for the buttons and holes. The calendar was drawn using a rectangle shape with curves added, as well as text effects and gradients (see Chapter 4).

These two images demonstrate converting a bitmap company logo into a scalable and printable vector logo (see Chapter 4).

One of Fireworks' unnatural strokes, text leading, and a Motion Trail plug-in effect were applied to this banner (see Chapter 2).

This logo was made with a custom gradient, which is fully editable (see Chapter 2).

The logo on the left was made using the Text On A Path command and using text leading and orientation options (see Chapter 2). The company logo on the right was designed using clip art in conjunction with custom gradients and specialized text.

This seaside image was made by placing two images on top of each other and punching the text out of the top layer, revealing the water behind it (see Chapter 2).

A custom stroke was applied to this plate of salad, producing a unique effect. The texture used for this stroke is provided on this book's CD-ROM (see Chapter 2).

The bitmap selection tools can be used to retouch your artwork. In Chapter 5, you will learn how to improve the top image by removing the woman's wrinkles and whitening her teeth by using the bitmap selection tools, Blur filter, and the Hue and Saturation filter.

This image was a bit dull and lifeless. By using the Levels panel and learning to read the histogram, each of the RGB channels was altered producing a sharper image.

This image, which has sharper detail, shows the same figure after tonal adjustments were made using the histogram in the Levels panel (see Chapter 5).

Finally, the image was colorized to add a bit of green to the scene using the Hue and Saturation filter along with levels to keep the snow white (see Chapter 5).

Tonal adjustments can be made using different techniques in Fireworks (see Chapter 5). The bottom image shows how the tonal range was altered on this happy couple by adjusting the highlight and shadow points via the Levels panel, which also removed the haze.

Making seamless compositions is easy in Fireworks (see Chapter 5). Both of these compositions (the larger images) contain multiple bitmaps (the smaller images), which blend together by use of gradient transparency masks and layer opacity settings.

This image shows the green slicing guidelines that are placed in preparation for slicing this document (see Chapter 6).

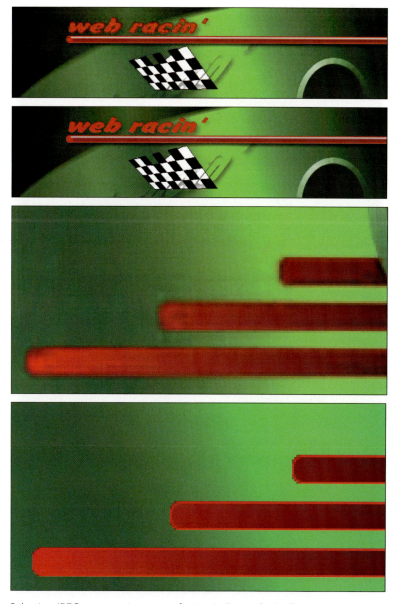

Selective JPEG compression, a new feature in Fireworks 4, allows you to use two different compression settings in the same slice (see Chapter 6).

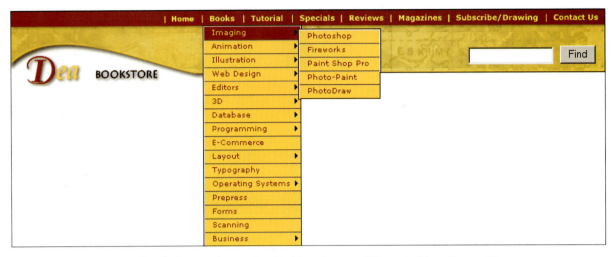

A complete navigation interface built using the new Pop-Up Menu feature of Fireworks 4 (see Chapter 7).

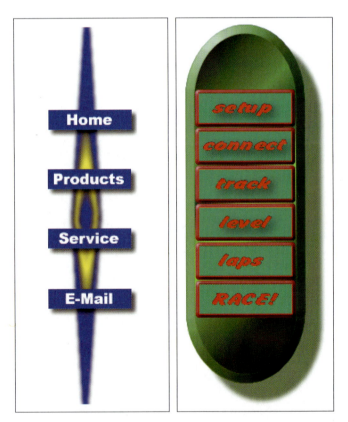

The navigation bar on the left was made into a symbol and can be added to a Web page with a click of the mouse. The navigation bar on the right was made using only the shape tools and combine commands (see Chapter 3); the buttons are made into a symbol in Chapter 7.

Both of these images use the Fireworks animation features discussed in Chapter 8. The quarter in the top image spins around in a complete circle using the animation tools. The company logo in the second image relies heavily on the timing of the frames and moving along a motion trail.

This composition uses edge effects that ship with Fireworks or that are included as demos on this book's CD-ROM (see Chapter 10).

The carousel image on the right (original on the left) was repaired using the demo version of AutoEye (supplied on this book's CD-ROM, see Chapter 10).

The left image uses a preset watercolor "stack" from the Segmentis plug-in. The right image also uses the Segmentis plug-in, but it has a Radial Simplifier filter applied (see Chapter 10).

The lizards were selected and colorized using bitmap selection tools and Adjust color features, and then the Xenofex Baked Earth plug-in (demo supplied) was applied to the background (see Chapter 10).

By taking charge of Fireworks' powerful bitmap tools such as the Gaussian Blur and Rubber Stamp tool, you can have reflections, even in the desert (see Chapter 5).

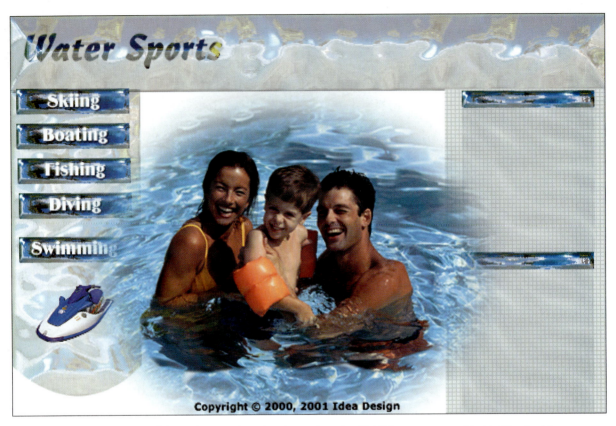

A plug-in called Primus inspired this Web page. Complete instructions for this Web page are provided in Chapter 10.

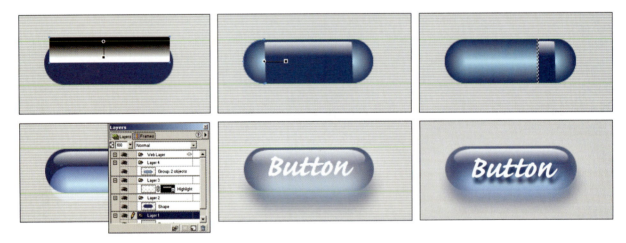

The very popular gel or plastic buttons can be done in Fireworks using the vector shape tools, gradients, and layers (see Appendix D).

Chapter 8

On the Move

This chapter will teach you how to make an animated logo and a banner ad. You will get hands-on experience controlling an animation's timing, looping, and opacity, and will find out how to export your animation as an animated GIF or SWF file for use in Flash. A detailed description of how to deconstruct an animation will teach you how to evaluate other animations, enabling you to reproduce them yourself.

Animations

Animations are often used to communicate an idea; unfortunately, they sometimes are used for no good reason at all, and end up only annoying users. The challenge you face when producing animations is to get the illusion of motion in as few frames as possible to keep the file size to a minimum. If an animation takes too long to download, it takes away from its intended purpose.

You probably remember using a flipbook as a child, a book containing many images that appeared to move as you flipped the pages with your thumb. That's the basic foundation of GIF animations: many images shown in sequence to give the illusion of motion—minus the thumb.

With the emergence of more Web-friendly animation technologies, Fireworks 4 has incorporated many features that aid you in producing high-quality GIF animations. The ability to use Photoshop and Illustrator layered files, Live Effects such as drop shadows, patterns, and beveling, and optimization tools such as comparing two to four different optimization settings at a time are just a few of the better features Fireworks 4 offers.

As you work, you'll have to decide whether to use a GIF animation or another technology such as Flash. Some of the determining factors will be your audience and the intended purpose of the animation, along with your budget and how frequently you produce animations. One of the major benefits of using Fireworks to produce GIF animations is the cost factor—no additional purchase is required for specialized software. If you only produce a limited number of animations or only short or small ones, then Fireworks 4 is more than suitable for the job. Another benefit to using GIF animations that may weigh heavily in the decision is that no additional plug-in is required to view the animations, and the learning curve is extremely short. Incorporating a GIF animation into an HTML Web page doesn't require any special coding; GIF animations are inserted just like any other image. Some of the drawbacks include a limited color palette of 256 colors, making GIF animations unsuitable for gradients, 3-D, or photographic animations; larger file sizes; and no streaming capabilities. Because all the frames of the animation need to be downloaded in the browser before it plays properly, the first time it runs, it may look jerky. After weighing the pros and cons, you may want to use GIF animations in some cases.

Working with Symbols and Instances

Understanding symbols and instances in Fireworks is the foundation of producing animations. *Symbols* represent an object, a group of objects, or a text block. A symbol may contain many objects, layers, and frames. They are either graphics, animations, or buttons; each of these symbols will be discussed in this section. When an object is converted into a symbol, the original symbol is accessed from the Library panel. Symbols are extremely useful when you want to reuse the same elements. In Fireworks, symbols are necessary, not optional, for producing GIF animations. Symbols are similar to what other programs call "sprites"; they animate independently and can be used multiple times throughout an animation.

Instances symbol. After an object is converted into a symbol, the object ʲ laced with an instance. The original symbol is stored ꞏꞏ a library anꞇ through the Library panel. Wherever a symbol is used in the docuꞯ. ꞏꞏy or an instance of the original symbol. If you edit the original symꞇ ꞏnce is automatically changed to the edited version, thereby streamlinꞇ ꞏflow.

Animated Symbols

If you decide to make GIF animations, the animated symboꞇ ꞏt likely be the most used option. An animated symbol plays independently, ꞏꞏ you to produce GIF animations that have more than one symbol interacꞇꞏ together. For instance, you may have text moving across the screen while a graphic is fading in and out in the background. To make a new animated symbol, follow these steps:

1. Choose Insert|New Symbol (Ctrl+F8/Cmd+F8).

2. The Symbol Properties dialog box opens, shown in Figure 8.1, in which you type a name for your symbol.

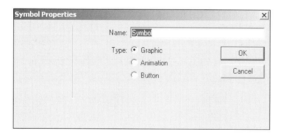

Figure 8.1
The Symbol Properties dialog box.

3. Choose the Animation option under the Type choices, and click OK.

4. The Symbol Editor window opens, in which you can draw either a vector object (discussed in Chapters 3 and 4) or a bitmap object (discussed in Chapter 5). Close the Symbol Editor when you are done.

5. You can now add frames to your symbol in the Object panel (Alt+F2/Option+F2); see "Adding and Deleting Frames," later in the chapter, for more information on adding frames.

To convert an existing object to an animated symbol, follow these steps:

1. Select an object.

2. Choose Modify|Animate|Animate Selection (Alt+Shift+F8/Option+Shift+F8).

3. The Animate dialog box opens, in which you choose your settings (see the following section for details). A bounding box is now around the object, and the symbol will appear in the Library panel.

Editing Symbol Properties

You can edit the properties of a symbol using either of two methods: Open the Object panel (Alt+F2/Option+F2), or use the Modify|Animate|Settings option, which opens the Animate dialog box and is available to all three types of symbols—animated, graphic, and button symbols. Each method has slightly different choices, as shown in Figures 8.2 and 8.3.

Figure 8.2
(Left) The Object panel symbol properties.

Figure 8.3
(Right) The Animate symbol properties.

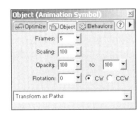

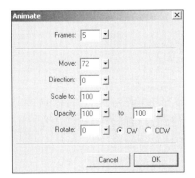

The Object Panel Options

The Object panel is where you specify how your animation will perform. You determine how many frames you need, what scaling is required, the opacity range, and any rotation you may want:

• *Frames*—Specifies how many frames you'd like in the animation. The slider in the drop-down list only goes to 250, but you can type in any number you'd like. The default is 5.

• *Scaling*—Specifies the percentage change in size from the beginning to the end of the animation. The default is 100 percent scaling, which keeps the animation at its original size, but it can be set to scale up to 250 percent of the original size.

• *Opacity*—Specifies the percentage change in the opacity from the beginning to the end of the animation. This is used to do the fade-in and fade-out effects. At 0 percent opacity, you'll see no image at all; at 100 percent opacity, you'll see the image with no transparency.

• *Rotation*—Determines the amount in degrees that the symbol rotates from the beginning to the end of the animation. The values range from 0 to 360 degrees; 0 is the default. You also have the option of having the animation rotate CW (clockwise) or CCW (counter-clockwise).

Note: The Object panel is one way to specify animation settings but not necessarily the best one. The Animate dialog box gives you additional settings and is always available. The Object panel doesn't always make the animation options available. For instance, if you convert an object to a symbol (Insert|Convert To Symbol), the Object panel does not give you the option to select Frames, Scaling, and so forth.

The Animate Properties

The Animate properties dialog box is available by selecting an instance and choosing Modify|Animate|Settings or Animate Selections. It includes the same options as the Object panel, plus two more:

- *Move*—Specifies the amount of movement in pixels that each object will move. The value range is from 0 to 250 pixels; the default is 72.

- *Direction*—Specifies the amount in degrees that the object will move. The value range is 0 to 360 degrees. The default setting is 0.

Editing Symbol Motion Paths

An animated symbol, when selected, will show a bounding box and a motion path, which is attached to it. This path indicates the direction in which the symbol will move. The green dot indicates the starting point and the red dot indicates the ending point. The blue dots in between represent the frames within the path. The Move and Direction values can be changed by dragging the handles in the bounding box in your document. You can move the green handle to change the beginning point and the red one to change the ending point. To constrain the movement to 45-degree increments, hold down the Shift key as you drag. Figure 8.4 shows a symbol with a motion path.

Figure 8.4
A motion path of a symbol.

PROJECT Making an Animated Symbol

To demonstrate how to convert a graphic into an animated symbol, you will produce an animated globe that will be used in another project in this chapter. Open the file called smallglobe.png, located in the toasterimages subfolder of the Chapter 8 folder on this book's CD-ROM. Follow these steps to animate this small globe, making it move and change size:

1. Select the globe and choose Insert|Convert To Symbol. When the Symbol Properties dialog box appears, select Animation for the type and click OK.

2. In the Animate dialog box, enter Frames 4, Move 52, Direction 57, Scale To 200, Opacity 100 to 100, and Rotate 0, choose CW (clockwise),

Figure 8.5

The motion path of the globe.

and click OK. The new motion path of the globe is shown in Figure 8.5. If you don't have the Library panel open, choose Window|Library (F11). Notice that the new animated symbol has been added to the library.

3. To see the animation in your workspace, click the Play button from the document window or the Preview mode. To view in a browser, choose File|Preview In Browser.

Graphic Symbols

Graphic symbols are objects that you may want to use in your animation multiple times. They can contain Live Effects, such as drop shadows, fills, and bevels. Graphic symbols can be accessed in the Library panel. If you want to use the symbol again, just drag an instance of the symbol from the Library panel onto your document. To make a new graphic symbol, follow these steps:

1. Choose Insert|New Symbol (Ctrl+F8/Cmd+F8).

2. The Symbol Properties dialog box opens. Choose Graphic from the Type option.

3. The Symbol Editor window opens. You can draw either a vector object (discussed in Chapters 3 and 4) or a bitmap object (discussed in Chapter 5). You can also open any image you want to use as a symbol and drag it into the Symbol Editor. Close the Symbol Editor when you are done drawing or dragging your object.

To convert an existing object to a graphic symbol, follow these steps:

1. Select an object.

2. Choose Insert|Convert To Symbol (F8).

3. In the Symbol Properties dialog box, choose your settings. A bounding box is now around the object, and the symbol will appear in the Library panel.

Editing Graphic Symbols

You can easily edit the underlying graphic of a symbol by using any of the drawing, text, or color tools. Because the graphic you are editing is a symbol, all instances of the symbol will be changed as well. To edit a graphic symbol, follow these steps:

Note: If you ever want to add a motion path, scaling, or any of the Animate properties to the graphic, simply choose Modify|Animate| Animate Settings and choose the options you want.

1. Double-click the graphic symbol to open the Symbol Editor.

2. Make any modifications to text, strokes, fills, or effects.

3. Close the Symbol Editor, and the changes will appear in your document.

Importing and Exporting Symbols

If you have symbols that you want to use in other projects or share with someone, you can save them as a library from the Library panel where they are stored in each document. You can also import libraries you have previously exported for use in your current document.

Exporting Libraries

To save a library of symbols from your current document, follow these steps:

1. Open the Library panel by choosing Window|Library.

2. Click the right pointing arrow and, from the pop-up menu, choose Export Symbols.

3. Select the symbols you want to export: If you want them all, choose Select All; if you want several in a row, Shift+click; if you want to pick and choose, press Ctrl/Option+click on the desired symbols. When you are done, click Export.

4. Name your library and choose where you want to save it; click Save.

> **Note:** For libraries you think you may use often, save them or move them to the Fireworks Library folder, which is in Macromedia\Fireworks 4\Configurations\Libraries. By placing your file here, it can be accessed by choosing Insert|Libraries.

Importing Libraries

To use a saved library in your current document, you will need to import it. To import a saved library, follow these steps:

1. Open the Library panel; if it isn't already, open choose Window|Library.

2. From the pop-up menu, choose Import Symbols.

3. Locate your saved library and choose Open.

4. The Import Symbols dialog box opens with the list of symbols in the library you selected to save. Choose the ones you want and click Import.

Button Symbols

Button symbols are made when you use the Button Editor, which is discussed in detail in Chapter 7. They are mentioned here because they are one of the animation types listed in the Symbol Properties dialog box. Refer to Chapter 7 to learn how to design button symbols.

Working with Frames

The Frames panel is where most of the designing is done when producing animations. What is included on each frame determines how the animation will play. By default, the Frames panel is grouped with the Layers panel and the History panel. When working on animations with the Frames panel, you will find it is easier to use if you can see the Layers panel and the Frames panel side by side, instead of having to click back and forth between their tabs. To do this, click the Frames tab and drag it out to the screen. You can now arrange the Layers panel and the Frames panel side by side for use in developing animations. If you want to return the Frames panel to the group, simply click and drag it back.

The Frames panel, shown in Figure 8.6, is the "control center" for your animation production. From the Frames panel, you can add, delete, move, and duplicate frames, use Onion Skinning, and set the looping options.

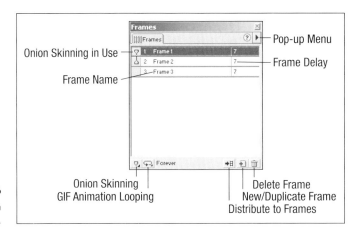

Figure 8.6
The Frames panel with labeled icons.

Adding and Deleting Frames

To add frames, you can add one at a time or enter a specified number of frames to add. If you have too many frames or decide you don't like or need a particular frame, you can delete one or more frames.

To add one frame, click the New/Duplicate Frame icon (refer to Figure 8.6).

To add multiple frames, click the right-pointing arrow to access the pop-up menu and choose Add Frames.

> **Note:** The name of this icon is misleading. You will not get a duplicate of the previous layer with this option; a new blank frame will be added.

When deleting a frame, you delete all of its content, with the exception of a frame that has been distributed to Frames (discussed in detail later in this chapter). Deleting a frame that contains a shared frame will not affect other frames that are using the shared frame. To delete a frame or frames, click the frame or Shift+click multiple frames and then use any of the following options:

- Click the trash can icon

- Click and drag the frame/frames on top of the trash can icon

- Click the right-pointing arrow in the Frames panel and choose Delete Frame

Moving and Duplicating Frames

Moving frames works the same way as moving layers; you click and drag the frame to the desired position. If you double-click the frame name, you can rename it. This is a change from Fireworks 3. In Fireworks 3, when you moved a numbered frame, the number changed to the new position it was moved to. In Fireworks 4, you can give your frames unique names. Moving the frames does not change the names or the numbers assigned.

Duplicating frames is a good way to save time by altering only the elements changing in each frame, instead of redrawing every frame from scratch. Another advantage to duplicating frames is that it makes it easier to reverse an animation. (Instead of an animation going through its frames and then starting at the beginning again, you can easily reverse the order and have it play backward to the beginning before starting over again. Oftentimes this results in a smoother animation.) When you Shift+select multiple frames and make a duplicate, the duplicate automatically starts with a duplicate of the last frame in the selection.

Figure 8.7

The Duplicate Frame dialog box.

To duplicate a frame, click the right-pointing arrow in the Frames panel and choose Duplicate Frame. Figure 8.7 shows the positioning options, from which you choose where you want the duplicate frame placed.

Distributing to Frames

The Distribute To Frames option of the Frames panel is used when you have multiple objects on one layer that you want in individual frames. Shift+select each object and click the Distribute To Frames icon. Each object will automatically be placed in its own frame.

Sharing Layers Across Frames

The ability to share layers across frames is important, because without it, you would have to insert repeating elements, such as a background image, into every frame, which would be very inefficient and time consuming. Sharing layers across frames will automatically place the contents of the selected layer onto every frame present and to all frames added. When you choose to share layers, this warning will open, "Sharing Layer 1 [or whatever layer] will delete any objects on that layer in frames other than the current frame. OK to proceed?" One caveat exists, though: Sharing layers is an all-or-nothing proposition—the layer will be shared on all layers; you cannot pick and choose which layers you want to share with. Later in the chapter, the project "Designing an Animated Company Logo" will show you how to overcome this obstacle if you have a few frames that you don't want the selected frame added to. To share a layer across all frames, follow these steps:

1. Double-click the layer you want to share.

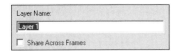

Figure 8.8

The frame name dialog box.

2. In the dialog box that appears (see Figure 8.8), name the layer and check Share Across Frames.

3. Repeat Steps 1 and 2 for any other layer you want to share.

4. To disable sharing of a particular frame, double-click the layer and uncheck the Share Across Frames option.

Onion Skinning

The Onion Skinning option allows you to see other frames of your animation through the current frame, aiding in placement of objects. This option is very handy if you need to align an object in one frame with an object in a frame above or below the current frame. Using Onion Skinning is like placing tracing paper over the individual frames, because you can see through to the other frames. One advantage of using the Onion Skinning feature is that you can select the faded objects (you see a faded version of the frames that are Onion Skinned) on frames other than the selected one and edit them without having to switch between frames. To use Onion Skinning, follow these steps:

1. Click the Onion Skinning icon (refer to Figure 8.6).

Figure 8.9

The Onion Skinning options.

2. From the Onion Skinning options, shown in Figure 8.9, choose Before And After. Frames that are using Onion Skinning have an icon next to them that resembles an elongated hourglass, as shown in Figure 8.10. If the No Onion Skinning option had been selected, this icon would be collapsed and look like a squashed hourglass, appearing only on the selected frame. To try it, click the Onion Skinning icon and choose No Onion Skinning.

3. If you tried the No Onion Skinning option, go back and change it to the Before And After option. In the Frames panel, click the gray square to the left of Frame 3, and notice how the icon expands to include this frame as well. If you click the Onion Skinning icon, you will notice that the option has automatically changed to Custom.

Figure 8.10

Onion Skinning icon indicating which frames are using Onion Skinning.

4. Click any object on your canvas; you can edit any of the frames, not just the object in the active frame. The frames made visible by Onion Skinning are faded.

Looping

The looping options set the number of times your animation will repeat. You can have it play over and over again indefinitely, choose a specific number of times to loop, or choose not to have it loop at all. Choosing No Looping simply means the animation plays one time and stops. To set the looping options, click the GIF animation looping icon (refer to Figure 8.6), which is next to the Onion Skinning icon, and select No Looping, a number, or Forever. No Looping is the default.

Frame Delay

The frame delay determines how long each frame is visible before the next frame appears. The delay settings are specified in hundredths of a second. For example, a setting of 10 would cause a 10 one-hundredths of a second (or a one-tenth of a second) delay before the next frame appears, and a setting of 100 would cause a 1-second delay before the next frame appears. To set the frame delay settings, double-click the last column in the Frames panel where you see a number. Enter the delay time you want and click outside of the dialog box to close it. You can set the delay for each frame individually or for multiple frames. To set the delay time for multiple frames, Shift select, then double-click the delay time number. Enter the number you want and click outside the dialog box to close it.

Tweening

At first glance, tweening appears to produce the same action as the motion paths you saw in the "Animated Symbols" section at the beginning of this chapter. In fact, it can do a lot more. Tweening is a traditional cartooning term that refers to the drawings done between the key frames of the animation. In the past, all that work was done by hand, usually by an assistant. Today the computer does this work for you. All you have to do is indicate a starting point and an ending point of an animation that you define by using instances. The computer generates the drawings in between the beginning and ending points with interpolated attributes; hence the term *tweening*, which derives from the word *between*.

You can do some extremely interesting things with tweening that you can't do using the Modify|Animate options. You will see in this section that the tweening methods for altering position, opacity, scale, and rotation achieve the exact same effect as they would in a motion path. Effects tweening—having an effect gradually change from the beginning instance to the end—can't be accomplished using a motion path. You can only achieve this effect using tweening. Tweening in Fireworks is performed on two or more instances of the same symbol. Using the same symbol is a key factor, but you can trick Fireworks, as you will discover in the second exercise.

Another interesting use of tweening is to replicate a duplication of objects, called *blending* in other vector programs. Blending works by having two objects and selecting how many steps in between you want to add. The objects added are sized according to the two objects selected, very similar to the way tweening works. Fireworks doesn't have a blend method per se, but tweening the objects will often produce similar results. In Chapter 3, a project that makes a spider web uses this technique.

Avoiding Jittery Animations

A trick that works on some animations is to set the first frame a bit longer than normal, allowing extra time for the rest of the animation to load. The biggest drawback to this trick is that when the animation loops, there will be a longer delay than normal each time. This isn't a problem in some animations.

Note: The types of tweening available in Fireworks are position, opacity, scale, rotation, and effects. You cannot do shape tweening, also known as *morphing*, which is a gradual changing of one shape into another, where your starting point is one graphic and the ending point is another. You can achieve a type of shape tween by using the Transform option and altering a shape by choosing Modify|Transform|Skew.

Applying a Multiple Tween

In this exercise, you will tween applying opacity, position, and scale by following these steps:

1. Open a new document (File|New) with a size of 300 pixels by 300 pixels.

2. Select any one of the drawing tools and draw an object, such as a circle, star, and so forth.

3. With the object selected, choose Insert|Convert To Symbol (F8). The symbol has been added to the library and an instance is in your document, which is indicated by the little arrow in the corner.

4. For the second symbol, select the instance and press Alt/Option. Click and drag a copy to the desired location, thereby producing a duplicate instance and the ending point of the tween.

5. Select just the ending point instance of the symbol, choose Modify| Transform|Scale, and drag one of the corners to increase the size.

6. To change the opacity, select the starting instance and, in the Layers panel, move the Opacity slider to 0. This will make the beginning instance invisible, with a gradual increase to 100 percent at the ending instance.

7. Shift+select the beginning and ending symbol instances and choose Modify|Symbol|Tween Instances, which opens the Tween Instances dialog box, shown in Figure 8.11. The default number of Steps is set to 10; you can change this number if you'd like. Be sure to check the Distribute To Frames checkbox. This will put each in-between instance on its own frame. If you neglect to check this option, all the in-between instances will be in the same frame.

Note: This exact same effect can be achieved with one animated symbol and using the Symbol Properties dialog box to set the Move, Direction, and Opacity settings.

Figure 8.11
The Tween Instances dialog box.

8. To preview the animation, click the Play button (white, right-pointing triangle) at the bottom of your document window. (It looks similar to VCR controls.) When you are done, click the black square (the white arrow turned into a black square).

PROJECT Distributing Objects to Frames

To practice distributing an object to frames, open the distribute.png file from the Chapter 8 resources folder on the book's CD-ROM and follow these steps:

1. Select the Porsche and choose Insert|Convert To Symbol; choose Graphic, and click OK.

2. Press Alt/Option and drag a copy of the Porsche to the far right of the document.

3. Shift+select both instances of the Porsche and choose Modify|Symbol| Tween Instances. Type in 6 Steps, don't check the Distribute To Frames checkbox, and click OK. Figure 8.12 shows what happens if you don't select the Distribute To Frames checkbox.

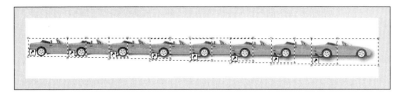

Figure 8.12
The Distribute To Frames option left unchecked produces this document.

4. Choose Edit|Undo Tween Instances. To do it properly, Shift+select the two instances, choose Modify|Symbol|Tween Instances, type in 6 Steps, and check the Distribute To Frames option. Look in the Frames panel and you will now see a total of eight frames—the two original frames and the six tweened ones.

Tween Live Effects

Tweening Live Effects is the method that cannot be produced using the animated symbol in the Animate dialog box. This little-known feature can produce some pretty amazing results. This exercise will demonstrate the basic technique of tweening Live Effects. To tween Live Effects, follow these steps:

1. Open a new document (File|New) with a size of 300 pixels by 300 pixels.

2. Select any one of the drawing tools and draw an object, such as a circle, star, and so on.

3. With the object selected, choose Insert|Convert To Symbol (F8); you can select Graphic or Animation. The symbol has been added to the library and an instance is in your document, indicated by the little arrow in the corner.

4. For the second symbol, press Alt/Option and click and drag a copy to the desired location, thus producing a duplicate instance and the ending point of the tween.

5. Here is where using tweening starts to vary from using a motion path. Select the beginning instance and open the Effect panel (Alt+F7/ Option+F7). From the down-pointing arrow, choose Adjust Color|Color Fill and select a color you like, but one that is different from the ending symbol. You may be wondering at this point how this can be done. You may recall that tweening can only be performed on two instances of the "same" symbol, and you just altered one. If you were to try to tween these two instances right now, it would not work. To make the two instances the same, the same effect has to be applied to both, which you'll do in the next step.

6. Select the ending instance and, from the Effect panel, choose Adjust Color|Color Fill (the same Effect you added to the beginning instance). This is where you fool Fireworks into thinking that both symbols are the same. The same effect is added; just move the Opacity slider to 0, and the not "visible" effect is applied.

7. Shift+select the beginning and ending symbol instances, choose Modify|Symbol|Tween Instances, accept the default frames, check the Distribute To Frames option, and click OK. Play your animation and you will see the gradual color change.

> **Note:** You can use more than two instances of a symbol when tweening. If you place instances in other locations, the tween will follow a path according to the stacking order; the closest to the canvas is the beginning point of the tween. Just remember that when you tween Live Effects, you must apply the effects whether they are invisible or not to every instance. You can make transformations, such as width, height, and skew, or opacity and blending modes, separately to individual instances.

PROJECT Tweening Using a Drop Shadow

To demonstrate and practice tweening Live Effects, you'll use an image from the Hemera Photo Objects 50,000 Premium Images Collection. It is in the Chapter 8 resources folder of this book's CD-ROM and is named porsche.png. Open it and follow these steps:

1. Open a new document (File|New) and use a white canvas at 600 pixels by 100 pixels.

2. With the object selected, choose Insert|Convert To Symbol (F8). The symbol has been added to the library and an instance is in your document, indicated by the little arrow in the corner.

3. For the second symbol, press Alt/Option and click and drag a copy to the desired location, thereby producing a duplicate instance and the ending point of the tween.

4. In the Effect panel, click the down arrow and choose Shadow And Glow|Drop Shadow. Enter a Distance of 0 and a Softness of 0, producing an invisible shadow.

5. Select the ending instance and, from the Effect panel, choose Shadow And Glow|Drop Shadow; enter a Distance of 7 and a Softness of 7, and set Opacity to 75 percent. Figure 8.13 shows the beginning and ending instances.

Figure 8.13
The beginning and ending instances of the Porsche.

6. Shift+select the beginning and ending instances, choose Modify|Symbol|Tween Instances, type in 6 frames, check the Distribute To Frames option, and click OK.

7. Play your animation and see how it starts with no shadow and ends with a shadow.

This exercise gives you just a sample of the possibilities available by tweening Live Effects.

Using Numeric Transform

Transforming the size of an object can produce interesting effects. The Numeric Transform option can be used to change the size of an object frame by frame or to distort the shape. To access the Numeric Transform dialog box, simply select the object you want to transform and choose Modify|Transform|Numeric Transform. Then, enter the parameters you want.

PROJECT Making a Quarter Spin

To make a quarter spin around from front to back, follow these steps:

1. Open a new document (File|New) with a size of 150 pixels by 150 pixels and a transparent background.

2. Open quarterfront.png from the Chapter 8 resources folder on this book's CD-ROM and drag it onto the new canvas. With the quarter selected, choose Edit|Copy.

3. Make the new document the active one. Open the Frames panel, click the right-pointing arrow, and choose Add Frames. In the Add Frames dialog box that opens, enter "10" for the Number, select the After Current Frame option, and click OK.

4. Choose Edit|Paste in each frame from Frame 1 to Frame 5 to add the quarter front.

5. Click Frame 2 (be sure the object is selected) and choose Modify|Transform|Numeric Transform. In the Numeric Transform dialog box, shown in Figure 8.14, uncheck the Constrain Proportions option, enter "75" for the height, and click OK.

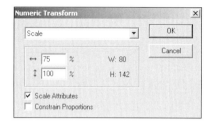

Figure 8.14
The Numeric Transform dialog box.

6. Select Frame 3 (be sure the object is selected) and choose Modify|Transform|Numeric Transform. In the Numeric Transform dialog box, uncheck the Constrain Proportions option, enter "50" for the height, and click OK.

7. Select Frame 4 (be sure to select the object) and choose Modify|Transform|Numeric Transform. Uncheck the Constrain Proportions option, enter "25" for the height, and click OK.

8. Select Frame 5 (select the object) and choose Modify|Transform|Numeric Transform. Uncheck the Constrain Proportions option, enter "10" for the height, and click OK.

9. Open the quarterback.png file from the Chapter 8 resources folder. Copy (Edit|Copy) and paste (Edit|Paste) it into Frame 6.

10. Align the quarter's back with the full-size image of the quarter. To see the images on the other layers, turn on the Onion Skinning feature by clicking the Onion Skinning icon (first icon to the left on the bottom of the Frames panel) and choosing Show All Frames.

> **Note:** In this example, you may not have to adjust the positioning because the canvas size is just a tad bigger than the quarter and the positioning is already correct.

11. After the quarter is aligned, select it and copy and paste it into Frames 7 through 10. Select Frame 7 and repeat Steps 5 through 8.

12. Select Frame 1 and copy (Ctrl+C/Cmd+C) the quarter front and then paste (Ctrl+V/Cmd+V) it into Frame 11.

13. To set the timing of the spin, double-click Frame 1 on the number 7 and enter "20"; repeat for all the frames with two exceptions: Set Frame 6 at 30 and Frame 11 at 100. Optionally, you can Shift+select all the frames and change to 20, and then go back and alter just Frames 6 and 30. Adjust the timing to your liking if this doesn't work for you.

14. To preview your animation, click the Play icon in the VCR-like control panel at the bottom of your document.

A copy of the completed animation named quarterspin.png is in the Chapter 8 resources folder of this book's CD-ROM.

Importing and Exporting

You will find various reasons to import and export your animations. To use your animation in a Web page, for example, you'll need to export it as a GIF animation. When you or a co-worker has made an animation from another program, you may want to import it into Fireworks to edit or to deconstruct to learn how it was made. Importing and exporting your GIF animations may be the easiest step in the whole process of developing the animation.

Importing

You can import GIF animations from other programs or users into Fireworks, where you can edit them or deconstruct them for learning purposes. If you import an existing GIF animation into a current document, it loses its frame delay settings and becomes a symbol of the current document. If you want to retain the frame delay settings of the original GIF animation, open it instead of importing it.

To import a GIF animation, follow these steps:

1. Choose File|Import.

2. Locate the file, select it, and click Open.

3. The cursor will turn into a corner shape; click in the document to place it. Any additional frames will be added.

Exporting

To export your animation with motion, you need to be sure that you have set it as an animated GIF. Open the Optimize panel and choose Animated GIF. The Optimize panel is also the place to reduce your colors as much as possible to reduce the file size. To export as a GIF animation, follow these steps:

1. Choose Animated GIF in the Optimize panel.

2. Choose File|Export.

3. In the Export dialog box, name the animation, choose where you want to export it, and click Save.

Your animation can be used in Flash and further edited there. To export as a Flash SWF file, follow these steps:

1. Choose File|Export.

Note: In the Export dialog box, the Save As Type box will show Images Only; this is correct. Your animation will export properly with motion if you remembered to choose Animated GIF in the Optimize panel prior to exporting.

2. Choose where you want to save the file.

3. Type in the name of your animation.

4. Click the down arrow under Save As Type and select Macromedia Flash SWF.

5. Click the Options button, choose the options you want, and click OK.

6. Click Save.

PROJECT Designing an Animated Company Logo

This project will walk you through every step involved in animating the Blue Toaster's logo. If you'd like to see the end result, open the bluetoaster.gif file from the Chapter 8 resources folder on the book's CD-ROM. The one step that isn't included is the conversion of the logo into vector elements. If you need to know how to make vector images, refer to Chapters 3 and 4. Some of the pieces being used in this project were completed in other projects.

Jeffrey Roberts did the vector conversion and the animation sequence. These instructions were all prepared by deconstructing the animation by using the Layers panel, the Frames panel, and the various dialog boxes containing the settings used, and then putting it back together. Please note, this is a logo for a real company and is copyrighted. Blue Toaster has graciously allowed us to provide the source files for you to practice on. To put all the pieces together and produce this animation, follow these steps:

1. Open a new document (File|New) with a white background and the size of 160 pixels by 100 pixels.

Note: This project uses the Layers panel and the Frames panel extensively, often changing back and forth between the two in the same step. Please read carefully when you are performing the steps.

2. From the Chapter 8 toasterimages folder on the book's CD-ROM, open toaster.png and drag it into the lower-left corner of the new document you just opened.

3. In the Layers panel (F2), double-click Layer 1, name the layer "Toaster", and then put a checkmark in the Share Across Frames option. This will allow the toaster to be on all the frames of the animation.

4. Open the Frames panel and drag the tab out from the Layers panel so that you can view both panels at the same time. Click Frame 1 and you will see the toaster. Click the New/Duplicate Frame icon to add a new frame.

5. In the Layers panel, click the New/Duplicate layer icon to add a layer, open toast.png from the toasterimages folder, and drag and position the toast over the toaster (see Figure 8.15). The Layers panel will show the toast on Layer 2, and the Frames panel will show the toast in Frame 2. Click the New/Duplicate Frame icon to add another frame.

Figure 8.15
The toast in position over the toaster.

6. Click Frame 3, open toast2.png from the toasterimages folder, and drag the toast onto the toaster. In the lower-left corner of the Frames panel, click the Onion Skinning icon and choose Show Before And After. Position toast2.png below the toast.png image and have it sitting on the toaster. Click the Onion Skinning icon and check No Onion Skinning. You want to keep the toast in this position for the next frame, so click the right-pointing arrow in the Frames panel and choose Duplicate Frame.

7. Click Frame 4 and notice that the toast is in it. Open lines.png from the toasterimages folder and place it according to Figure 8.16. From the pop-up menu in the Frames panel, choose Duplicate Frame.

8. Click Frame 5 and open frame5path.png from the toasterimages folder. Look in the Layers panel; you will see that frame5path.png has a curved design and a rectangle. The curve and the rectangle are grouped together right now to make moving the file easier. Drag this grouped image into position and place it according to Figure 8.17. The white rectangle is covering most of the path that a globe will follow in the next frame. Drag this group below everything else in Layer 2. In the Frames panel, from the pop-up menu, choose Duplicate Frame, and then choose After Current Frame. Type in "3" and click OK.

9. Choose File|Import, navigate to the Chapter 8 resources folder on this book's CD-ROM, and choose smallglobe.png. (This globe was animated in a previous project.) Your cursor will turn into a half rectangle; click the canvas to place it in the document, and then drag the globe into position, as shown in Figure 8.18. In the Layers panel, drag the animated symbol from Layer 1 into Layer 2 and put it just before the rectangle and path object. Select Layer 1 and click the trash can icon to delete it.

10. Click Frame 6; you will see the globe move up a bit and enlarge slightly. Click Frame 7; the globe is up higher and is larger. This is where you want to see the little path that is covered up. In the Layers panel, in Layer 2, select the rectangle and delete it.

11. Click Frame 8. In the Layers panel, delete the rectangle again. Open the largeglobe.png file from the toasterimages folder. Click the Onion Skinning icon in the bottom-left corner of the Frames panel and choose Before And After. Drag largeglobe.png directly on top of the ending globe from the animation symbol. You are doing this so that the large globe will be present for the rest of the animation. The large globe will be behind the ending tweened globe; line it up carefully. From the pop-up menu, choose Duplicate Frame, and choose After Current Frame.

Figure 8.16
The placement of lines around the toaster.

Figure 8.17
The positioning of the rectangle and the image it covers.

Figure 8.18
The positioning of the small globe.

12. Click Frame 9. Open the blob.png file from the toasterimages folder and place it behind the large globe. From the pop-up menu, choose Duplicate Frame and select After Current Frame (see Figure 8.19). Click Frame 10. Open computer.png from the toasterimages folder and drag it into position, as shown in Figure 8.19. From the pop-up menu, choose Duplicate Frame, and choose After Current Frame.

Figure 8.19
The placement of the blob and small computers.

13. Click Frame 11. Drag the computer into position, as shown in Figure 8.19. From the pop-up menu, choose Duplicate Frame, and choose After Current Frame. Click Frame 12. Drag the computer into position, as shown in Figure 8.19. Click the New/Duplicate Frame icon.

14. The next part of the animation doesn't use the toaster, and this is the one object shared across all the layers. Because sharing layers is an all-or-nothing proposition, you need to cover the toaster. Select the Rectangle drawing tool. From the color well at the bottom of the toolbox, select white for the fill color. Draw a rectangle big enough to just cover the whole toaster image, shadow and all.

15. Select the Text tool and click the canvas. Select Arial for the font and a size of 12. Click the color well and type in Hex #000099 (dark blue). Click the B for bold and the I for Italic, and choose Smooth Anti-Alias. Type "Hosted By . . ." and then click OK.

16. Center the text by dragging it into position. Choose Modify|Animate| Animate Settings. In the Animate properties dialog box, type in Frames 8, Move 0, Direction 0, Scale 150, Opacity 20 to 100, and Rotation 0; select CW; and click OK. When asked whether to automatically add additional frames, click OK.

17. If you check Frames 14 through 20 right now, you will see that the toaster is showing. The only way to solve this is to select Frame 13 and, in the Layers panel, select the rectangle and copy it (Edit|Copy or Ctrl+C/Cmd+C). Now click Frame 14, and in the Layers panel in Layer 2, paste the rectangle (Edit|Paste or Ctrl+V/Cmd+V). Repeat through Frame 20. Click the New/Duplicate Frame icon. Copy the rectangle again, select Frame 21, and paste the rectangle into Layer 2.

18. Select the Text tool and click the canvas. Select Arial for the font and a size of 12. Click the color well and type in Hex #000099 (dark blue). Click the B for bold, the I for Italic, and the U for underline, and choose Smooth Anti-Alias. Type in the words "Blue Toaster" and click OK.

19. To set the timing of the frames, double-click the Timing Delay column in the Frames panel and type in the amount of time you want. To see

how this animation's timing was set for each frame, open the completed file bluetoaster.png from the Chapter 8 resources folder.

20. Double-check the Optimize panel to be sure you have Animated GIF
    selected. Choose File|Export. In the Export dialog box, name the anima-
    tion, choose where you want to export it, and click Save.

Your animation is now ready to play.

PROJECT Deconstructing an Animated Banner

In this project, you will deconstruct an animated banner for the
IDea Bookstore that you worked on in Chapter 4. To view the completed animation, open the bookstore.gif file in the Chapter 8 resources folder
on the book's CD-ROM. To deconstruct this banner, follow these steps:

1. To deconstruct an animated GIF, you need to have the source file
   open; for this project, it is in the Chapter 8 resources folder and is
   named bookstore.png. Arrange the Layers panel and the Frames panel
   side by side for easy access. Figure 8.20 shows the animation you are
   going to deconstruct.

Figure 8.20
IDea Bookstore animated banner.

2. Click Frame 1. You will see two layers other than the special Web layer.
   The first one is named Shared Layer and the second is called Layer 1
   (the default name). The first thing to do is get a copy of what is on the
   Shared Layer. To do this, Shift+select all the object groups and choose
   Edit|Copy. Then, choose File|New, accept the defaults, click OK, and
   choose Edit|Paste. You now have the objects to reuse. Choose File|Save
   As and save in a practice folder of your choice. This is saved as
   shared.png in the Chapter 8 bookstoreimages folder.

3. This banner background is not a rectangle object the size of the banner,
   which you can tell by the images you just copied. The background color
   is that of the canvas. To set the canvas size and color, choose Modify|
   Canvas Size and then Modify|Canvas Color.

4. With Frame 1 still selected, you have one more element to deconstruct;
   it is on Layer 1 and is called Animation Symbol. To have a copy of the
   symbol, copy and paste the same way you did in Step 2. When the
   dialog box opens asking whether to add additional frames, click OK. To
   see the settings used in this symbol, choose Modify|Animate|Animate
   Settings. The Animate properties dialog box gives you all the informa-

tion you need to reproduce the symbol. If you follow the instructions on how to produce an animated symbol and use these settings and the graphic used here, you can reproduce the effect exactly. To get just the graphic and not the settings, choose Modify|Animate|Remove Animation, and then save the image only so that you can add the settings yourself.

5. Click each frame and watch Layer 1 in the Layers panel to see when a new element has been added. You will see that there are no changes in Layer 1 until Frame 24 (up to this point it's the same symbol moving along a motion path); the rest of the frames contain the computer-generated motion path. In Frame 24, the book image has changed. In the Layers panel, in Layer 1, select the group of objects, copy and paste the group into a new document, and save as "booksdown.png". A copy is in the bookstoreimages folder. When you reconstruct, you simply open the booksdown.png file and either drag into Layer 1 while Frame 24 is selected or paste the file into Layer 1.

6. Frame 26 contains a new animation symbol; it is the logo on a new motion path, but this time it is retreating. To copy it, select the anima-tion symbol from Layer 1 in the Layers panel and paste it into a new document. To see the settings used, choose Modify|Animate|Animate Settings, and the Animate properties dialog box will display all the settings used. To remove the settings and keep just the graphic, choose Modify|Animate|Remove Animation, choose File|Save As, and save the file as "retreat.png". A copy is in the bookstoreimages folder.

7. Frame 33 is named End Retreat, but a new symbol is introduced as well. In Layer 1, select and copy (Edit|Copy) the animation symbol and paste it into a new document. Save it as "lightbulb.png" (a copy is in the bookstoreimages folder). To see the animation settings used, choose Modify|Animate|Animate Settings, and the Animate properties dialog box reveals all the settings used.

8. Frame 34 introduces three additional animated symbols. The procedure to deconstruct the rest of this animation is the same as Steps 1 through 7. All the images are provided for you in the bookstoreimages folder if you need them, but you shouldn't need them if you follow these steps.

Using these deconstruction techniques, you can learn how others have de-signed their animations.

Moving On

By now, you understand what a symbol and an instance are and how to use each of them to produce animations in Fireworks. You've learned how to use frames, tween objects, and the Numeric Transform command.

In Chapter 9, you will learn how to incorporate Fireworks images and HTML code that you have exported into an external HTML visual editor. Special attention will be given to incorporating the code generated for the new pop-up menus and placing it into your HTML visual editor. You will also discover an impressive array of file formats that can be imported into Fireworks.

Chapter 9

Incorporating Fireworks 4 HTML Code into Other Applications

This chapter shows you how to get your Fireworks 4 HTML code into a Web design program such as Dreamweaver, GoLive, or FrontPage and how to make the result compatible with both Internet Explorer and Netscape browsers. Fireworks 4 pop-up menu placements are also dealt with in detail, helping you to position these menus so that they appear where you want them.

Fireworks Integration

Fireworks is great for generating your Web-ready images. These images and their code then need to be moved to a Web design program or HTML editor to prepare them for Web presentation.

Dreamweaver is the preferred choice of many developers because of its tight integration with Fireworks. In this chapter, you will discover the many ways Dreamweaver makes getting your Fireworks designs onto the Web easy. Dreamweaver is not the only HTML editor discussed, however. Fireworks HTML code can also be used in other WYSIWYG editors, such as GoLive and FrontPage.

Exporting Fireworks HTML Code for Use in HTML Editors

Fireworks uses a generic code for exporting your finished images to use in Web pages. When you choose to export using the HTML And Images option, the images and the HTML code are generated. The HTML code includes the table that puts the image slices back together, as well as any JavaScript code used for features such as rollovers and navigation bars.

To prepare for the subjects discussed in this chapter, you will export a sample file in several different ways. By doing this, you will have the sample files at your fingertips and will be able to put them into a Web page instead of just reading about how to do it. All the images and HTML files needed for these exercises can be found in the Chapter 9 folder on this book's CD-ROM.

Exporting Generic HTML and Images

For ease of explanation and step-by-step instruction, you should set up a folder to contain all the sample exports and files used for this chapter. You will benefit the most by doing each exercise. If you already are comfortable with a section and want to skip it, you can find the entire structure of the export folder on this book's CD-ROM in the exportingsamples folder. To use the completed structure and files, copy the entire exportingsamples folder and then paste or drag it onto your hard drive.

To export an image as a generic "HTML and Images" file, follow these steps:

1. In Fireworks, open the navbarsample.png file. You can find it in the Chapter 9 exportingsamples folder. Figure 9.1 shows the simple image file you will be exporting.

2. Open the Optimize panel (Window|Optimize) and choose GIF, WebSnap Adaptive, and 32 colors (see Figure 9.2). The file you will be exporting consists of button symbols, which were made in Chapter 7. In this chapter, you will not be slicing this image; you will just let

Figure 9.1

The buttons that are being exported.

Fireworks generate the slices needed other than the buttons. (They already have slices from a previous exercise.) Detailed instructions are given in Chapter 6 on the best techniques to use to slice an image.

3. Choose File|Export. In the Save In box, choose a place on your hard drive to save these exercises. Click the Create New Folder icon (the solid-yellow folder) and name the folder "exportingsamples". Double-click this folder to open it, click the solid-yellow icon again, and name this folder "generic". Double-click it to open it so that you can save files in this folder.

Figure 9.2
The Optimize settings for the sample export.

4. In the Save As Type box, choose HTML And Images. In the HTML box, choose Export HTML File. In the Slices box, choose Export Slices. Check Include Areas Without Slices, and check Put Images In Subfolder. Don't browse for a folder, because a new folder named images will be automatically added. Click the Save button. Figure 9.3 shows the settings used.

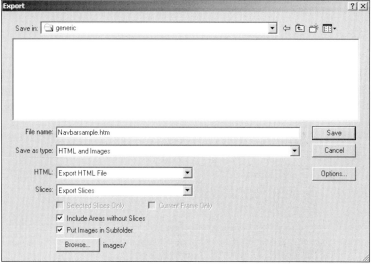

Figure 9.3
The export settings used for the generic export.

If you look in the generic folder, you will see a file called navbarsample.htm (Windows) and a separate folder named images. This image and its code are ready to be used in a Web page.

PROJECT Exporting a Pop-Up Menu

Fireworks 4 pop-up menus are exported using the generic HTML And Images method. You will need the file resulting from this project in placement exercises later in this chapter. Fireworks 4–generated pop-up menus present some challenges, which will be discussed in "Positioning Fireworks 4 Pop-up Menus," later in this chapter. To export a pop-up menu, follow these steps:

Figure 9.4
Button image sliced in
four pieces.

1. In Fireworks, open the popupsample.png file found in the Chapter 9 exportingsamples folder on this book's CD-ROM.

2. A slice and a small pop-up menu have been added to the Products image. If you move your cursor over the Products button, you will see how the menu has been aligned to the side of the button. You can export and include the areas without slices or use the slice tool and make four slices out of this image (refer to Chapter 6 for slicing instructions). Figure 9.4 shows the image with four slices.

3. You can select each slice now and add URLs and alternative text in the Object panel (Window|Object), or you can do it in Dreamweaver. Choose File|Export. In the Export dialog box, in the Save In area, navigate to the exportingsamples folder. Double-click it to open it. Click the solid-yellow folder icon to add a new folder, and name it "popup". Double-click the popup folder.

4. Name the file; this one is being named "popupsample.htm". In the Save As Type box, choose HTML And Images. In the HTML box, choose Export HTML File. In the Slices box, choose Export Slices. Check only the Put Images In Subfolder option, unless you didn't slice the sample file, in which case you should also check the Include Areas Without Slices option. Click Save. This menu is ready to be inserted into a Web page.

Exporting Images Only

The images in this exercise are just the images of the previous exercise with no slices. To export just the images, follow these steps:

1. In the Chapter 9 resources folder, open the exportimages.png file.

2. Right-click each image and choose Insert Slice (or go through the menu—Insert|Slice).

3. In the Optimize panel, select GIF and set the Colors setting to 16.

4. Choose File|Export. Navigate to your exportingsamples folder, add a new folder (click the solid-yellow folder icon), and name it "imagesonly". Double-click to open the folder.

5. Name your file. In the Save As Type box, choose Images Only. In the Slices box, choose Slices Only. Uncheck the Include Areas Without Slices option. Click Save. Four images are now in the imagesonly folder, ready for use in a Web page.

Exporting as a Library Item

If you want to use your image as a Library item in Dreamweaver, follow these steps:

1. In Fireworks, open the Navbarsample.png file. You can find it in the Chapter 9 exportingsamples folder.

2. Open the Optimize panel (Window|Optimize) and choose GIF, WebSnap Adaptive and 32 colors.

3. Choose File|Export. In the Save As Type box, choose Dreamweaver Library. A message will open telling you to have a Library folder in the root (see Figure 9.5); click OK. In the new window that opens, click the Create New Folder icon (the solid-yellow folder) and name the folder "library". Click Open.

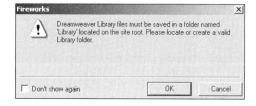

Figure 9.5
Library folder message.

4. In the Slices box, choose Export Slices. Check the Include Areas Without Slices box and check the Put Images In Subfolder box.

5. Double-click the library folder to export into it.

Exporting Image Maps

The only kind of image map that Fireworks can produce is a client-side image map. When you export this type of image map, the graphics and the HTML file containing the map coordinates, hotspots, and URLs are generated. To export an image map, follow these steps:

1. Prepare the image map by defining the hotspots, assigning the URLs, and choosing the optimization options. Then choose File|Export.

2. No sample of an image map is provided, so navigate to the folder you would like to export an image map into, and name the file.

3. In the Save As Type box, choose HTML And Images. In the HTML box, choose Export HTML File. So far, the options you are choosing are the same as those you choose when doing a generic export; however, this changes with the Slice box options. For the Slices option, choose None, because hotspots don't have slices.

4. If you want the images put in a separate folder, check that option and click the Save button.

> **Note:** Fireworks 4 pop-up menus cannot be exported as a Library item. A workaround exists if you want to use it as a Library item, as explained in "Pop-Up Menus as a Library Item," later in this chapter.

Placing Exported HTML and Images

Most of the directions and explanations in this chapter are for Dreamweaver 4, not because it is the only program that Fireworks is compatible with, but because it is the editor that the author uses and is most familiar with, and because it is so tightly integrated with Fireworks 4 that it really is a timesaver. A demo of Dreamweaver 4 is included on this book's CD-ROM. Even if you don't use or don't want to use Dreamweaver, it may benefit you to evaluate the code and placement techniques for use in other editors. When the term *Dreamweaver* is used, it refers to any application of Dreamweaver 4 or Dreamweaver UltraDev 4, standalone, demo, or studios. The Dreamweaver portion is the same in all of the variations. General information for using GoLive 5 and FrontPage 2000 also will be given.

Preparing a Dreamweaver Web Page

You can place your Fireworks code into any existing Web page or use the Fireworks-generated HTML file as your template. To make all the exercises in this chapter easier to follow along with, you will be given instructions when to add a new folder and what to name it. If you want to skip that part, you can use everything in the Chapter 9 exportingsamples folder. A practice file called DWsample.htm is included.

For some of the inserted code to be recognized, the site's root directory has to be defined. Also, for correct placement of inserted images, you will set your margins to 0 so that no margin exists in the browser. To define the site and set the margins, follow these steps:

1. Open Dreamweaver 4 (if you don't have it, a demo is supplied on this book's CD-ROM). Choose Modify|Page Properties. The only things to be concerned about for this exercise are the Left Margin and Top Margin settings; type in "0" for both. This will assure that no browser border appears around your placed images. Even though both margins are blank before you enter 0, a 2-pixel default border exists when using Dreamweaver. A 2 should be shown in the box, but it isn't, so you have to specifically enter 0.

2. Now you need to define this site so that some of the examples in the rest of this chapter will work, such as using the Library item you exported in the previous section. Choose Sites|Define Sites and click the New button. In the window that opens, click the yellow folder icon to locate the exportingsamples folder, and then click Select. Click OK. A window will open saying that the cache will be created; click OK, and then click Done.

> **Note:** If you didn't start at the beginning of this chapter, you will need the folders and files included on this book's CD-ROM to complete all the exercises and projects in this chapter. Copy the entire exportingsamples folder in the Chapter 9 folder to your hard drive.

3. Choose Insert|Table or use the Object Inspector's Common category (see Figure 9.6). In the window that opens, type in 1 Row, 2 Columns, 100%, and a Border of 0. Click the OK button.

4. Place your cursor over the dotted vertical lines in the center of the table, and click and drag to the left. Figure 9.7 has an arrow pointing to the lines to move. To view the code and see the design area at the same time, click the Show Code And Design Views icon, which the cursor is pointing to in Figure 9.7.

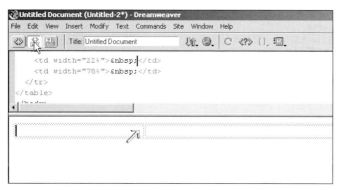

Figure 9.6
The Object Inspector in Dreamweaver.

Figure 9.7
The Design view, the line being moved, and the Show Code And Design Views icon.

5. Place your cursor in the first column and click. Figure 9.7 shows the portion of the code visible when you clicked in the first cell. Notice the code that looks like this:

```
<td width="22%"> </td>
<td width="78%"> </td>
```

Your numbers will vary, but this is the code to look for. Highlight the 22% (or whatever percentage you have in the first **<TD>** tag) and change it to 200. The code will now look like this:

```
<td width="200"> </td>
<td width="78%"> </td>
```

You have made the first column a fixed width, and the second column is a percentage. By keeping the second column a percentage, it will stretch to fit a browser's size. By having the first column fixed, whatever is placed in it will always remain in the same position no matter the browser size. This is particularly important for placing Fireworks 4 pop-up menus later in this chapter.

That is the important part of this Web page. You can save this file or you can use the one done for you in the exportingsamples folder, named DWsamplefile. htm. The DWsamplefile.htm file includes a simple text layout so that you can see how it stretches in some of the exercises you will use this file in.

Placing Fireworks 4 HTML Code into a Dreamweaver 4 Web Page

A few different ways exist to get your Fireworks code into a Dreamweaver Web page. You can simply use an insert command, or you can copy and paste it into the correct areas.

Inserting the Fireworks 4 HTML Code into Dreamweaver

To insert the Fireworks code of the pop-up menu you exported earlier in the "Exporting a Pop-Up Menu" project (files are in the popup folder in the exportingsamples folder), follow these steps:

1. Open Dreamweaver 4, choose File|Open, and navigate to the exportingsamples folder on your hard drive (or you can open the one on this book's CD-ROM). Choose DWsamplefile.htm and click Open. Figure 9.8 shows the file the way it looks so far.

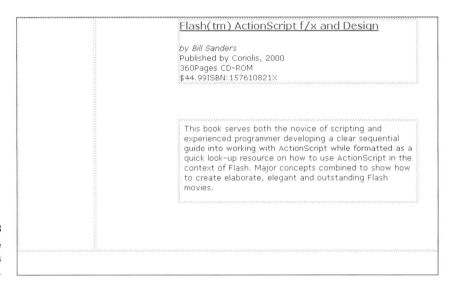

Flash(tm) ActionScript f/x and Design

by Bill Sanders
Published by Coriolis, 2000
360Pages CD-ROM
$44.99ISBN:157610821X

This book serves both the novice of scripting and experienced programmer developing a clear sequential guide into working with ActionScript while formatted as a quick look-up resource on how to use ActionScript in the context of Flash. Major concepts combined to show how to create elaborate, elegant and outstanding Flash movies.

Figure 9.8
The appearance of the sample Web page before Fireworks code is inserted.

Figure 9.9
The Insert Fireworks HTML icon.

2. Place your cursor in the first column and click. Choose Insert|Interactive Images|Fireworks HTML. Or you can use the Insert Fireworks HTML icon in the Common section of the Object Inspector, as shown in Figure 9.9.

3. In the window that opens, click the Browse button. Navigate to the exportingsamples folder and open the popup folder. Click the popupsample.htm file. Don't select the Delete File After Insertion option, because you will be using it again. If you were doing this on a real Web page, you would usually want to delete the file after it was placed because the code is now integrated into the file you placed the Fireworks HTML into. When you are finished, click OK. The completed file is shown in Figure 9.10.

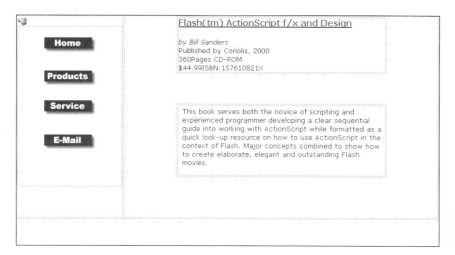

Figure 9.10
The sample Web page with the
Fireworks 4 HTML code added.

4. Choose File|Preview In Browser or click on the Globe icon on the same
row as the HTML code icons below the menu bar, and select the browser
you want preview in. Pass your cursor over the Products button. The
menu will pop out, but notice the red X in Internet Explorer or a blank
square in Netscape next to the first menu's items. The instructions had
you use DWsamplefile.htm in the exportingsamples folder. This was
done to demonstrate this point. You see the X or blank area because the
arrow image that goes in the menu is missing. It's in the image folder
of the popup folder. The files accessing the pop-up menus need to be in
the same folder as the fw_menus.js file and the image folder. Choose
File|Save As and save this file in the popup folder. Now if you preview,
the arrows will be there. A copy of the file has been saved for you in the
popup folder and is called popupinserted.htm.

Using the Fireworks 4 HTML File

If you think inserting the Fireworks 4 HTML code was easy, you'll find using
the native Fireworks 4 HTML file even easier. If you don't yet have a current
Web page you want to insert into, then you can simply open the HTML file
that Fireworks generated when you exported. You can use the Fireworks 4 HTML
file as a Dreamweaver template. Of course, you can use this file as a template
in any editor that supports templates.

Copying and Pasting Fireworks 4 HTML Code into Dreamweaver

Copying and pasting Fireworks 4 HTML code into Dreamweaver is the same as
it is for GoLive or other applications. When you are going to use Fireworks 4
HTML, you need to choose the generic Export As HTML And Images option. To
copy and paste the pop-up menu you exported in the "Exporting a Pop-Up
Menu" project, follow these steps:

1. In Dreamweaver, choose File|Open, navigate to the exportingsamples folder, select DWsamplefile.htm (the copy without any menus inserted), and click Open.

2. Click the second icon below the menu bar, Show Code And Design Views, to view the code and the Web page. Choose File|Open, navigate to the popup folder inside the exportingsamples folder, select the popupsample.htm file, and click Open. To see just the HTML code in this file, click the first icon below the menu bar, called Show Code View. Listing 9.1 shows the top portion of the HTML code.

Listing 9.1   The **<HEAD>** portion of the HTML code of the pop-up menu.

```
<title>popupsample.gif</title>
<meta http-equiv="Content-Type" content="text/html;">
<!-- Fireworks 4.0  Dreamweaver 4.0 target.  Created Mon Jan 22
12:45:36 GMT-0600 (Central Standard Time) 2001-->
<script language="JavaScript">
<!--
function MM_findObj(n, d) { //v3.0
  var p,i,x;  if(!d) d=document;
if((p=n.indexOf("?"))>0&&parent.frames.length) {
    d=parent.frames[n.substring(p+1)].document;
n=n.substring(0,p);}
  if(!(x=d[n])&&d.all) x=d.all[n]; for
(i=0;!x&&i<d.forms.length;i++) x=d.forms[i][n];
  for(i=0;!x&&d.layers&&i<d.layers.length;i++)
x=MM_findObj(n,d.layers[i].document); return
}
function MM_nbGroup(event, grpName) { //v3.0
  var i,img,nbArr,args=MM_nbGroup.arguments;
  if (event == "init" && args.length > 2) {
    if ((img = MM_findObj(args[2])) != null && !img.MM_init) {
      img.MM_init = true; img.MM_up = args[3]; img.MM_dn =
img.src;
      if ((nbArr = document[grpName]) == null) nbArr =
document[grpName] = new Array();
      nbArr[nbArr.length] = img;
      for (i=4; i < args.length-1; i+=2) if ((img =
MM_findObj(args[i])) != null) {
        if (!img.MM_up) img.MM_up = img.src;
        img.src = img.MM_dn = args[i+1];
        nbArr[nbArr.length] = img;
      } }
  } else if (event == "over") {
    document.MM_nbOver = nbArr = new Array();
    for (i=1; i < args.length-1; i+=3) if ((img =
MM_findObj(args[i])) != null) {
      if (!img.MM_up) img.MM_up = img.src;
      img.src = (img.MM_dn && args[i+2]) ? args[i+2] :
```

```
args[i+1];
      nbArr[nbArr.length] = img;
    }
  } else if (event == "out" ) {
    for (i=0; i < document.MM_nbOver.length; i++) {
      img = document.MM_nbOver[i]; img.src = (img.MM_dn) ?
img.MM_dn : img.MM_up; }
  } else if (event == "down") {
    if ((nbArr = document[grpName]) != null)
      for (i=0; i < nbArr.length; i++) { img=nbArr[i]; img.src
= img.MM_up; img.MM_dn = 0; }
    document[grpName] = nbArr = new Array();
    for (i=2; i < args.length-1; i+=2) if ((img =
MM_findObj(args[i])) != null) {
      if (!img.MM_up) img.MM_up = img.src;
      img.src = img.MM_dn = args[i+1];
      nbArr[nbArr.length] = img;
  } }
}


function MM_preloadImages() { //v3.0
 var d=document; if(d.images){ if(!d.MM_p) d.MM_p=new Array();
  var i,j=d.MM_p.length,a=MM_preloadImages.arguments; for(i=0;
i<a.length; i++)
  if (a[i].indexOf("#")!=0){ d.MM_p[j]=new Image;
d.MM_p[j++].src=a[i];}}
}


function fwLoadMenus() {
  if (window.fw_menu_0) return;
    window.fw_menu_0_1 = new Menu("Product 1",77,17,"Verdana,
Arial, Helvetica, sans
serif",10,"#0000cc","#009900","#009900","#0000cc");
    fw_menu_0_1.addMenuItem("Sample 1");
    fw_menu_0_1.addMenuItem("Sample 2");
    fw_menu_0_1.hideOnMouseOut=true;
    window.fw_menu_0_2 = new Menu("Product 2",81,17,"Verdana,
Arial, Helvetica, sans
serif",10,"#0000cc","#009900","#009900","#0000cc");
    fw_menu_0_2.addMenuItem("Sample 1");
    fw_menu_0_2.addMenuItem("Sample  2");
    fw_menu_0_2.hideOnMouseOut=true;
  window.fw_menu_0 = new Menu("root",76,17,"Verdana, Arial,
Helvetica, sans
serif",10,"#0000cc","#009900","#009900","#0000cc");
  fw_menu_0.addMenuItem(fw_menu_0_1);
  fw_menu_0.addMenuItem(fw_menu_0_2);
  fw_menu_0.hideOnMouseOut=true;
  fw_menu_0.childMenuIcon="images/arrows.gif";

  fw_menu_0.writeMenus();
} // fwLoadMenus()
```

```
//-->
</script>
<script language="JavaScript1.2" src="fw_menu.js"></script>
</head>
```

The area that is grayed out is the code that you copy from the Fireworks 4 HTML–generated code and paste into the **<HEAD>** section of
the Web page you want to use it in. Paste this code below the **<TITLE>**
and **<META>** tags but before the **</HEAD>** (end head) tag. The code
you are copying and pasting is the JavaScript for the rollovers.

3. The next section to copy and paste is only needed when images are
   coded to preload. Listing 9.2 shows the code from the pop-up menu
   sample you are using. If this code is not present in a document you are
   copying, skip this step. The top gray area shown in Listing 9.2 is the
   only part you are copying right now.

Listing 9.2   The code in the body background section and the
              table code.

```
</head>
<body topmargin="0" leftmargin="0" marginheight="0"
marginwidth="0" bgcolor="#ffffff"
 onLoad="MM_preloadImages('images
popupsample_r2_c2_f2.gif','images
popupsample_r2_c2_f3.gif','images
popupsample_r6_c2_f2.gif','images
popupsample_r6_c2_f3.gif','images
popupsample_r8_c2_f2.gif','images/popupsample_r8_c2_f3.gif');">
<script language="JavaScript1.2">fwLoadMenus();</script>

<table border="0" cellpadding="0" cellspacing="0" width="200">
<!-- fwtable fwsrc="popupsample.png" fwbase="popupsample.gif"
fwstyle="Dreamweaver" fwdocid = "742308039" fwnested="0" -->

  <tr>
   <td><img src="images/spacer.gif" width="43" height="1"
border="0"></td>
   <td><img src="images/spacer.gif" width="116" height="1"
border="0"></td>
   <td><img src="images/spacer.gif" width="41" height="1"
border="0"></td>
   <td><img src="images/spacer.gif" width="1" height="1"
border="0"></td>
  </tr>

  <tr>
   <td colspan="3"><img name="popupsample_r1_c1" src="images
popupsample_r1_c1.gif" width="200" height="12" border="0"></td>
```

```
      <td><img src="images/spacer.gif" width="1" height="12"
border="0"></td>
  </tr>
  <tr>
    <td rowspan="8"><img name="popupsample_r2_c1" src="images
popupsample_r2_c1.gif" width="43" height="288" border="0"></td>
    <td><a href="#" onMouseOut="MM_nbGroup('out');"
onMouseOver="MM_nbGroup('over','popupsample_r2_c2','images
popupsample_r2_c2_f2.gif','images
popupsample_r2_c2_f3.gif',1);"
onClick="MM_nbGroup('down','navbar1','popupsample_r2_c2','images
popupsample_r2_c2_f3.gif',1);" ><img name="popupsample_r2_c2"
src="images/popupsample_r2_c2.gif" width="116" height="45"
border="0"></a></td>
    <td rowspan="8"><img name="popupsample_r2_c3" src="images
popupsample_r2_c3.gif" width="41" height="288" border="0"></td>
    <td><img src="images/spacer.gif" width="1" height="45"
border="0"></td>
  </tr>
  <tr>
    <td><img name="popupsample_r3_c2" src="images
popupsample_r3_c2.gif" width="116" height="15" border="0"></td>
    <td><img src="images/spacer.gif" width="1" height="15"
border="0"></td>
  </tr>
  <tr>
    <td><a href="#" onMouseOut="FW_startTimeout();"
onMouseOver="window.FW_showMenu(window.fw_menu_0,149,83);"
><img name="popupsample_r4_c2" src="images
popupsample_r4_c2.gif" width="116" height="44" border="0"><
a></td>
    <td><img src="images/spacer.gif" width="1" height="44"
border="0"></td>
  </tr>
  <tr>
    <td><img name="popupsample_r5_c2" src="images
popupsample_r5_c2.gif" width="116" height="14" border="0"></td>
    <td><img src="images/spacer.gif" width="1" height="14"
border="0"></td>
  </tr>
  <tr>
    <td><a href="#" onMouseOut="MM_nbGroup('out');"
onMouseOver="MM_nbGroup('over','popupsample_r6_c2','images
popupsample_r6_c2_f2.gif','images
popupsample_r6_c2_f3.gif',1);"
onClick="MM_nbGroup('down','navbar1','popupsample_r6_c2','images
popupsample_r6_c2_f3.gif',1);" ><img name="popupsample_r6_c2"
src="images/popupsample_r6_c2.gif" width="116" height="45"
border="0"></a></td>
    <td><img src="images/spacer.gif" width="1" height="45"
border="0"></td>
  </tr>
  <tr>
```

```
    <td><img name="popupsample_r7_c2" src="images
popupsample_r7_c2.gif" width="116" height="19" border="0"></td>
    <td><img src="images/spacer.gif" width="1" height="19"
border="0"></td>
  </tr>
  <tr>
    <td><a href="#" onMouseOut="MM_nbGroup('out');"
onMouseOver="MM_nbGroup('over','popupsample_r8_c2','images
popupsample_r8_c2_f2.gif','images
popupsample_r8_c2_f3.gif',1);"
onClick="MM_nbGroup('down','navbar1','popupsample_r8_c2','images
popupsample_r8_c2_f3.gif',1);" ><img name="popupsample_r8_c2"
src="images/popupsample_r8_c2.gif" width="116" height="45"
border="0"></a></td>
    <td><img src="images/spacer.gif" width="1" height="45"
border="0"></td>
  </tr>
  <tr>
    <td><img name="popupsample_r9_c2" src="images
popupsample_r9_c2.gif" width="116" height="61" border="0"></td>
    <td><img src="images/spacer.gif" width="1" height="61"
border="0"></td>
  </tr>
</table>
```

The code to copy is located in the body background area. The code to locate in the target Web page is similar to this:

```
<body bgcolor="#FFFFFF" text="#000000" leftmargin="0"
topmargin="0">
```

Delete the last > tag and paste the two grayed lines of code, as shown in Listing 9.2, starting with onLoad and ending with </**SCRIPT**>.

4. The last chunk of code to copy and paste contains the buttons and their table. The second gray area in Listing 9.2 is where you copy all the way through the </**TABLE**> tag. Locate the code (it's close to the <**BODY**> tag) and then paste what you just copied, just before the </**TD**> that you see in this portion of code:

```
<table width="100%" border="0">
<tr>
<td width="200
" valign="top">  </td>
```

You have just pasted the table containing the buttons and surrounding image slices into the first column.

Placing Fireworks 4 HTML Code into GoLive

To use Fireworks 4 HTML code in GoLive, you need to export from Fireworks using the generic HTML And Images option. To copy and paste into GoLive, follow the same steps as described in "Copying and Pasting Fireworks 4 HTML Code into Dreamweaver," earlier in this chapter.

Placing Fireworks 4 HTML Code into FrontPage

To use Fireworks 4 HTML code in FrontPage, you need to export from Fireworks using the generic HTML And Images option. FrontPage does not separate the JavaScript into the **<HEAD>** section of a Web page. So, when copying and pasting, copy the JavaScript from the **<HEAD>** section and paste it into Notepad or another text editor. Then, copy the **<BODY>** code and paste it into Notepad. Select all the code in Notepad (or another text editor) and paste it below the **<BODY>** tag in a FrontPage Web page.

Using Exported Dreamweaver Library Objects

Dreamweaver Library items simplify the process of editing and updating a frequently used Web site component, such as a navigation bar. A Library item is a portion of an HTML file located in a folder named library at your root site. Library items appear in the Dreamweaver Library palette. From this palette, you can drag a copy to any page in your Web site. To place a Library item in a Web page, follow these steps:

1. In Dreamweaver, open the Web page in which you want to place a Library item. For this exercise, open the DWsamplefile.htm file in the exportingsamples folder. Earlier in this chapter, you exported a sample Library item into the root folder of exportingsamples.

2. If the Library category isn't open, choose Window|Library or Window|Assets; in previous versions of Dreamweaver, the Library was in its own panel. Now it is a category in the Assets panel. If you did the "Export as a Library Item" section earlier in this chapter, you will see the Navbarsample in the Library. Drag either the image or the text (which one doesn't matter) into the first column. That's all there is to it. Using Dreamweaver really is the simplest way to integrate your Fireworks 4 HTML code.

You cannot edit a Library item directly in the Dreamweaver document; you can only edit the master Library item. Then, you can have Dreamweaver update every copy of that item as it is placed throughout your Web site by using the Update option found by clicking the right-pointing arrow in the Library panel.

Using Exported Images Only

At the beginning of this chapter, you exported a file as images only. A copy is in the imagesonly folder in the exportingsamples folder. To add images only to a Dreamweaver page (or to any other editor using similar steps), follow these steps:

1. Open the DWsamplefile.htm file located in the exportingsamples folder.

2. Place your cursor in the first column (left side) and click. From the Object Inspector, click the Insert Image icon (a little tree) or choose Insert| Image. Navigate to the imagesonly folder in the exportingsamples folder, select the first image—navbarsample_rw2_c2.gif—and click Select.

3. Press the Enter/Return key, click the Insert Image icon again, choose the second image, and click Select. Repeat for the last button.

4. Select the first button and, if the Property Inspector isn't open, choose Window|Properties. Figure 9.11 shows the Property Inspector with the Home button selected. Add your link and alternative text here.

Figure 9.11
The Property Inspector.

5. Repeat Step 4 for each button.

Positioning Fireworks 4 Pop-Up Menus

To place the pop-up menus generated by Fireworks 4, you use the same methods as you use to insert regular Fireworks HTML code. A special section is devoted to placing the pop-up menus not because the placement is any different, but because some of the problems you may encounter need to be discussed. Centering the pop-up menus on the page is a common problem. Some of the options of how to center pop-up menus will be discussed in this section. But, just in case you decide to skip portions of the introductory explanations, you should know before you start experimenting that you cannot center the image containing pop-up menus or the table you place them into.

Absolute Positioning

The first thing to understand about the Fireworks 4 pop-up menus is that they use absolute positioning. Fireworks 4 generates a JavaScript file, which generates CSS layers. The JavaScript code assigns absolute positioning of each pop-up menu CSS layer. This is done to keep the menus and the submenus in the same

Browser Compatibility

At the time the browser compatibility tests in this chapter were done, they worked in IE5, and some worked in Netscape 6. Hopefully, by the time you try this, Netscape 6 (maybe 7) will be more compatible. Always be sure to test your menus in the major browsers. The pop-up menus will not work in the Opera browser. The positioning may be a bit different in Internet Explorer and Netscape browsers. Making these pop-up menus compatible to both platforms is the most challenging part of using them. As a designer, you need to evaluate the pros and cons of one browser versus another and whether or not the new Fireworks pop-up menus will be suitable to your audience.

location in relation to the buttons they are linked to. When the button is moved to another location, the menus stay where they were designed to be. The coordinates that are written into the HTML code of the pop-up menus are relative to the position of 0px from the top-left corner of the browser. If it's not the same position in the Web page, then the menus will not be positioned correctly. Several options are available to solve some of these problems, and you can choose which one works best for your situation.

Changing the Coordinates

Changing the coordinates of the menu's positioning via the HTML Inspector in Dreamweaver is easy. If you are using another HTML editor, then open the HTML file generated for your pop-up menu and alter the coordinates there. To change the coordinates, follow these steps:

1. To change the coordinates in Dreamweaver, open the HTML Inspector. If you are using version 4 or the demo on this book's CD-ROM, then click the Show Code And Design Views icon (the cursor is pointing to it in Figure 9.12). Locate the line of code that is highlighted in Figure 9.12. You can find it in the **<BODY>** part of the code, not in the **<HEAD>** part. The following is the code you are looking for:

   ```
   onMouseOver="window.FW_showMenu(window.fw_menu_0,145,82);"
   ```

   This is the code from the exercise where you inserted the pop-up menu code into the sample HTML page. The saved file is in the Chapter 9 exportingsamples, popup folder and is named insertedpopup.htm.

2. The second two sets of numbers in the preceding code represent the X, Y coordinates of the menu. You can change them according to where you would like the menus positioned. Along these lines, you can open the file in Fireworks and use the Info panel to determine the exact location of the menu, and use these coordinates.

3. You may ask, "How do I know what to change the coordinates to?" Good question. Open the file you designed; in Fireworks, open the Info panel (Window|Info), and place your cursor in the top-left corner of a menu. Look in the Info panel and you will see the X, Y coordinates.

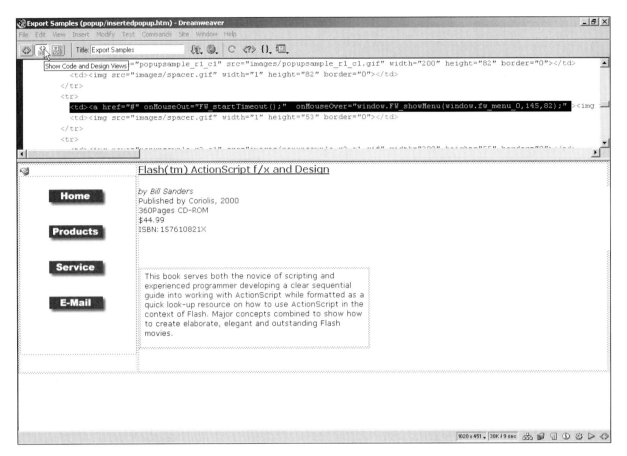

Figure 9.12

The Code and Design views of the sample Web page.

Designing in Fireworks

Another option is to place the menus in Fireworks in the location you want them to appear in the Web page. In other words, if your menu will start at perhaps 200 pixels down the Web page, then start your design in Fireworks at that point. Then, when the page is exported and placed in an editor, the menus will be positioned properly. This technique works great for centering a top navigation bar.

Trial and Error

You could also reopen the menu in Fireworks, move the position of the menu, export it again, insert it into the Web page again, and then preview. Repeat this process until the menu is where you want it.

Using Layers and Coordinates

This procedure worked every time it was tested in IE5 and Netscape 4.5, 4.7, and 6. Follow these steps to use a layer:

1. Open the DWsamplefile.htm located in the exportingsamples folder. Place your cursor in the first column on the left and click to set the cursor location.

2. Choose Insert|Layer. When the layer is placed, click and drag it over the first column. In the Code Inspector, locate this code:

```
<div id="Layer1" style="position:absolute; width:209px;
    height:108px; z-index:1; left: 11px; top: 10px"></div>
```

3. The only reason you dragged the layer a bit was to add the **left:** and **top:** code. If you didn't drag the layer, these coordinates won't be in your code and you'll have to add them by hand-coding. The numbers will vary, of course. In this example, change the **left: 11px** to **0px**, and change the **top: 10px** to **0px**.

4. If you are using Dreamweaver, place your cursor in the layer, click to place your cursor in the correct position, and choose Insert|Interactive Images. Locate the file you want to insert, and click OK.

Pop-Up Menus as a Library Item

You cannot export a Fireworks 4 pop-up menu as a Library item. However, Macromedia Technical Support offers a workaround that appeared in the Fireworks' forum to convert the pop-up menus into a Library item. There was talk of making this workaround a technote at Macromedia's Fireworks support center. The technotes and the forum are both wonderful resources; be sure to use them. As with any workaround, you should try it, test it, and play with it to make it do what you want. To begin this workaround, which starts in Dreamweaver, follow these steps:

1. You need to define a site in Dreamweaver. Choose Site|Define Sites and navigate to the site you want to use the Library item in.

2. In Fireworks 4, export your pop-up menu into the library folder of the site you just defined. Export as HTML And Images, *not* as a Dreamweaver Library. In the Export dialog box, check the Put Images In Subfolder option; don't browse to select a folder, let Fireworks generate it.

3. In Dreamweaver, open a new page (File|New) and then choose File|Save As. Navigate to the library folder of the site you just defined, name your file, and type in the ".lbi" extension to save it as a Library item.

4. Choose Insert|Interactive Images, navigate to the library folder, and select the popupsample.htm that you exported there in Step 2. Choose File|Save (it is still being saved in the library folder as a Library item).

5. Open a new page (File|New) and then choose File|Save As. Name it what you'd like and save it in the root folder, not the library folder.

6. If the Library isn't open in Dreamweaver, choose Window|Library. Drag the pop-up menu, which is now a Library item, onto the canvas.

Note: You can also place a top navigation bar in a layer in a fixed center cell (not a centered table) to center a header. This should also work in Netscape browsers, but always check. A lot depends on how you designed the top navigation bar in Fireworks and your coordinates.

Positioning Facts

The pop-up menus will not display properly if you center the main table or a nested table that you insert the menu into. If you use a percentage table and don't set a fixed-width cell or column, then the pop-up menu will reposition as a browser resizes, causing the menus to be incorrectly positioned. Be sure that the cell or table you place the Fireworks 4 pop-up menu code into has an absolute placement and is not centered.

7. If you see any code highlighted in yellow, just select it and delete it. Be sure not to delete the little yellow icon, because it contains a JavaScript command. To preview, choose File|Preview In Browser and select each browser to test. This technique was tested several times in IE5 and Netscape 4.7, and the menu worked every time. The menus still need to be positioned according to the instructions in the earlier "Positioning Fireworks 4 Pop-Up Menus" section.

The preceding instructions are for a pop-up menu that uses HTML for the menus. If you used images instead, you will have to change the links to the images in Dreamweaver. Look in the <**HEAD**> section and locate the code that looks like this (the sizes may be different):

```
fw_menu_0.bgImageUp="images/fwmenu1_110x18_up.gif";
fw_menu_0.bgImageOver="images/fwmenu1_110x18_over.gif";
```

Add the word "Library" and a "/" in front of **images**. The code should look like this when you are done:

```
fw_menu_0.bgImageUp="Library/images/fwmenu1_110x18_up.gif";
fw_menu_0.bgImageOver="Library/images/fwmenu1_110x18_over.gif";
```

Working with Images in Dreamweaver

The integration between Fireworks 4 and Dreamweaver 4 allows you to edit Fireworks source files without leaving Dreamweaver. If you are using the Fireworks 4 and Dreamweaver 4 Studio, the integration files are added to Dreamweaver.

In previous versions of Fireworks and Dreamweaver, if you installed Fireworks before Dreamweaver, the integration files were not added to Dreamweaver. To solve this problem, you had to reinstall Fireworks before you'd be ready to edit Fireworks files without leaving Dreamweaver. Apparently, this is no longer the case, according to Macromedia Technical support. If you do run into problems, use the workaround just described.

Optimizing Images from within Dreamweaver

You can optimize an image without leaving Dreamweaver. If you decide you'd like to change the optimization settings, you can access a version of Fireworks' optimization settings by following these steps:

1. Open a Web page in Dreamweaver that has images that you made in Fireworks, or make a new one. If you make a new page, save it at least once before trying to edit images.

2. Select an image and choose Commands|Optimize Image In Fireworks. If a window opens telling you that you need to save, then you didn't save in Step 1.

Note: The first time you use this command, you may be asked to enter the Fireworks serial number again. If you can't get your hands on it quickly, open Fireworks and choose Help|About Fireworks. Click in the area that scrolls, and your serial number will be displayed.

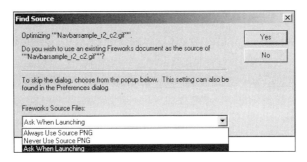

Figure 9.13
The Find Source dialog box.

3. A Find Source dialog box opens (see Figure 9.13) asking you if you want to use the source image; you also have the option of selecting Always Use Source PNG, Never Use Source PNG, or Ask When Launching. Dreamweaver will try to find the source file; if it can't, you can browse to locate the PNG or any other format yourself.

4. A version of the Optimize panel opens. Figure 9.14 shows how many options are available without leaving Dreamweaver. When you are done making changes, click the Update button. The changes you made are now updated in Dreamweaver.

> **Fireworks Source Files**
>
> It's a good idea to select Always Use Source PNG when the Find Source dialog box opens. This is particularly important when working with a JPEG image. Every time you save a JPEG image, you lose more detail and quality. For instance, the first time you saved as a JPEG file, the compression method threw out details of your image, to compress it to a smaller size. When you save again, the same compression throws out more information. You'll get a much better image if you optimize the original first. If you don't have the source file, then try for the best image you can get.

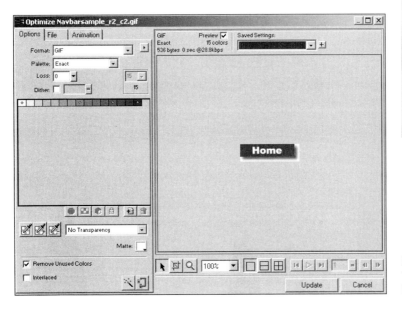

Figure 9.14
The Optimize window in Dreamweaver.

Editing Images in Dreamweaver

You can change anything in your image that you want. You can change the fill, effect, style, or whatever else suits your needs. To edit an image while in Dreamweaver, follow these steps:

1. Open a page in Dreamweaver and click an image to edit.

2. In the Property Inspector (Window|Properties), click the Edit button. Fireworks opens and you are given the opportunity to locate the image file.

3. Make any changes as you normally would in Fireworks. Notice that the top bar of the document you are editing your image in says Editing From Dreamweaver on it (see Figure 9.15). When you are done making changes, click the Done button.

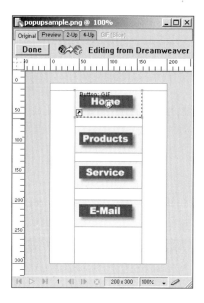

Figure 9.15
The Editing From Dreamweaver label displayed in Fireworks.

4. Changes you've made in Fireworks will be updated in Dreamweaver, except for one: If you changed the physical size of the image, it doesn't get automatically updated in the Dreamweaver code. The image may appear distorted or blurry. In the past, you had to manually change the size, but a great new feature has been added in Dreamweaver 4. Figure 9.16 shows the Property Inspector, which now has a button on it called Reset Size. Click it, and the size is changed for you.

Figure 9.16
The Property Inspector's Reset Size button.

Other Applications that Integrate Well with Fireworks

Sometimes, you may have files you produced in another program that you want to use in Fireworks. Or a client may give you a file in a format other than Fireworks to work with. Fireworks can open or import a wide range of files. This section gives a brief description of the various formats that can be used in Fireworks 4.

Photoshop and Fireworks Files

Fireworks can open Photoshop PSD files, including Photoshop 6, and maintain editing capability. Photoshop can also open Fireworks PNG files and maintain editing capability. When you export a Fireworks file as a PSD file, you can choose which is more important to you, better editing capability or better appearance. To open and use a PSD file, choose File|Open and open it like any other file.

> **Note:** Photoshop 6 PSD files only open in Fireworks 4, not in earlier versions.

Using Illustrator, FreeHand, and CorelDRAW Files

Fireworks can open Illustrator, FreeHand, and CorelDRAW files, with some exceptions. Illustrator files are limited to files made with Illustrator 7 and 8. Illustrator 9 files will not open or import into Fireworks 4.

You can open and edit FreeHand files, including Freehand 9 files.

CorelDRAW 7 or 8 files can be opened in Fireworks and edited. Many of the blends and effects applied in CorelDRAW will be lost, though. Fireworks isn't very friendly with regard to CorelDRAW.

When you open one of the vector program files, a Vector File Options dialog box opens, similar to Figure 9.17. You can choose how you want the imported image to look.

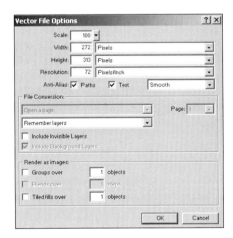

Figure 9.17
The Vector File Options dialog box.

Other Formats

Some of the other file types that Fireworks can open include BMP, TIF, EPS, and WBMP.

Moving On

You should now be fully equipped to insert your Fireworks 4 HTML code into a Web page editor such as Dreamweaver, GoLive, or FrontPage. You've seen the drawbacks of the new pop-up menus in Fireworks 4 and the solutions to positioning the menus. You have also discovered how easy it is to optimize and edit images from within Dreamweaver 4.

In Chapter 10, you will see how to use third-party plug-ins and filters to enhance your images. Chapter 10 includes all kinds of great and fun tools to try out, including special edge effects and free and demo plug-ins.

Chapter 10
Using Special Effects

In this chapter, you will look at some of the remaining options in the Xtras menu, including the Unsharp filter and some special plug-in filters. You will also explore using freely distributed commands and plug-ins, as well as third-party, for-sale plug-ins.

The Xtras Menu

You used the Xtras menu to do color adjustments and corrections in Chapter 5. The Xtras menu has a few remaining items that need to be discussed, mainly the use of Blur filters, Sharpen filters, and plug-ins.

The Other options on the Xtras menu won't be detailed here. The Convert To Alpha option is a holdover from an earlier version of Fireworks in which the new masking techniques weren't available, meaning that this option now is obsolete. The Find Edges option doesn't offer any apparent benefits except for possibly the rare special effect. This doesn't mean that a Find Edges filter is useless. In Photoshop, you can do some pretty cool things with the Find Edges filter, but because the Find Edges filter in Fireworks isn't a selection, you can't inverse it, which limits its usability. Maybe you can find something neat to do with it. If you do, feel free to send any ideas to the author at this book's companion Web site.

Using the Blur Filters

The Blur filters are helpful in many retouching situations. In Chapter 5, you saw how using a Blur filter can help to reduce facial wrinkles in a photo. Blurring can also be applied to an image that looks scratchy, speckled, or a bit dirty. Before you start blurring an image that you are repairing, make a duplicate layer; you can always delete it later if you don't need it. But if you blur too far and want more detail, you can put the duplicate layer on top of the blurred layer and lower the duplicate layer's opacity just enough to add detail but not to reveal the flaws you were trying to cover.

If you want just a little bit of blur, choose Xtras|Blur. If you want a bit more, choose Xtras|Blur More. The best Blur filter by far is Gaussian Blur, because it gives you full control over how much blur is applied. To apply Gaussian Blur, choose Xtras|Gaussian Blur and type in the amount of blur (or use the slider) you want (see Figure 10.1).

Figure 10.1
The Gaussian Blur dialog box.

Note: The Gaussian Blur filter has an option to preview the blur amount. The preview in real time only works if you use the slider to select a setting. If you type in a setting, you have to press the Enter/Return key to see the result.

 Making a Reflection Using the Gaussian Blur Filter

This is a really simple way to make a reflection that looks realistic. (Well, as realistic as a desert scene that is reflected on water can be.) To make a reflection using the Gaussian Blur filter, follow these steps:

1. Open a new document (File|New) with a size of 400 pixels by 600 pixels.

2. Open the cactusoriginal.png file from the Chapter 10 resources folder on this book's CD-ROM. Drag the picture of the cacti to the new document and place it at the top.

3. With the cacti picture selected, choose Edit|Clone, and then choose Modify|Transform|Flip Vertical. Move the flipped version below the original image and line up the bottoms perfectly.

4. With the bottom image selected, choose Xtras|Gaussian Blur and type in "3" or "4" (3 was used in this example). Figure 10.2 shows the image with the blur added.

Figure 10.2
The cacti image with Gaussian Blur applied.

5. Open the water.png file from the Chapter 10 resources folder. Drag it onto the bottom image object. Click and drag the points on the water object, and enlarge the water to cover the entire bottom image. In the Layers panel, set the Opacity to 30% and press the Enter/Return key. You now have a water texture for your reflection.

6. The cacti scene is now reflecting in the water. The only thing that remains is to blend the line between the water and the top image. Double-click the Rubber Stamp tool to open the Rubber Stamp tool options, shown in Figure 10.3. Choose Aligned for the Source and Document for the Sample. This allows you to sample from one object and stamp onto another, treating both objects as one.

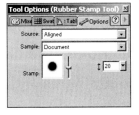

Figure 10.3
The Rubber Stamp tool options.

7. To soften the transition of the reflection line, press the Alt/Option key above the reflection to set the sampling point, and then click on top of the reflection. Do this sporadically along the line. You can sample above and below the dividing line, but be careful not to stamp in a pattern. (Refer to Chapter 5 for more details on using the Rubber Stamp tool.) Figure 10.4 shows the finished reflection.

Figure 10.4
The reflected cacti image.

Using the Sharpen Filters

The Sharpen and Sharpen More filters are automatic adjustments that don't leave you in control. What the Sharpen filters do, especially the Unsharp Mask filter, is improve the appearance of images' sharpness by working with contrast. The contrast is emphasized in an image based on the selections you make in the Unsharp Mask dialog box. The following are the three selections to enter:

- *Sharpen Amount*—Specifies the intensity, or how much neighboring pixels affect one another. The Sharpen Amount setting is affected by the Radius and Threshold amounts as well, so you may have to adjust this setting. The best setting for the Sharpen Amount is between 50% and 100%.

- *Pixel Radius*—Similar to a feather effect, this setting determines how many pixels are evaluated. The larger the number you select, the more pronounced the contrast. The Pixel Radius setting's range should be .5 percent to 1.5 percent of the dpi of the image. So, for a 72 dpi image, the Pixel Radius should be in the range of .35 pixel to 1 pixel. If your image is busy and has low contrast, use the high end of the Pixel Radius

---

Gaussian Blur and Unsharpen Mask Hints

After you apply the Gaussian Blur filter or the Unsharpen Mask filter, the effect may be too much. Or, it may be too much just in certain areas. To help lessen the effect, you can apply a small blur. If you need just a bit of sharpening added back to either an image with blur or an image with sharpen and blur applied, follow these steps:

1. Make a duplicate of the original layer or object (for a sharpened image, duplicate the sharpened layer or object). Or, if just a certain area needs more detail put back, such as eyes, you can copy just the portion you need (for example, eyes) of the original or sharpened image.

2. Put the duplicate layer or the layer with a duplicate part of an image on top of the object or image that has too much blurring.

3. Lower the Opacity of the duplicate layer in the Layers panel until the image looks the way you want it to look.

---

settings. If the image is not so busy and has high contrast, use the low end of the settings.

- *Threshold*—Determines which pixels are affected. Which pixels are affected is based on the number of levels of difference in the surrounding pixels. If the number of levels is greater than the Threshold, sharpening will be applied based on the settings for Radius and Sharpen Amount. The higher the Threshold number, the fewer pixels are affected. The Threshold is based on how the pixels work against each other, which is based on their differences. For instance, a Threshold of 0 allows neighboring pixels to affect one another, whereas a high threshold of 255 prevents pixels from affecting each other.

  The Threshold setting is normally 0 to 5, but most often 0 is the best choice. If you have an image with a lot of noise, a Threshold of 1 or 2 is the better choice because it will prevent the noise from being sharpened. The noisier the image, the higher the Threshold setting should be. Settings above 5 are used only when you want to emphasize the contrast of image elements.

To use the Unsharp Mask filter, select the object or make a selection of a portion of an object. Choose Xtras|Sharpen|Unsharp Mask. Enter the settings for the Sharpen Amount, Pixel Radius, and Threshold and click OK.

Using Plug-ins

Fireworks 4 is compatible with most third-party, Photoshop-compatible plug-ins, but not with Photoshop 6 native plug-ins. If you happen to have Photoshop, you don't have to reinstall the plug-ins into Fireworks, because you can tell Fireworks where to find them. To use Photoshop-compatible plug-ins, choose Edit|Preferences and click the Folders tab in the Preferences dialog box, shown in Figure 10.5.

Select the Photoshop Plug-ins option and click the Browse button. Locate the folder containing your plug-ins and then click Open. You don't have to have Photoshop to use this option. You can put all of your Photoshop-compatible

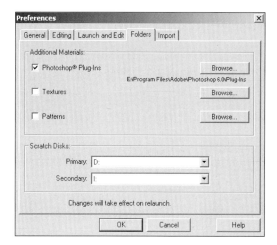

Figure 10.5

The Preferences dialog box.

plug-ins into one folder and use this method to tell Fireworks where to find them. Or, if Fireworks is the only program you will use the plug-ins in, you can directly install new plug-ins into Fireworks. When you are asked where to install, locate Fireworks4\Configuration\Xtras. Remember, any new plug-ins or newly located plug-ins won't be available for use until the next time you open Fireworks.

Fireworks 4 ships with Eye Candy 4000 LE (Alien Skin Software), which contains three filters. See Appendix C for more information on the full version of Eye Candy 4000 and other third-party plug-ins. To use any of the plug-ins, simply choose Xtras|Plug-in and make your choices in the various dialog boxes.

Projects Using a Variety of Plug-ins

Fireworks ships with only one plug-in (Eye Candy 4000 LE). If you want to really use the power of plug-ins, try some of the demos available on this book's CD-ROM. This section and Appendix C will also point you to some free, shareware, or for-sale plug-ins.

Eye Candy 4000 Plug-in

The three filters included with this plug-in are Bevel Boss, Motion Trail, and Marble. This first project uses the Bevel Boss filter.

PROJECT Using the Eye Candy 4000 LE Bevel Boss Plug-in Filter

Alien Skin plug-ins usually offer plenty of options to customize the effects you are looking for. To make a button using the Bevel Boss plug-in, follow these steps:

1. Open a new document (File|New) with a size of 200 pixels by 200 pixels.

2. Select the Rectangle tool and draw a rectangle in the shape of a button.

3. Open the Fill panel and choose a Fill category of Pattern and a Pattern name of Illusion. Choose Xtras|Eye Candy 4000 LE|Bevel Boss. A dialog box will open saying that vectors will be converted to a bitmap; click OK. Figure 10.6 shows the opening dialog box for the Bevel Boss filter.

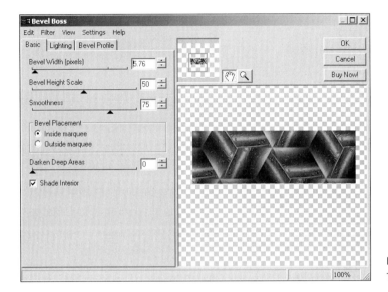

Figure 10.6
The Bevel Boss filter dialog box.

4. The first tab is Basic. This example uses a Bevel Width of 16.15 and a Bevel Height Scale of 64. Click the Lighting tab and change the Direction to 138; the Inclination will set itself according to the Direction setting you use.

5. Click the Bevel Profile tab. This is really an interesting tab. You can click any of the names in the list for some preset bevels, or you can drag the curve around and form your own. If you really like a new setting that you make, you can add it to the list, as well, by clicking the Add button, naming the new preset, and clicking OK. Figure 10.7 shows the new curve used for this example.

6. Click OK to finish the button bevel. Select the Type tool and click anywhere on the button. In the Text dialog box, type "Tools" and select your font. In this example, the font Ruach with a size of 77 was used, with Bold and a color of white. This particular font uses all lowercase. To get the capital *T*, the lowercase *t* was highlighted and the font Staccato555 BT was selected with a size of 90. Click OK when you get the look you want.

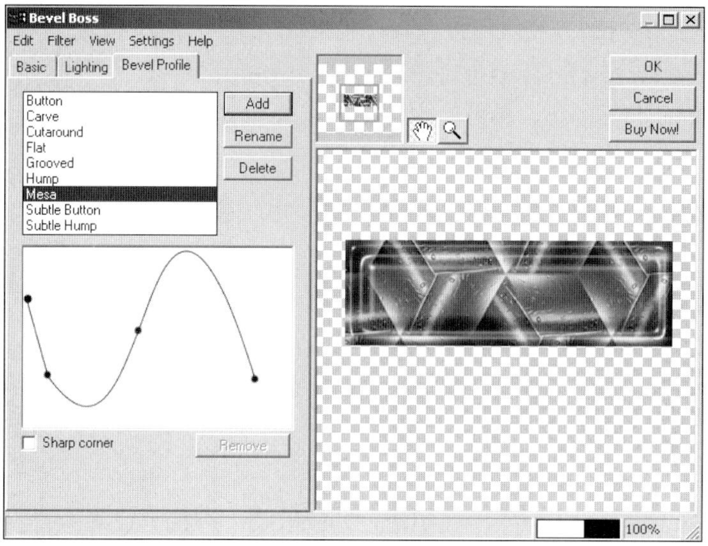

Figure 10.7
The custom preset in the Bevel Profile tab.

7. Open the Effect panel and choose Bevel And Emboss|Raised Emboss, with a Width of 3 and a Softness of 2. Open the Stroke panel and choose Charcoal, Soft, color of black, and a Tip size of 3. Press Enter/ Return. Figure 10.8 shows the completed button.

Figure 10.8
A button with the Bevel Boss plug-in filter applied.

PROJECT Using Eye Candy 4000's Motion Trail Filter

The Motion Trail filter uses the color of the object to give the illusion of motion. To use this filter, follow these steps:

1. Open a new document (File|New) with a size of 205 pixels wide by 175 pixels high and a canvas color of White.

2. Open the water.png file from the Chapter 10 resources folder of this book's CD-ROM. Drag it on top of your new document. Drag the corner points of the water image to fill the entire canvas. In the Layers panel, set the Opacity of the water to 70%.

3. Open the boat.png image from the Chapter 10 resources folder. Drag the boat to the new document. Open the Info panel and place the boat with an X coordinate of 15 and a Y coordinate of 0.

4. Choose Xtras|Eye Candy 4000 LE|Motion Trail. Figure 10.9 shows the Motion Trail dialog box and the settings used for this example: Direction 225, Length 108, Taper 40, and Overall Opacity 95. Click the OK button to apply. Figure 10.10 shows the final image.

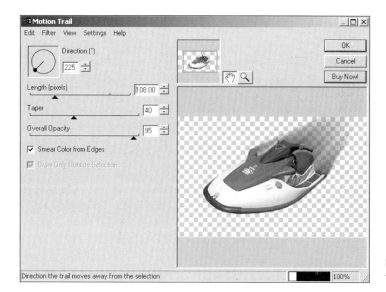

Figure 10.9
The Motion Trail dialog box.

Figure 10.10
The boat with the Motion Trail plug-in filter applied.

Free Plug-ins

Because Fireworks doesn't ship with very many plug-ins, you may want to find some other plug-ins to experiment with. If you search the Internet for Photoshop-compatible plug-ins, you will find plenty to try out. Some will work and some won't. If a plug-in doesn't work, the problem is likely the plug-in, not Fireworks. That's the risk you take with using "freebies." (The worst I've ever had happen while using a freebie is a computer lockup and corresponding wasted time.)

Be sure to check Appendix C for links to a few free plug-in resources. Plenty more free plug-ins are available. Just enter "Free Photoshop plug-ins" into a search engine, and all kinds of sites will be listed.

Primus

Primus, made by Flaming Pear Software, has both free and demo software. The Web site is **www.flamingpear.com**. Download the Primus plug-in and place it into a folder with your other plug-ins. You will be prompted to register for your free activation code about a minute after you start using it for the first time. The code will be sent promptly to your email address. Enter the code and you are all set. If Fireworks is open when you add the plug-in, you will need to close Fireworks and reopen it to have the plug-in available in the Xtras menu.

PROJECT Designing a Web Page Using the Primus Plug-in

The Primus plug-in was so inspiring that this project uses only one of the plug-in's options to design this Web page, shown in Figure 10.11.

Copyright © 2000, 2001 Idea Design

Figure 10.11

A Web page using primarily the Primus plug-in.

No new techniques are used in this project; everything done to produce it has been demonstrated in this book. In keeping with the format of the rest of this book, you will be given instructions on how to complete the entire Web page, not just use the filter. The following is a list of the techniques used in this project, along with the chapter number references in case you need additional information:

• Selection and drawing tools: Chapter 5

• Changing a straight path to a curved path: Chapter 4

• Opacity settings: Chapter 1

• Appling patterns, effects, and strokes: Chapter 2

• Making button symbols and nav bars: Chapter 7

• Adjusting hue and saturation: Chapter 5

- Feathering a selection: Chapter 5

- Using the Lasso Polygon tool and Marquee tools: Chapter 5

- Rubber Stamp techniques: Chapter 5

To make this Web page, follow these steps:

1. Open a new document (File|New) with a size of 600 pixels by 400 pixels and a White canvas.

2. Draw a rectangle. Using the Info panel, change the size to 600 pixels wide by 75 pixels high and place the rectangle at the top of the canvas.

3. Choose Xtras|Flaming Pear|Primus. The dialog box that opens, shown in Figure 10.12, has a lot of really interesting effects. Click the circle in the second row, third from the left. The cursor at the bottom of the dialog box shows the setting to use; click OK. The Opacity of this image was lowered to 40% in the Layers panel.

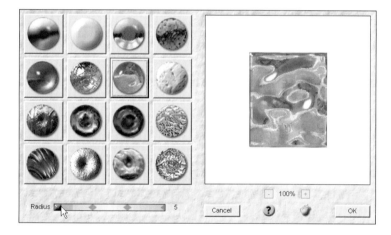

Figure 10.12
The Primus dialog box.

4. Draw a rectangle and make it about 160 by 315 pixels. Choose Edit|Duplicate. Place a rectangle on the right and left sides below the top rectangle. For the left rectangle, ungroup it and use the Subselection tool to change the bottom-right point to a curve; pull the Bézier handle to make the curve. Apply the Primus plug-in the exact same way as it is applied in Step 3.

5. Draw a rectangle the size you'd like your buttons to be, and apply the Primus filter as in Step 3, but don't lower the Opacity. Make your buttons into symbols or a navigation bar and add the text. The text here has a Raised Emboss with a Width of 1 and a Softness of 1.

6. Fill the rectangle on the right (the one you placed in Step 4) with a solid fill of gray (the color in this project was sampled from the top bar after

the Primus filter was applied) and add a Hatch 4 Texture at 50 percent. Draw another rectangle, 130 by 155 pixels. This rectangle goes on top of the large rectangle you just filled with gray on the right side. Fill the small rectangle by using a pattern. (Any pattern you like that adds a subtle texture is fine. The one used in this sample was located years ago on the Internet; unfortunately, it can't be supplied to you because of the inability to get permission.) Lower the Opacity, and change the Hue and Saturation to blend with the background. A pattern with large clouds might work well here. Add a small rectangle to the top of the rectangle, and apply the Primus plug-in. Group the smaller top rectangle containing the Primus filter effect and the larger rectangle and make a duplicate (Edit|Duplicate). Drag the duplicate below the first set, as shown previously in Figure 10.11.

7. Open the boat image, boat.png, located in the Chapter 10 resources folder, and drag it onto the Web page. Select the Type tool, click the canvas, and type the name ("Water Sports" is used here) into the Text dialog box. Choose your font and size and click OK. The Primus plug-in was applied to this text as well (repeat Step 3, but don't lower the Opacity).

8. Add whatever you'd like for the center. This image is from the Comstock Vacations-Resorts CD. The desired result was to have the water overlap the two sidebars a bit. Using the original image and resizing it didn't work because the people were too big for the desired result. Getting this particular image to fit the way it does in this sample was a bit more complicated, but not too difficult. The original image was opened. Using the Lasso Polygon tool, the people and their shadows were selected, copied to a new document, and cut from the original image, leaving part of the image empty. The empty area's edges were then filled with the surrounding water using a large rubber stamp. An Oval Marquee selection of the water was made with a Feather of 40 and then positioned on the Web page. The people were resized smaller (Modify|Image Size) and placed over the water on the Web page. The completed file, watersports.png, is in the Chapter 10 resources folder.

Tachyon

Tachyon is another plug-in from Flaming Pear Software; it reverses the brightness and keeps the colors. Figure 10.13 shows the before image, baby.png, located in the Chapter 10 resources folder on the book's CD-ROM. Select the image and choose Xtras|Flaming Pear|Tachyon. It's an automatic filter with no settings. The results are shown in Figure 10.14 and in the Color Section.

Figure 10.13
(Left) The image before the Tachyon filter is applied.

Figure 10.14
(Right) The image after the Tachyon filter is applied.

Third-Party Demo Plug-ins

Many plug-ins are available for sale. The ones that follow are some of the most popular and useful.

AutoEye and Photo/Graphic Edges Demos (Auto FX Software)

The AutoEye demo is a fully functional time-limited demo. The Photo/Graphic Edges demo includes sample effects in the Edge, Light, Tiles, Texture, and Distort categories. The demo can be found on this book's CD-ROM.

PROJECT Making a Composition Using the Photo/Graphic Edges Demo

Because only a limited number of effects are included in the demo, making a whole composition with just what is available can be quite challenging, but it is possible. For more choices than you could possibly use, consider looking into the full version. The Photo/Graphic Edges package really does offer a lot for the money. To make a composition using the demo version of Photo/Graphic Edges, follow these steps:

1. Open the trees.png file from the Chapter 10 resources folder. This is an image taken with a Nikon CoolPix 800 digital camera.

2. Choose Xtras|Auto F/X|Photo/Graphic Edges. Click the picture in the Select Edge area. Depending on how and where you installed the plug-in, the folder may come up in the dialog box that opens. If not, locate the AutoFX folder, select the PGE40 folder, click to open the Tiles folder, select tile number Afs068, and click OK. Figure 10.15 shows the result.

3. This makes the tree image unrecognizable, but it makes a decent background effect. While you are in this dialog box, play with some of the other settings available. For instance, click any of the tabs; a window will open telling you what the settings in each tab are for. When you are done with the Photo/Graphic Edges dialog box, click Apply.

Background Alternative

You can use the effect in Step 2 as is for a background, or you can open the Effect panel, choose Shadow And Glow| Drop Shadow, choose a Distance of 4 and a Softness of 3, and check Knock Out. It produces a pretty nice effect.

Figure 10.15
A tile applied to the tree image.

4. Open the 2girls.jpg file (provided by Comstock from the Diversity Lifestyles CD Collection). Choose Xtras|Auto F/X|Photo/Graphic Edges. Click the picture in the Select Edge area. Locate the AutoFX folder, select the PGE40 folder, and then click to open the Edges folder. Select the edge number Af321, change the Border to 3, click the color and choose a dark green, and click OK. Drag the image onto your composition.

5. In the Layers panel, click the yellow folder icon to add a new layer. Select the Rectangle tool and draw a rectangle in the center portion of the 2girls image. In the Stroke panel, choose Pencil, 1-Pixel Hard, and a dark green color. In the Fill panel, choose Solid and a color of black. In the Texture area, choose Scanlines and adjust to 100%. In the Layers panel, set the Opacity to 20%.

6. Open baby.png (taken with a Nikon CoolPix 800), select the image, and choose Xtras|Auto F/X|Photo/Graphic Edges. Click the picture in the Select area. Locate the AutoFX folder, select the PGE40 folder, and then click to open the Light folder. Select the light number Af131 and click OK.

7. Open 2children.png (provided by Comstock from the Diversity Lifestyles CD Collection). Choose Xtras|Auto F/X|Photo/Graphic Edges. Click the picture in the Select Edge area. Locate the AutoFX folder, select the PGE40 folder, and then click to open the Light folder. Select the light number Af035 and click OK. Select the Oval Marquee tool and draw a selection around the two girls. Choose Modify|Marquee|Feather, enter between 10 and 20 for the feathering, and click OK. Choose Edit|Copy, select the composition, and choose Edit|Paste. Move this image wherever it looks good to you.

8. Open the soccer.png file from the Chapter 10 resources folder and drag it into the composition. Open the skates.png file. Select the Rectangle tool and draw a rectangle over the skates. Open the Fill panel and choose Radial, Black and White. Shift+select the ball object and choose Modify|Mask|Group As Mask. To adjust the gradient, select it and click the gradient icon in the Layers panel. To adjust the color position of the gradient, click the Edit button and move the Black color well over to the right some. Click near the White color well to add another color and fill it with a dark gray. Adjust the gradient until you get the look you want. (Refer to Chapter 2 for more information on working with gradients.) Drag the skates into the composition. The ball and skates are part of the Hemera Photo Objects 50,000 Premium Collection.

9. The lines in the background look a bit busy. To lessen the effect, open the trees.png file again and drag a copy onto the composition. In the Layers panel, click and drag the trees layer to just above the background layer, and lower the Opacity to 50% or so. Figure 10.16 shows the composition.

Figure 10.16
A composite image made using demo plug-ins.

PROJECT Using the AutoEye Demo Plug-in

The AutoEye plug-in offers a great deal of flexibility. It works much differently than the Auto Levels or the Auto Curves from the Adjust Color options. With AutoEye, you can manually make changes or use the Automatic feature. Figure 10.17 shows the options available if you choose to use the Manual options.

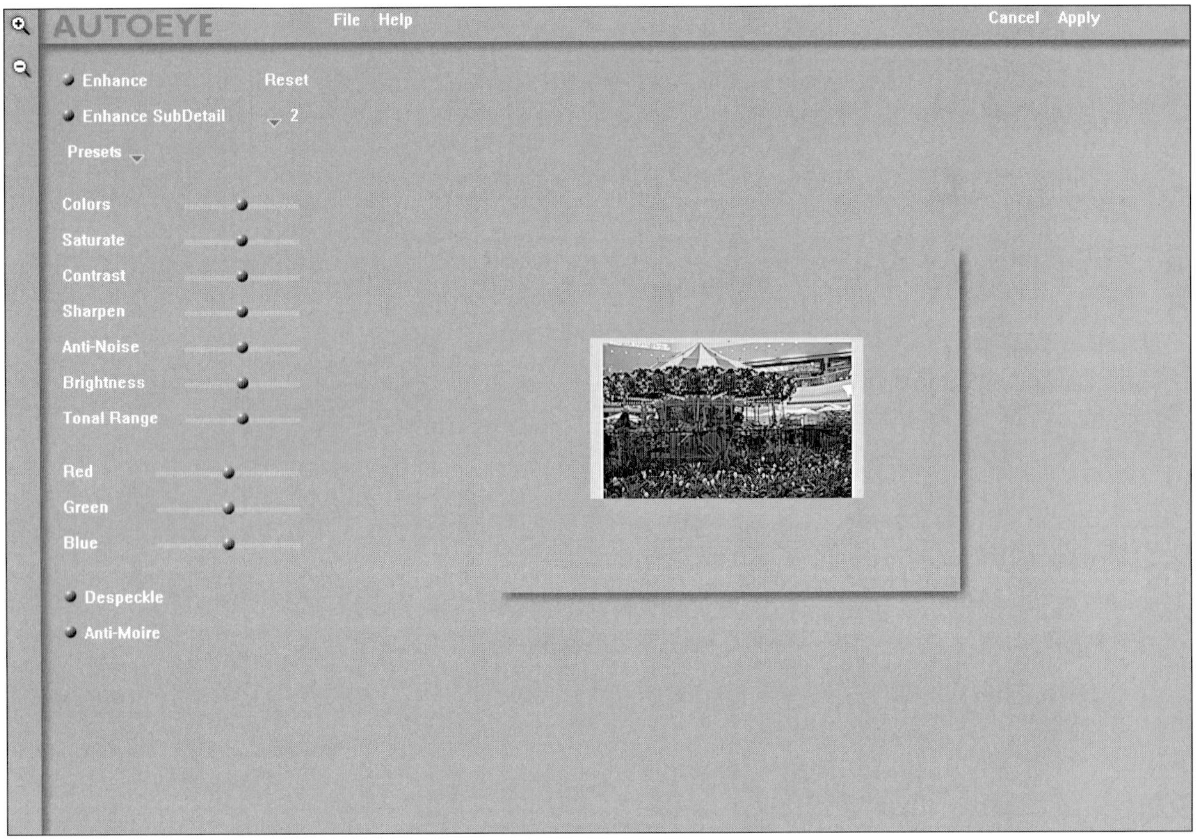

Figure 10.17

The Manual options in AutoEye.

To bring out the detail in an extremely dark image, follow these steps:

1. Open the carousel.tif file from the Chapter 10 resources folder. This image was taken while learning how to use the settings on a Kodak DC 3400 Digital Zoom Camera. It was chalked up as a ruined picture. You may be surprised at how much detail is really in this image. Figure 10.18 shows the carousel before it is enhanced.

2. Select the image and choose Xtras|AutoFX|AutoEye. A window opens giving you the option to use Automatic or Manual. Click Automatic. Figure 10.19 shows the Automatic options.

3. This image is extremely dark, so choose the Enhance Very Dark Image option, and then click Automatic again. Figure 10.20 shows the enhanced image. It is a great deal better.

Xenofex and Eye Candy 4000 Demos (Alien Skin)

These two full-version plug-in packages offer a lot of room for innovative designs. The demos give previews of all the plug-ins, but only a few of the plug-ins are fully functional. The Xenofex fully functional filters are Crumple and Stain. The Eye Candy 4000 fully functional filters are Marble, Glass, and Shadowlab,

Figure 10.18
The carousel "before" image.

Figure 10.19
Automatic options for AutoEye.

Figure 10.20
The carousel enhanced "after" image.

the latter two of which are different from the samples that ship with Fireworks 4 in the Eye Candy 4000 LE version.

PROJECT Using a Xenofex Plug-in Filter

Install the demo of the Xenofex filters, which is in the Alienskin folder on this book's CD-ROM. This project uses a photograph taken with the Kodak DC 3400 Digital Zoom Camera. To drastically change the appearance and add a special effect, follow these steps:

1. Open the lizard.png file in the Chapter 10 resources folder. Figure 10.21 shows the beginning image.

2. One part of this image needs retouching. If you look in the Color Section of this book, you'll see that the rock in the back-left corner is blue, probably because of the ultraviolet lights used in the terrarium. Select

Figure 10.21
The image of lizards before any
filter or touchup is applied.

the blue area using the Lasso tool or the Polygon Lasso tool (refer to Chapter 5) and choose Xtras|Adjust Color|Hue And Saturation. To get a gray color, use these settings: Hue –180, Saturation –100, and Lightness 18.

3. To make the lizards stand out and to add back their natural color, make a selection around just the lizards. The Polygon Lasso tool works best for this selection. Choose Xtras|Adjust Color|Hue And Saturation. The settings used here are a checkmark in the Colorize box, Hue 86, Saturation 23, and Lightness –24.

4. You want to apply a plug-in filter to everything except the lizards. To invert the selection, choose Modify|Marquee|Invert Select Inverse. Everything is selected now except the lizards.

5. Choose Xtras|Xenofex|Baked Earth. In the Baked Earth dialog box, choose Crack Length 25, Crack Width 2, Variations 50, Highlight Brightness 39, and Sharpness 9. Click the checkmark when done. The result is shown in Figure 10.22.

Note: Because this is a demo version, the preview is as far as you can go with the Baked Earth filter. It won't be applied to the final image, but the interface shows a preview so you can see what the effect would look like. The Xenofex demo has two fully functional filters, Crumple and Stain.

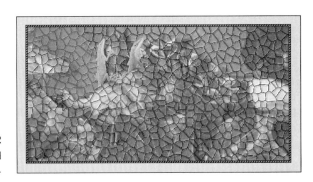

Figure 10.22
The lizard image with the Baked
Earth plug-in applied.

BuZZ.Professional 1.03 (Segmentis Limited)

You can download a fully functional demo of BuZZ.Lite or BuZZ.Professional from **www.segmentis.com**. The demo will work on 20 images. This is a unique plug-in filter and works differently than anything you may have seen. It makes your image look like artwork, and it gives you an amazing amount of control. One of the methods used is a Simplifier filter, which removes detail while preserving the important features of a picture. You choose how much detail to take out. You will use the preset "stacks" in this next project. For more information on this plug-in, see Appendix C.

PROJECT Using BuZZ.Professional 1.03 to Simulate a Watercolor Image

BuZZ.Professional 1.03 is used in this project. If you haven't installed it yet, do it now. It will automatically locate the Photoshop plug-ins folder if you have it; otherwise, click the Browse button to locate the folder you want to install into. To turn an image into a watercolor painting, follow these steps:

1. Open the carouselfixed.png file from the Chapter 10 resources folder.

2. Choose Xtras|BuZZ.Professional|Watercolor. You will see a separate window with preset stacks in it. You can add or remove effects; for this project, don't do anything with that window. The preview window has a few options in it. In the Simplifier One Removes area, change the number of colors to remove to 100. In the Edge Detect Colour area, type "57" and click OK. Figure 10.23 shows the result.

Figure 10.23
The carousel image with a Watercolor plug-in applied.

3. You can save this if you like, or choose Edit|Undo and try one more filter. If you saved the image, open the carousel.png file again, choose Xtras|BuZZ.Professional|RadialSimplifier, accept the defaults, and click OK. Figure 10.24 shows the result.

Figure 10.24
The carousel with the Radial Simplifier filter applied.

Using the Commands Menu

In this section, you will use the Creative options and some freely available command scripts.

Creative Options

The following are the three choices in the Creative menu:

- *Convert To Grayscale*—When you want to totally get rid of all color and have a grayscale image, this option is quick and easy. To convert an image or object to grayscale, simply select it and choose Commands| Creative|Convert To Grayscale.

- *Convert To Sepia*—Sepia-colored images have become popular in recent years. Sepia gives the appearance of an old-fashioned image. To convert an image or object to sepia, choose Commands|Creative|Convert To Sepia.

- *Create Picture Frame*—This is a fun way to enhance an image very quickly. Open any image (the one in Figure 10.25 was taken with a Kodak DC 3400 Digital Zoom Camera), choose Commands|Creative|Create Picture Frame, enter the number of pixels you'd like your frame size to be, and click OK.

> **Note:** If you want a two-color image similar to sepia but using a different color, you can also choose Xtras|Adjust Color|Hue And Saturation. Check the Colorize box and choose the color you want.

Figure 10.25
The Create Picture Frame command applied.

Using Free Commands

You have used a few utility-type commands throughout this book to do such things as finding overlapping slices, making a copyright notice, or drawing a dashed line. In this section, you will discover some fun but functional commands to expand your commands collection. Be sure to check Appendix C to find the URLs for sites from which you can download more commands. The commands used in this section are provided in the Commands Brian Baker folder.

PROJECT Making Automatic Glass Buttons

Brian Baker, a Macromedia specialist who is active in the Fireworks Forum, gave permission to include this command on this book's CD-ROM, so you don't have to download it. Be sure to check Appendix C for the link to his site, because he has quite a few more commands available. To make instant glass type buttons, follow these steps:

1. Copy the GlassButtonMaker.jsf file located in the Commands\Brian Baker folder on this book's CD-ROM.

2. Locate the Fireworks 4\Configuration\Commands folder and paste the GlassButtonMaker.jsf file into it. It will be immediately available in the Commands menu.

3. Open a new document (File|New) and use any size you'd like.

4. Choose Commands|GlassButtonMaker. The dialog box shown in Figure 10.26 will open. Type in the width of your button (110 is used here), followed by a comma, the width of your button (30 is used here), another comma, and the roundness of the button ends (50 is used here). Click OK.

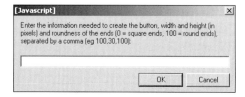

Figure 10.26

Dialog box to enter the parameters for the glass buttons.

5. Another dialog box will open, allowing you to choose the color of button you'd like. Type in the number that represents the color you'd like, and click OK. Figure 10.27 shows the finished button.

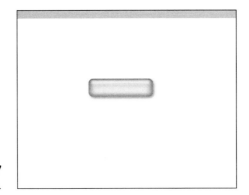

Figure 10.27
The finished glass button.

PROJECT Making Spirals

Spirals can be very handy when designing Web sites. You could make your own by tweening circles, cutting the paths in half, and nudging one half of the cut circles to meet up with the next line. Or, you could simply use this wonderful spiral command. To make instant spirals, follow these steps:

1. Locate the spirals.jsf file in the Commands\Brian Baker folder on this book's CD-ROM and copy it.

2. Paste the spirals.jsf in the Fireworks 4\Configuration\Commands folder.

3. Open a new document (File|New) of any size you'd like.

4. Choose Commands|Spiral to open the dialog box shown in Figure 10.28. Type how many turns you'd like, followed by a comma, and then how many pixels you want between the turns. This project uses 4 turns with 30 pixels between each turn.

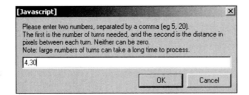

Figure 10.28
The spiral commands dialog box.

5. In the Color section of the toolbar, you will see the pencil icon. If the color well has the same color as your canvas, be sure to change it or you won't see the object drawn.

6. Have some fun with your spiral by adding some cool strokes. Open the Stroke panel, select Unnatural in the Stroke category, and in the Stroke name category, choose Outline. Change the Tip size to a size that works well with the stroke selection you made. This example uses a tip size of 20 (see Figure 10.29).

7. With the spiral selected, add some texture. In the Stroke panel, drag the Texture slider up (100% is used here). Choose a texture type (DNA is used here, shown in Figure 10.30). Try some of the grid textures, which are quite interesting.

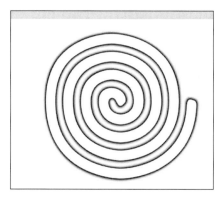 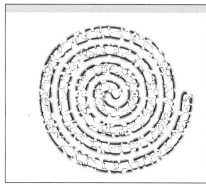

Figure 10.29
(Left) Spiral with an Unnatural, Outline stroke applied.

Figure 10.30
(Right) A spiral with an Unnatural, DNA stroke applied.

Try these spirals:

• To make another spiral, repeat Steps 2 through 5. In the Stroke category, choose Unnatural, a Stroke name of Chameleon, and a color of Hex #3300FF. This produces an interesting blend of colors.

• To make an @ symbol, repeat Steps 2 through 4, but change the number of turns to 2 and the number of pixels between turns to 20. Repeat Step 5. For Step 6, choose the Stroke category of Calligraphy and a Stroke Name of Quill. The tip size here is 10. If you want to alter the spiral, you can choose the Subselection tool and move any point you'd like. Figure 10.31 shows an example of the @ spiral.

Figure 10.31
A spiral representing the @ symbol.

Moving On

You have just finished exploring many demo and free plug-ins, and using freely available commands and commands that ship with Fireworks. Your images don't have to have boring edges with these tools at your disposal. Have fun with them, and be sure to check Appendix C for Web addresses to find even more.

Appendix A

Fireworks Panels

In this appendix, you will see screen shots of all the panels in Fireworks and most of their pop-up menus. Fireworks 4 now contains 19 pop-up menus.

Fireworks 4 Panels

Fireworks 4 has 20 panels containing different options for all the tools and actions you perform in your document. With this many panels, finding something could get quite confusing. However, Macromedia has grouped panels together in a logical manner. Often, the default groupings work just fine. But you can ungroup and regroup the panels anyway you choose.

To remove a panel from any grouping, just click its tab and drag it out to the screen or onto another grouping. An example of a time when you'd want to move a panel is when you work with animations. Animations involve the Layers panel and the Frames panel, which are located in the same panel group. It's easier if you can see both panels at the same time. Simply drag the Frames panel off on its own.

Fireworks 4 Toolbars

In Fireworks, toolbars are used to gain easier access to the most commonly used functions. To open them, choose Window|Toolbars|Main or Window|Toolbars|Modify. They will open in your workspace. You can dock them below the Menu by clicking and dragging them below the Menu:

- *The Main Toolbar*—Contains the basic commands that are in the File and Edit menus (see Figure A.1).

- *The Modify Toolbar*—Contains the functions from the Modify menu that deal with the position and shape of an object (see figure A.2).

Figure A.1
The Main toolbar.

Figure A.2
The Modify toolbar.

All of Fireworks' drawing and editing tools can be accessed from the Tools panel (see Figure A.3). Tools that are similar to each other are grouped together. You can tell tools that are grouped together by the little triangle in the lower right corner of the icon. You access the additional tools by clicking and holding on the triangle; a flyout will open, and then you move your cursor over the tool you want and release the mouse button.

Fireworks 4 Panels in Their Default Groupings

Other than the Tools panel (Figure A.3), Fireworks 4 has 19 other panels. The Window menu shows all the panels; they are arranged in the Window menu by the group in which Fireworks has placed each panel. If you want to move a panel, simply click and drag it to another group or to the workspace to be a free-floating panel.

Figure A.3
The Tools Panel.

A list of the panels and their main functions follows:

- *Fill panel*—Has options such as a solid fill and a selection of gradient fills, patterns, and textures (see Figure A.4).

- *Effect panel*—Where Live Effects such as shadows and bevels as well as some third-party plug-in filters are accessed (see Figure A.5).

- *Info panel*—Shows the size of an object and its X, Y coordinates as well as color information (see Figure A.6).

- *Stroke panel*—Contains options for determining how the edge of an object or image will appear (see Figure A.7).

- *Behaviors panel*—Where JavaScripts that act when triggered by an event are accessed (see Figure A.8).

- *Optimize panel*—Contains the options for optimizing images (see Figure A.9).

- *Object panel*—Changes according to the type of object selected. The choices in the Object panel control how the object interacts with the canvas and other objects (see Figure A.10).

- *Color Mixer panel*—Where the color space can be changed and where custom colors are mixed (see Figure A.11).

- *Swatches panel*—Shows all the available colors in the selected color space. The Web safe colors are the default (see Figure A.12).

- *Color Table panel*—Shows all the colors in use in the current 8-bit or less image in the Preview mode (see Figure A.13).

- *Tool Options panel*—Gives additional tool functions to some tools; this panel is accessed by double-clicking on a tool icon in the Tools panel. If it is blank, then no additional options are available (see Figure A.14).

- *Layers panel*—Manages the placement and grouping of images and objects (see Figure A.15).

- *Frames panel*—Manages the frames of an animation or rollover (see Figure A.16).

- *History panel*—Shows actions that have been performed in a document. This panel is also used for making commands and repeating steps (see Figure A.17).

- *Styles panel*—Contains preset styles that ship with Fireworks that allow users to apply instant Live Effects to objects. It is also where custom-made styles are stored (see Figure A.18).

- *URL panel*—Contains the most frequently used URL addresses. It can be accessed while using the Pop-Up Menu Wizard to add URLs longer than the wizard allows (see Figure A.19).

- *Library panel*—Contains any symbols that have been made (see Figure A.20).

- *Find And Replace panel*—The control center for finding (and replacing) items such as text, URLs, fonts, and colors (see Figure A.21).

- *Project panel*—Records every changed document and interacts closely with the Find And Replace panel (see Figure A.22).

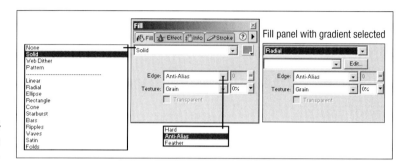

Figure A.4

The Fill panel with various pop-ups.

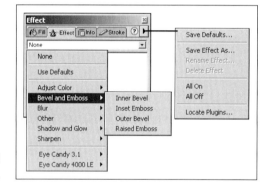

Figure A.5

The Effect panel with pop-ups.

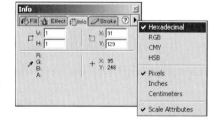

Figure A.6

The Info panel.

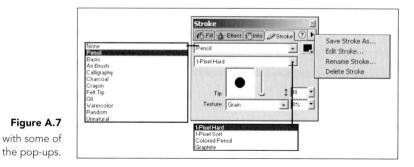

Figure A.7

The Stroke panel with some of the pop-ups.

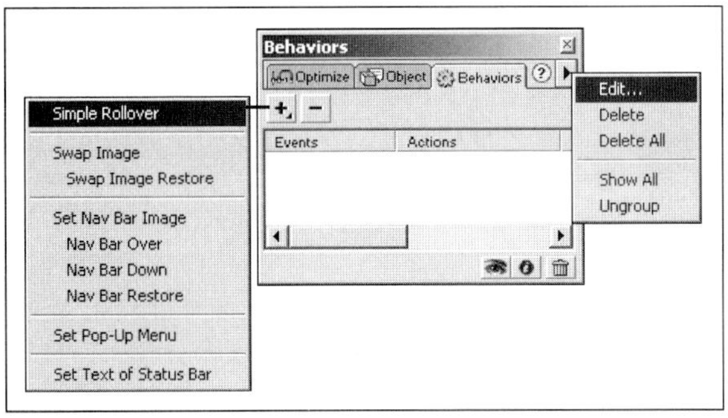

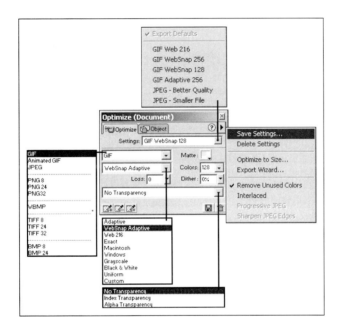

Figure A.8

The Behaviors panel with pop-ups.

Figure A.9

The Optimize panel showing the pop-up options.

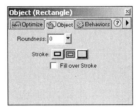

Figure A.10

The Object panel.

Figure A.11

The Color Mixer panel and its pop-up menu.

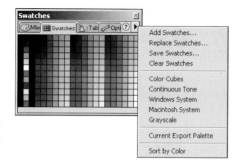

Figure A.12
The Swatches panel and its pop-up menu.

Figure A.13
The Color Table panel in its default appearance.

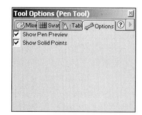

Figure A.14
The Tool Options panel with the Pen tool options.

Figure A.15
The Layers panel with the layer options.

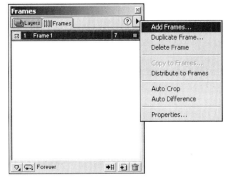

Figure A.16
The Frames panel with the Frames options.

Figure A.17
The History panel with its pop-up menu.

Figure A.18
The Styles panel with its pop-up menu.

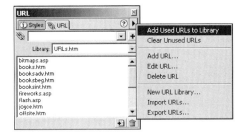

Figure A.19
The URL panel with its pop-up menu.

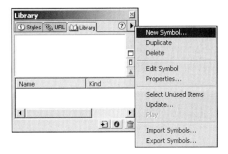

Figure A.20
The Library panel with its pop-up menu.

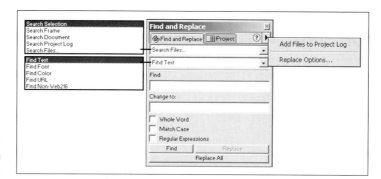

Figure A.21

The Find And Replace panel with its pop-up menu.

Figure A.22

The Project panel in its default state and its pop-up menu.

Appendix B

Using Keyboard Shortcuts

This appendix lists the keyboard shortcuts available in Fireworks 4. A list of shortcuts for Photoshop and other applications is also included, as well as instructions on how to customize your own keyboard shortcut sets.

Using Shortcuts from Other Applications in Fireworks

If you want to use familiar shortcuts from Photoshop, Freehand, Illustrator, or Fireworks 3, you can load them and customize them in Fireworks 4 (see "Customizing Shortcuts" in the next section). Macromedia Standard is the default set of keyboard shortcuts in Fireworks 4.

To select a different set of keyboard shortcuts, follow these steps:

1. Open Fireworks and choose Edit|Keyboard Shortcuts. Figure B.1 shows the Keyboard Shortcuts dialog box.

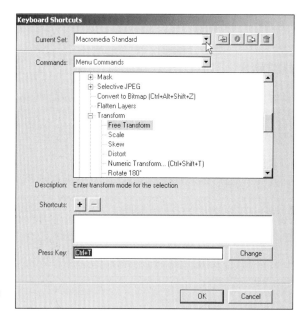

Figure B.1
The Keyboard Shortcuts dialog box.

2. Click the down arrow in the Current Set box and choose Photoshop, Illustrator, Freehand, or Fireworks 3.

3. If you want to customize any shortcut, you can do it now (see the next section, "Customizing Shortcuts"). Click OK after you have made your selection.

Customizing Shortcuts

Any set of keyboard shortcuts can be customized. You need to know only a few rules, which consist of the following:

*   PC menu commands must use the Control modifier key, and Macintosh menu commands must use the Command modifier key. You can use Shift and Alt (Shift/Option) with the Control key. The exception to the modifier key rule, is the use of function keys, if any are available (F2 through F12).

- Tool shortcuts can't include any modifier keys; they use a single letter or a number.

To customize the shortcuts, follow these steps:

1. Choose the set of shortcuts you want to customize; this exercise is using Photoshop. You could alter the set that Fireworks supplies, but it is probably better to use a copy with a new name. This way, if you ever want to use the original again, it is still intact.

2. Figure B.1 shows the Keyboard Shortcuts dialog. In the top-right corner are some icons. From left to right, they are as follows: Duplicate Set, Rename Set, Export Set As HTML, and Delete Set. Click the first one, Duplicate Set.

3. Name the new set in the window that opens; the set's name plus the word *copy* is the default name. Click OK.

4. Notice in the Shortcuts area of the Keyboard Shortcuts dialog window that the + and – signs are grayed out right now. You can practice by adding a shortcut command (which will activate the + and – signs in the Shortcuts area) that I find very useful. Locate the Modify section of the Photoshop Commands, click the + sign next to Modify, scroll down to Transform, and click the + sign next to Transform. Select Free Transform (refer to Figure B.1).

5. Click the + sign in the Shortcuts area; the cursor will move to the Press Key box. You can't type the shortcut in this box. To set the shortcut, you actually press Ctrl/Cmd+T and then click the Change button. In case you are wondering what the white box below the Shortcut area is used for, it's where you delete an existing shortcut. To try it out, click a menu command with a shortcut. Notice the shortcut is present in the box below Shortcuts and the – sign is now activated.

You can really speed up your workflow by customizing keyboard shortcuts to the way you work.

File Menu

New	Ctrl+N
Open	Ctrl+O
Close	Ctrl+W
Save	Ctrl+S
Save As	Ctrl+Shift+S
Import	Ctrl+R
Export	Ctrl+Shift+R
Export Preview	Ctrl+Shift+X

Preview in Browser Pop-up Menu Options

Preview in Browser	F12
Preview in Secondary Browser	Shift+F12
Print	Ctrl+P
Exit	Ctrl+Q

Edit Menu

Undo	Ctrl+Z
Redo	Ctrl+Y, Ctrl+Shift+Z
Cut	Ctrl+X
Copy	Ctrl+C
Copy HTML Code	Ctrl+Alt+C
Paste	Ctrl+V
Clear	Backspace, Delete
Paste Inside	Ctrl+Shift+V
Paste Attributes	Ctrl+Alt+Shift+V
Deselect	Ctrl+D
Duplicate	Ctrl+Alt+D
Clone	Ctrl+Shift+D
Find and Replace	Ctrl+F
Preferences	Ctrl+U

View Menu

Zoom In	Ctrl+=, Ctrl+Num +, Ctrl+Shift+=
Zoom Out	Ctrl+–, Ctrl+Num –
Hide Selection	Ctrl+L
Show All	Ctrl+Shift+L
Rulers	Ctrl+Alt+R

Magnification Pop-up Menu Options

50%	Ctrl+5
100%	Ctrl+1
200%	Ctrl+2
400%	Ctrl+4
800%	Ctrl+8
6400%	Ctrl+6
Fit Selection	Ctrl+Alt+0
Fit All	Ctrl+0
Full Display	Ctrl+K

Grid Pop-up Menu Options

Show Grid	Ctrl+Alt+G
Snap to Grid	Ctrl+Alt+Shift+G
Show Guides	Ctrl+;
Lock Guides	Ctrl+Alt+;
Snap to Guides	Ctrl+Shift+;
Slice Guides	Ctrl+Alt+Shift+;
Hide Panels	F4, Tab

Insert Pop-up Menu Options

New Symbol	Ctrl+F8
Convert to Symbol	F8
Hotspot	Ctrl+Shift+U
Slice	Alt+Shift+U

Modify Menu

Trim Canvas	Ctrl+Alt+T
Fit Canvas	Ctrl+Alt+F
Edit Bitmap	Ctrl+E
Exit Bitmap Mode	Ctrl+Shift+E
Group	Ctrl+G
Ungroup	Ctrl+Shift+G

Animate Pop-up Menu Options

Animate Selection	Alt+Shift+F8

Symbol Pop-up Menu Options

Tween Instances	Ctrl+Alt+Shift+T

Marquee Pop-up Menu Options

Select Inverse	Ctrl+Shift+I
Convert to Bitmap	Ctrl+Alt+Shift+Z

Transform Pop-up Menu Options

Numeric Transform	Ctrl+Shift+T
Rotate 90° CW	Ctrl+9
Rotate 90° CCW	Ctrl+7

Arrange Pop-up Menu Options

Bring to Front	Ctrl+Shift+Up
Bring Forward	Ctrl+Up
Send Backward	Ctrl+Down
Send to Back	Ctrl+Shift+Down

Align Pop-up Menu Options

Left	Ctrl+Alt+1, Ctrl+Alt+Num 1
Center Vertical	Ctrl+Alt+2, Ctrl+Alt+Num 2
Right	Ctrl+Alt+3, Ctrl+Alt+Num 3
Top	Ctrl+Alt+4, Ctrl+Alt+Num 4
Center Horizontal	Ctrl+Alt+5, Ctrl+Alt+Num 5
Bottom	Ctrl+Alt+6, Ctrl+Alt+Num 6
Distribute Widths	Ctrl+Alt+7, Ctrl+Alt+Num 7
Distribute Heights	Ctrl+Alt+9, Ctrl+Alt+Num 9
Join	Ctrl+J
Split	Ctrl+Shift+J

Text Menu

Bold	Ctrl+B
Italic	Ctrl+I

Align Pop-up Menu

Left	Ctrl+Alt+Shift+L
Center Horizontally	Ctrl+Alt+Shift+C
Right	Ctrl+Alt+Shift+R
Justified	Ctrl+Alt+Shift+J
Stretched	Ctrl+Alt+Shift+S
Attach to Path	Ctrl+Shift+Y
Convert_to_Path	Ctrl+M

Xtras Menu

Repeat Xtra	Ctrl+Alt+Shift+X

Window Menu

New Window	Ctrl+Alt+N
Stroke	Ctrl+Alt+F4
Fill	Shift+F7
Effect	Alt+F7
Info	Alt+Shift+F12
Object	Alt+F2
Behaviors	Shift+F3
Color Mixer	Shift+F9
Swatches	Ctrl+F9
Tool Options	Ctrl+Alt+O
Layers	F2
Frames	Shift+F2
History	Shift+F10
Styles	Shift+F11
Library	F11
URL	Alt+Shift+F10
Find and Replace	Ctrl+F

Help Menu

Using Fireworks	F1

Shortcuts for the Tools Panel

Pointer Tool	V, 0
Select Behind Tool	V, 0
Export Area Tool	J
Subselection Tool	A, 1
Marquee Tool	M
Oval Marquee Tool	M
Lasso Tool	L
Polygon Lasso Tool	L
Crop Tool	C

Magic Wand Tool	W
Line Tool	N
Pen Tool	P
Rectangle Tool	R
Rounded Rectangle Tool	R
Ellipse Tool	R
Polygon Tool	G
Text Tool	T
Pencil Tool	Y
Brush Tool	B
Redraw Path Tool	B
Scale Tool	Q
Skew Tool	Q
Distort Tool	Q
Freeform Tool	F
Reshape Area Tool	F
Path Scrubber Tool—additive	U
Path Scrubber Tool—subtractive	U
Eyedropper Tool	I
Paint Bucket Tool	K
Eraser Tool	E
Rubber Stamp Tool	S
Hand Tool	H
Zoom Tool	Z
Hide/Show Slices	2
Set Default Brush/Fill Colors	D
Swap Brush/Fill Colors	X

Miscellaneous

Clone and Nudge Down	Alt+Down
Clone and Nudge Down Large	Alt+Shift+Down
Clone and Nudge Left	Alt+Left
Clone and Nudge Left Large	Alt+Shift+Left
Clone and Nudge Right	Alt+Right
Clone and Nudge Right Large	Alt+Shift+Right
Clone and Nudge Up	Alt+Up
Clone and Nudge Up Large	Alt+Shift+Up
Fill Pixel Selection	Alt+Backspace
Page Down	Ctrl+Page Down
Nudge Down Large	Shift+Down
Nudge Left Large	Shift+Left
Nudge Right Large	Shift+Right
Paste Inside	Ctrl+Shift+V
Play Animation	Ctrl+Alt+P
Previous Frame	Page Up, Ctrl+Page Up

File Menu

New	Ctrl+N
Open	Ctrl+O
Close	Ctrl+W
Save	Ctrl+S
Save As	Ctrl+Shift+S
Save a Copy	Ctrl+Alt+S
Export	Ctrl+Shift+R
Export Preview	Ctrl+Shift+X
Page Setup	Ctrl+Shift+P
Print	Ctrl+P
Exit	Ctrl+Q

Edit Menu

Undo	Ctrl+Z
Redo	Ctrl+Shift+Z
Cut	Ctrl+X
Copy	Ctrl+C
Copy HTML Code	Ctrl+Alt+C
Paste	Ctrl+V
Clear	Delete, Backspace
Paste as Mask	Ctrl+Shift+V
Paste Attributes	Ctrl+Alt+V
Select All	Ctrl+A
Deselect	Ctrl+D
Clone	Ctrl+Shift+C
Crop Selected Bitmap	Ctrl+Alt+A
Preferences	Ctrl+K

View Menu

Zoom In	Ctrl+=
Zoom Out	Ctrl+−

Magnification Pop-up Menu

50%	Ctrl+5
100%	Ctrl+1
200%	Ctrl+2
400%	Ctrl+4
800%	Ctrl+8
3200%	Ctrl+3
6400%	Ctrl+6
Fit All	Ctrl+0

Macintosh Gamma	Ctrl+Y
Hide Selection	Ctrl+Shift+H
Show All	Ctrl+Shift+M
Rulers	Ctrl+R
Show Grid	Ctrl+'
Snap to Grid	Ctrl+Shift+'
Edit Grid	Ctrl+Alt+G
Show Guides	Ctrl+;

Lock Guides	Ctrl+Alt+;
Snap to Guides	Ctrl+Shift+;
Edit Guides	Ctrl+Alt+Shift+G
Slice Guides	Ctrl+Alt+Shift+;
Hide Edges	Ctrl+H

Insert Menu

New Symbol	Ctrl+F8
Hotspot	Ctrl+Shift+U
Layer	Ctrl+Shift+N

Modify Menu

Tween Instances	Ctrl+Alt+Shift+T
Exit Bitmap Mode	Ctrl+Shift+D
Select Inverse	Ctrl+Shift+I
Feather	Ctrl+Alt+D
Paste as Mask	Ctrl+Shift+V
Convert to Bitmap	Ctrl+Alt+Shift+Z
Flatten Layers	Ctrl+E
Numeric Transform	Ctrl+Shift+T
Rotate 90° CW	Ctrl+F9
Rotate 90° CCW	Ctrl+F7
Bring Forward	Ctrl+Shift+F
Send Backward	Ctrl+Shift+B
Send to Back	Ctrl+B
Left	Ctrl+Alt+1
Center Vertical	Ctrl+Alt+2
Right	Ctrl+Alt+3
Top	Ctrl+Alt+4
Center Horizontal	Ctrl+Alt+5
Bottom	Ctrl+Alt+6
Distribute Widths	Ctrl+Alt+7
Distribute Heights	Ctrl+Alt+9
Join	Ctrl+J
Split	Ctrl+Shift+J
Group	Ctrl+G
Ungroup	Ctrl+Shift+G

Text Menu

Plain	Ctrl+Alt+Shift+P
Bold	Ctrl+Alt+Shift+B
Italic	Ctrl+Alt+Shift+I
Underline	Ctrl+Alt+Shift+U
Left	Ctrl+Alt+Shift+L
Center Horizontally	Ctrl+Alt+Shift+C
Right	Ctrl+Alt+Shift+R
Justified	Ctrl+Alt+Shift+J
Stretched	Ctrl+Alt+Shift+S
Editor	Ctrl+Shift+E

Xtras Menu

Repeat Xtra	Ctrl+F
Auto Levels	Ctrl+Shift+L
Curves	Ctrl+M
Hue/Saturation	Ctrl+U
Invert	Ctrl+I
Levels	Ctrl+L

Window Menu

New Window	Ctrl+Alt+N

Tool Panel

Pointer Tool	A
Select Behind Tool	V
Export Area Tool	J
Subselection Tool	A
Marquee Tool	M
Lasso Tool	L
Polygon Lasso Tool	I
Crop Tool	C
Magic Wand Tool	W
Line Tool	L
Pen Tool	P
Rectangle Tool	U
Ellipse Tool	R
Polygon Tool	G
Text Tool	T

Pencil Tool	N
Brush Tool	B
Redraw Path Tool	B
Scale Tool	R
Distort Tool	T
Freeform Tool	F
Reshape Area Tool	F
Eyedropper Tool	I
Paint Bucket Tool	K
Eraser Tool	E
Rubber Stamp Tool	S
Slice Tool	Y
Hand Tool	H
Zoom Tool	Z
Set Default Brush/Fill Colors	D
Swap Brush/Fill Colors	X
Next Frame	Ctrl+Page Up
Nudge Down	Ctrl+Down
Nudge Down Large	Ctrl+Shift+Down
Nudge Left	Ctrl+Left
Nudge Left Large	Ctrl+Shift+Left
Nudge Right	Ctrl+Right
Nudge Right Large	Ctrl+Shift+Right
Nudge Up	Ctrl+Up
Nudge Up Large	Ctrl+Shift+Up
Previous Frame	Ctrl+Page Down

File Menu

New	Ctrl+N
Open	Ctrl+O
Close	Ctrl+W
Save	Ctrl+S
Save As	Ctrl+Shift+S
Import	Ctrl+R
Export	Ctrl+Shift+R
Export Preview	Ctrl+Shift+X
Preview in Secondary Browser	Shift+F12
Print	Ctrl+P
Exit	Ctrl+Q

Edit Menu

Undo	Ctrl+Z, Alt+Backspace
Redo	Ctrl+Y, Ctrl+Alt+Backspace
Cut	Ctrl+X, Shift+Delete
Copy	Ctrl+C, Ctrl+Insert
Paste	Ctrl+V, Shift+Insert
Clear	Backspace
Paste Inside	Ctrl+Shift+V
Paste Attributes	Ctrl+Alt+Shift+V
Select All	Ctrl+Shift+A
Superselect	Ctrl+Up
Subselect	Ctrl+Down
Duplicate	Ctrl+D
Clone	Ctrl+Shift+C
Find and Replace	Ctrl+Shift+F
Crop Selected Bitmap	Ctrl+Alt+C
Preferences	Ctrl+Shift+D

View Menu

Zoom In	Ctrl+=
Zoom Out	Ctrl+–

Magnification Pop-up Menu

50%	Ctrl+5
100%	Ctrl+1
200%	Ctrl+2
400%	Ctrl+4
800%	Ctrl+8
Fit Selection	Ctrl+0
Fit All	Ctrl+Alt+0
Full Display	Ctrl+K
Hide Selection	Ctrl+M
Show All	Ctrl+Shift+M
Rulers	Ctrl+Alt+M

Grid Pop-up Menu

Show Grid	Ctrl+'
Snap to Grid	Ctrl+Shift+;

Guides Pop-up Menu

Show Guides	Ctrl+;
Lock Guides	Ctrl+Alt+;
Snap to Guides	Ctrl+Alt+G
Edit Guides	Ctrl+Alt+Shift+G
Slice Guides	Ctrl+Alt+Shift+;
Hide Edges	Ctrl+H
Hide Panels	Ctrl+Shift+H, F12

Insert Menu

Convert to Symbol	Ctrl+F8
Hotspot	Ctrl+Shift+U
Empty Bitmap	Ctrl+Alt+Y

Modify Menu

Tween Instances	Ctrl+Alt+Shift+T
Edit Bitmap	Ctrl+E
Select Inverse	Ctrl+Shift+I
Group as Mask	Ctrl+Shift+G
Convert to Bitmap	Ctrl+Alt+Shift+Z
Scale	Ctrl+F10
Skew	Ctrl+F11
Numeric Transform	Ctrl+Shift+T
Rotate 90° CW	Ctrl+9
Rotate 90° CCW	Ctrl+7

Arrange Pop-up Menu

Bring to Front	Ctrl+F
Bring Forward	Ctrl+Alt+Shift+F
Send Backward	Ctrl+Alt+Shift+K
Send to Back	Ctrl+B

Align Pop-up Menu

Left	Ctrl+Alt+4
Center Vertical	Ctrl+Alt+9
Right	Ctrl+Alt+6
Top	Ctrl+Shift+Left
Center Horizontal	Ctrl+Alt+7
Bottom	Ctrl+Shift+Right
Join	Ctrl+J
Split	Ctrl+Shift+J
Group	Ctrl+G
Ungroup	Ctrl+U

Text Style Pop-up Menu

Plain	Ctrl+Alt+Shift+P, F5
Bold	Ctrl+Alt+B, F6
Italic	Ctrl+Alt+I, F7
Underline	Ctrl+Alt+U

Text Align Pop-up Menu

Left	Ctrl+Alt+Shift+L
Center Horizontally	Ctrl+Alt+Shift+M
Right	Ctrl+Alt+Shift+R
Justified	Ctrl+Alt+Shift+J
Stretched	Ctrl+Alt+Shift+S
Editor	Ctrl+Shift+E
Attach to Path	Ctrl+Shift+Y
Convert to Paths	Ctrl+Shift+P

Xtras Menu

Repeat Xtra	Ctrl+Alt+Shift+X

Window Menu

New Window	Ctrl+Alt+N
Tools	Ctrl+Alt+T
Stroke	Ctrl+Alt+L
Fill	Ctrl+Alt+F
Effect	Ctrl+Alt+E
Object	Ctrl+I
Behaviors	Ctrl+Alt+H
Color Mixer	Ctrl+Shift+9
Swatches	Ctrl+Alt+S
Tool Options	Ctrl+Alt+O
Layers	Ctrl+6
Frames	Ctrl+Alt+K
Styles	Ctrl+3
Find and Replace	Ctrl+Shift+F
Cascade	Shift+F5
Tile Vertical	Shift+F4

Tool Panel

Pointer Tool	V, 0
Select Behind Tool	V, 0
Export Area Tool	J
Subselection Tool	A, 1

Oval Marquee Tool	M
Lasso Tool	L
Polygon Lasso Tool	L
Crop Tool	C
Magic Wand Tool	W
Line Tool	N
Pen Tool	P
Rectangle Tool	R
Polygon Tool	G
Text Tool	T
Pencil Tool	Y
Brush Tool	B
Redraw Path Tool	B
Skew Tool	Q
Freeform Tool	F
Reshape Area Tool	F
Path Scrubber Tool—additive	U
Path Scrubber Tool—subtractive	U
Eyedropper Tool	I
Paint Bucket Tool	K
Eraser Tool	E
Rubber Stamp Tool	S
Hand Tool	H
Zoom Tool	Z
Set Default Brush/Fill Colors	D
Swap Brush/Fill Colors	X
Group as Bitmap Mask	Ctrl+Shift+G
Next Frame	Ctrl+Page Up
Nudge Down Large	Shift+Down
Nudge Left Large	Shift+Left
Nudge Right Large	Shift+Right
Nudge Up Large	Shift+Up
Paste Inside	Ctrl+Shift+V
Previous Frame	Ctrl+Page Down

File Menu

New	Ctrl+N
Open	Ctrl+O
Close	Ctrl+W
Save	Ctrl+S
Save As	Ctrl+Shift+S
Save a Copy	Ctrl+Alt+S
Revert	F12
Export	Ctrl+Shift+R
Export Preview	Ctrl+Shift+X
Page Setup	Ctrl+Shift+P
Print	Ctrl+P
Exit	Ctrl+Q

Edit Menu

Undo	Ctrl+Z
Redo	Ctrl+Shift+Z
Cut	Ctrl+X, F2
Copy	Ctrl+C, F3
Copy HTML Code	Ctrl+Alt+C
Paste	Ctrl+V
Clear	Backspace, Delete
Paste as Mask	Ctrl+Shift+V
Paste Attributes	Ctrl+Alt+V
Select All	Ctrl+A
Deselect	Ctrl+Shift+A
Clone	Ctrl+Shift+C
Crop Selected Bitmap	Ctrl+Alt+A
Preferences	Ctrl+K

View Menu

Zoom In	Ctrl+=
Zoom Out	Ctrl+−
50%	Ctrl+5
100%	Ctrl+1
200%	Ctrl+2
400%	Ctrl+4
800%	Ctrl+8
6400%	Ctrl+6
Fit Selection	Ctrl+Shift+Y
Fit All	Ctrl+Y
Full Display	Ctrl+0
Hide Selection	Ctrl+3
Show All	Ctrl+Alt+3
Rulers	Ctrl+R
Show Grid	Ctrl+'
Snap to Grid	Ctrl+Shift+'
Edit Grid	Ctrl+Alt+G
Show Guides	Ctrl+;
Lock Guides	Ctrl+Alt+;

Snap to Guides	Ctrl+Shift+;
Edit Guides	Ctrl+Alt+Shift+G
Slice Guides	Ctrl+Alt+Shift+;
Hide Edges	Ctrl+H
Hide Panels	Tab

Insert Menu

New Symbol	Ctrl+F8
Convert to Symbol	F8
Hotspot	Ctrl+Shift+U
Layer	Ctrl+Shift+N

Modify Menu

Image Size	Ctrl+Alt+P
Tween Instances	Ctrl+Alt+Shift+T
Select Inverse	Ctrl+Shift+I
Feather	Ctrl+Alt+D
Paste as Mask	Ctrl+Shift+V
Convert to Bitmap	Ctrl+Alt+Shift+Z
Flatten Layers	Ctrl+E
Free Transform	Ctrl+T
Numeric Transform	Ctrl+Shift+T
Rotate 90° CW	Ctrl+F9
Rotate 90° CCW	Ctrl+F7
Bring to Front	Ctrl+Shift+]
Bring Forward	Ctrl+]
Send Backward	Ctrl+[
Send to Back	Ctrl+Shift+[

Align Pop-up Menu

Left	Ctrl+Alt+1
Center Vertical	Ctrl+Alt+2
Top	Ctrl+Alt+4
Center Horizontal	Ctrl+Alt+5
Bottom	Ctrl+Alt+6
Distribute Widths	Ctrl+Alt+7
Distribute Heights	Ctrl+Alt+9

Join	Ctrl+J
Split	Ctrl+Shift+J
Group	Ctrl+G
Ungroup	Ctrl+Shift+G

Text Style Pop-up Menu

Plain	Ctrl+Alt+Shift+P
Bold	Ctrl+Alt+Shift+B
Italic	Ctrl+Alt+Shift+I
Underline	Ctrl+Alt+Shift+U

Text Align Pop-up Menu

Left	Ctrl+Alt+Shift+L
Center Horizontally	Ctrl+Alt+Shift+C
Right	Ctrl+Alt+Shift+R

Justified	Ctrl+Alt+Shift+J		Pen Tool	P
Stretched	Ctrl+Alt+Shift+S		Rectangle Tool	M
Editor	Ctrl+Shift+E		Ellipse Tool	L

Window Menu

New Window	Ctrl+Alt+N		Polygon Tool	G
Tools	Ctrl+Alt+T		Text Tool	T
Stroke	F5		Pencil Tool	N
Fill	Ctrl+Alt+F		Brush Tool	B
Effect	Ctrl+Alt+E		Redraw Path Tool	B
Behaviors	Ctrl+Alt+H		Scale Tool	R
Color Mixer	F6		Distort Tool	T
Tool Options	Ctrl+Alt+O		Freeform Tool	E
Layers	F7		Reshape Area Tool	F
Frames	Ctrl+Alt+K		Eyedropper Tool	I
History	F9		Paint Bucket Tool	K
Styles	Ctrl+Alt+J		Eraser Tool	E
URL	Ctrl+Alt+U		Rubber Stamp Tool	S

Tool Panel

			Slice Tool	Y
Pointer Tool	V		Hand Tool	H
Select Behind Tool	V		Zoom Tool	Z
Export Area Tool	J		Next Frame	Ctrl+Page Up
Subselection Tool	A		Nudge Down	Ctrl+Down
Marquee Tool	M		Nudge Down Large	Ctrl+Shift+Down
Lasso Tool	L		Nudge Left	Ctrl+Left
Polygon Lasso Tool	I		Nudge Left Large	Ctrl+Shift+Left
Crop Tool	C		Nudge Right	Ctrl+Right
Magic Wand Tool	W		Nudge Right Large	Ctrl+Shift+Right
Line Tool	L		Nudge Up	Ctrl+Up
			Nudge Up Large	Ctrl+Shift+Up
			Previous Frame	Ctrl+Page Down

File Menu

New	Ctrl+N
Open	Ctrl+O
Close	Ctrl+W
Save	Ctrl+S
Save As	Ctrl+Shift+S
Import	Ctrl+R
Export	Ctrl+Shift+R
Export Preview	Ctrl+Shift+X
Preview in Browser	F12
Preview in Secondary Browser	Shift+F12
Print	Ctrl+P
Exit	Ctrl+Q

Edit Menu

Undo	Ctrl+Z
Redo	Ctrl+Shift+Z
Cut	Ctrl+X
Copy	Ctrl+C
Paste	Ctrl+V
Clear	Backspace, Delete
Paste Inside	Ctrl+Shift+V
Paste Attributes	Ctrl+Alt+Shift+V
Select All	Ctrl+A
Superselect	Ctrl+Up
Subselect	Ctrl+Down
Deselect	Ctrl+D
Duplicate	Ctrl+Alt+D
Clone	Ctrl+Shift+C
Crop Selected Bitmap	Ctrl+Alt+C

View Menu

Zoom In	Ctrl+=
Zoom Out	Ctrl+−
50%	Ctrl+5
100%	Ctrl+1
200%	Ctrl+2
400%	Ctrl+4
800%	Ctrl+8
3200%	Ctrl+3
6400%	Ctrl+6
Fit Selection	Ctrl+0
Fit All	Ctrl+Alt+0
Full Display	Ctrl+K
Hide Selection	Ctrl+M
Show All	Ctrl+Shift+M
Rulers	Ctrl+Alt+R
Show Grid	Ctrl+'
Snap to Grid	Ctrl+Shift+'
Edit Grid	Ctrl+Alt+G

Show Guides	Ctrl+;
Lock Guides	Ctrl+Alt+;
Snap to Guides	Ctrl+Shift+;
Edit Guides	Ctrl+Alt+Shift+G
Slice Guides	Ctrl+Alt+Shift+;
Hide Edges	Ctrl+H
Hide Panels	Tab, Ctrl+Shift+H

Insert Menu

New Symbol	Ctrl+F8
Convert to Symbol	F8
Hotspot	Ctrl+Shift+U

Modify Menu

Empty Bitmap	Ctrl+Alt+Y
Tween Instances	Ctrl+Alt+Shift+T
Edit Bitmap	Ctrl+E
Exit Bitmap Mode	Ctrl+Shift+D
Select Inverse	Ctrl+Shift+I
Group as Mask	Ctrl+Shift+G
Convert to Bitmap	Ctrl+Alt+Shift+Z
Free Transform	Ctrl+T
Numeric Transform	Ctrl+Shift+T
Rotate 90° CW	Ctrl+9
Rotate 90° CCW	Ctrl+7
Bring to Front	Ctrl+F
Bring Forward	Ctrl+Shift+F
Send Backward	Ctrl+Shift+B
Send to Back	Ctrl+B

Align

Left	Ctrl+Alt+1
Center Vertical	Ctrl+Alt+2
Right	Ctrl+Alt+3
Top	Ctrl+Alt+4
Center Horizontal	Ctrl+Alt+5
Bottom	Ctrl+Alt+6
Distribute Widths	Ctrl+Alt+7
Distribute Heights	Ctrl+Alt+9

Text Menu

Join	Ctrl+J
Split	Ctrl+Shift+J
Group	Ctrl+G
Ungroup	Ctrl+U

Text Style

Plain	Ctrl+Alt+Shift+P, F5
Bold	Ctrl+Alt+Shift+B, F6
Italic	Ctrl+Alt+Shift+I, F7
Underline	Ctrl+Alt+Shift+U

Align

Left	Ctrl+Alt+Shift+L
Center Horizontally	Ctrl+Alt+Shift+C
Right	Ctrl+Alt+Shift+R
Justified	Ctrl+Alt+Shift+J
Stretched	Ctrl+Alt+Shift+S
Editor	Ctrl+Shift+E
Attach to Path	Ctrl+Shift+Y
Convert to Paths	Ctrl+Shift+P

Xtras

Repeat Xtra	Ctrl+Alt+Shift+X

Window

New Window	Ctrl+Alt+N
Tools	Ctrl+Alt+T
Stroke	Ctrl+Alt+B
Fill	Ctrl+Alt+F
Effect	Ctrl+Alt+E
Info	Ctrl+Alt+I
Object	Ctrl+I
Behaviors	Ctrl+Alt+H
Color Mixer	Ctrl+Alt+M
Swatches	Ctrl+Alt+S
Tool Options	Ctrl+Alt+O
Layers	Ctrl+Alt+L
Frames	Ctrl+Alt+K
Styles	Ctrl+Alt+J
URL	Ctrl+Alt+U

Tools

Pointer Tool	V, 0
Select Behind Tool	V, 0
Export Area Tool	J
Subselection Tool	A, 1
Marquee Tool	M
Oval Marquee Tool	M
Lasso Tool	L
Polygon Lasso Tool	L

Crop Tool	C
Magic Wand Tool	W
Line Tool	N
Pen Tool	P
Rectangle Tool	R
Ellipse Tool	R
Polygon Tool	G
Text Tool	T
Pencil Tool	Y
Brush Tool	B
Redraw Path Tool	B
Scale Tool	Q
Skew Tool	Q
Distort Tool	Q
Freeform Tool	F
Reshape Area Tool	F
Path Scrubber Tool—additive	U
Path Scrubber Tool—subtractive	U
Eyedropper Tool	I
Paint Bucket Tool	K
Eraser Tool	E
Rubber Stamp Tool	S
Hand Tool	H
Zoom Tool	Z
Swap Brush/Fill Colors	X
Group as Bitmap Mask	Ctrl+Shift+G
Next Frame	Ctrl+Page Up
Nudge Down Large	Shift+Down
Nudge Left	Left
Nudge Left Large	Shift+Left
Nudge Right	Right
Nudge Right Large	Shift+Right
Nudge Up	Up
Nudge Up Large	Shift+Up
Paste Inside	Ctrl+Shift+V
Previous Frame	Ctrl+Page Down

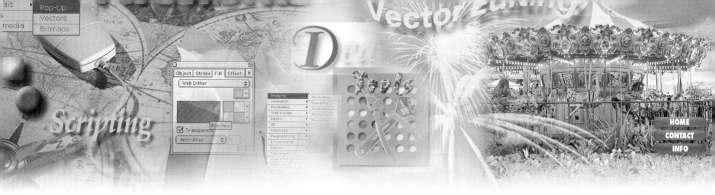

Appendix C

Resources

This appendix provides links to Fireworks resources, such as additional tutorials, commands, and plug-ins. You will also find a list of resources and product descriptions of software and hardware that can aid you in the design process. You will find links and short "reviews" of items such as digital cameras, easy 3D text applications, and third-party plug-ins.

Links to Fireworks Resources

The community of Fireworks users is growing each day. As the program develops and becomes more powerful, more and more designers are discovering they can't work without it. With the release of Fireworks 4, both experienced and new users of Fireworks are seeking answers and help with the program. New resources for Fireworks help are starting to crop up. Currently, the number of sites devoted solely or primarily to Fireworks is limited. The list that follows is as complete as possible as of February 2001. A few sites for Dreamweaver have been added as well because it is so tightly integrated with Fireworks.

Macromedia Fireworks Forum

The Macromedia Fireworks Forum should be on the top of your list when you run into a snag and need help. The Forum has very helpful and courteous people available to assist you. You frequently can find Macromedia technical support hanging out. In Fireworks, choose Help|Macromedia Online Forums, and select Fireworks from the list.

Commands/Tutorials

In this book, you've seen how to use commands and how useful they can be. The supply of Fireworks tutorials is scarce, but here are some sites with commands and tutorials for Fireworks 4, including the Web site I set up for this book.

Fireworks 4 f/x and Design Companion Web Site

www.je-ideadesign.com/fireworksbook.htm

Fireworks 4 f/x and Design updates, tutorials, and product reviews are provided on this site. Every attempt has been made to avoid errors in this book, but if any are found, corrections will be promptly posted at this site. I will also be adding additional tutorials, as time permits, and addressing user comments when it's appropriate or helpful to others.

Massimo Foti

www.massimocorner.com

This site has downloadable objects, behaviors, and other files related to Dreamweaver, Dreamweaver UltraDev, and Fireworks. Massimo won the Macromedia award for the Best Extension Developer.

Pretty Lady

http://dhtmlnirvana.com/#

When you arrive at this site, check out all the links. It has a lot of design information in addition to the Fireworks information. To get to the Fireworks area, click the Pretty Lady button. In that area, you'll find commands, styles, and interfaces you can download for Fireworks. Goodies for Dreamweaver can also be found on this page.

Playing With Fire

www.playingwithfire.com

The Playing With Fire site has a nice assortment of beginner's tutorials and a Fireworks bulletin board.

Project Fireworks

www.projectfireworks.com

Project Fireworks has an archive of downloadable commands, patterns, textures, and symbols.

International—Escogitando

www.escogitando.it

Japi Honoo owns this site, which is available in Italian, Spanish, and English, although the English version had no tutorials yet. Japi's site promises that you'll be "able to download textures, patterns, styles and PNG files of buttons and interfaces, FAQ's and links concerning Fireworks." (Japi provided the techniques I used to write the gel button tutorial in Appendix D.)

About.com

www.graphicssoft.about.com/computer/graphicssoft/cs/fireworks/

About.com provides a list of Fireworks tutorials and resources. Not much is available for Fireworks 4 yet, but check now and then to see what is available. Tutorials for Fireworks 3 will often work if you are familiar enough with the Fireworks work environment to know what has changed and where to find each tool.

Project VII Design

www.projectseven.com

Project VII Design is a Dreamweaver resource site; it contains tutorials, extensions, and templates for Dreamweaver.

Third-Party Plug-ins

Plug-ins that I have tested personally will be noted in this section. In addition, links are listed for you to explore on your own. Some of the plug-ins are free, some are demos, and some are for sale only.

Puzzle Pro 1.2

www.avbros.com

This is a very cool plug-in from AV Bros. that makes producing puzzles quick and easy. It offers a wide range of flexibility, with all kinds of options for puzzle shapes, bevels, and more. Figure C.1 shows the interface. Figure C.2 shows the second interface screen, which allows you to edit even further. The price is $39.95.

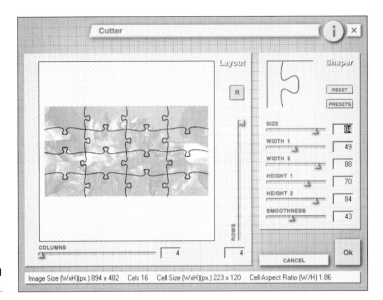

Figure C.1
The Puzzle Pro interface.

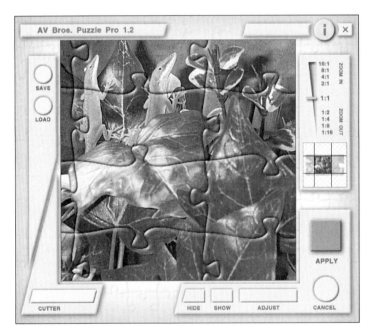

Figure C.2
The Puzzle Pro Edit interface.

Auto FX Software Plug-ins

www.autofx.com

Auto FX Software offers a variety of special-purpose plug-ins, some of which are listed here.

AutoEye

A demo of AutoEye is included on this book's CD-ROM, and a sample of its use is given in Chapter 10. AutoEye is similar to Auto Levels in Fireworks except that it uses a different algorithm and brings out detail a bit differently. In some

Figure C.3
The AutoEye plug-in.

cases, I found it has a tendency to oversharpen, but it brings out a tremendous amount of detail in very dark pictures.

Photo/Graphic Edges 10,000+

A demo of Photo/Graphic Edges 10,000+ is on this book's CD-ROM, and samples used from the demo can be seen in Chapter 10. This product has more edges than you could ever possibly use, but it is great to be able to pick from so many. The manual helps you locate the type of edge you'd like; after you have located the edge on the CD-ROM, you can alter it before it's applied to your image.

Figure C.4
Photo/Graphic Edges
10,000+ plug-in.

Studio Bundle Pro 2.0

Studio Bundle Pro 2.0 contains 11 of Auto FX Software's most popular products in one integrated package for $199.95. This package is worth over $1,250 if the products were purchased separately. The effects in this package include Typo/Graphic Edges; Ultimate Texture Collection, Volumes 1, 2, and 3; Photo/Graphic Patterns; Universal Animator; Universal Rasterizer; Photo/Graphic Frames, Volumes 1 and 2; Page/Edges; and WebVise Totality.

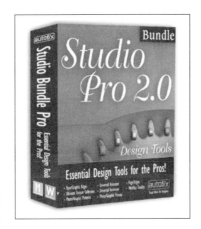

Figure C.5
Studio Bundle Pro plug-in.

Alien Skin Software Plug-ins

www.alienskin.com

Alien Skin Software is very well known for two of its spectacular products, Xenofex and Eye Candy 4000. These two plug-ins offer some really great effects that are fully customizable before you apply them to an image.

Eye Candy 4000

A demo version of Eye Candy 4000 by Alien Skin Software is on this book's CD-ROM. Samples are given in Chapter 10 using only the filters that ship with Fireworks 4. Eye Candy has many other great filters, so be sure to check out Alien Skin's Web site, which has a great interface enabling you to see each of the included 23 filters in use. The price of Eye Candy 4000 is $169, or an upgrade price of $69 is offered for registered users of Eye Candy 3.

Figure C.6
Eye Candy 4000 plug-in.

Xenofex

A demo of the Xenofex plug-in is included on this book's CD-ROM, and a sample is provided in Chapter 10. The Xenofex filters from Alien Skin have a collection of 16 filters and 160 presets. Be sure to check out the filters at its Web site. The price is $129.

Figure C.7
Xenofex filters.

Flaming Pear Software Plug-ins

www.flamingpear.com

Flaming Pear Software offers the free Primus plug-in that you may have tried in Chapter 10. The company has a very nice and innovative collection of plug-ins.

Tachyon

This filter reverses the brightness and keeps the colors. A sample of Tachyon in use is provided in Chapter 10. You can find Tachyon on Flaming Pear's site by clicking the Download link on its home page and going to the Free Plugins category.

SuperBladePro

In September 2000, Flaming Pear released SuperBladePro, adding new effects such as dust, moss, waterstains, and abrasion. Flaming Pear plans to offer more texture packs, presets, and tutorials for SuperBladePro, and to continue developing intriguing and useful plug-ins. SuperBladePro is available via download and online purchase for $30. Registered users of the original BladePro may purchase an upgrade for $15.

Helpful Accessories

When you work with graphics, a few additional items can make your job easier. I have tested some hardware and accessories, and only those worthy of mention (worth the money) will be listed here.

Matrox Millennium G450 32MB DualHead Graphics Card

www.matrox.com/mga

If you are tired of moving your panels and palettes around your screen all the time, you have to try dual monitors—it's great. I have Fireworks running on one monitor and the panels on another. Sometimes I keep Fireworks on one monitor and open Word on the other. It made writing this book much easier, because I could perform the projects on one monitor and write on the other.

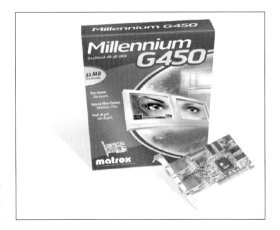

Figure C.8

Matrox Millennium G450 32MB DualHead Graphics Card.

Note: As of March 2001, the Matrox Millenium Group and G450 graphics cards now support full DualHead support in Windows 2000. You can now have separate resolutions on two monitors and can use DualHead instead of a virtual desktop. The Windows 2000 drivers are available at **www.matrox.com**.

Some of the highlights of the Matrox G450 are that you can use monitors with separate resolutions, or a monitor and a TV. The Matrox G450 is also compatible with LCD flat screens.

To read more about the benefits of this new chip, go to **www.matrox.com/ mga/archive_story/dec2000/work_g450vsg400.cfm**.

Wacom Graphire Tablet

www.wacom.com/graphire/index.html

A pressure-sensitive tablet comes in handy with a program like Fireworks. Many of the strokes and the Brush tool take advantage of pressure sensitivity, speed, and the direction you draw. What's nice about the Graphire tablet is that it takes up the same amount of desk real estate as a mouse pad. The price of $99.95, which includes the pen tool and cordless mouse, makes it a great deal for novice and occasional users. You can trace images on the tablet, design your own innovations, or sign your name. If you make the occasional map, a tablet makes the job much easier.

Figure C.9
Wacom Graphire tablet.

Key Features

- Tablet is connected to the computer via a cable to either the USB or serial port

- Patented cordless and battery-less pen and mouse

- Pen features pressure-sensitive tip, two side switches, and pressure-sensitive eraser

- Mouse features three buttons and rubberized scrolling wheel

- Ambidextrous mouse design

- No-ball mouse design always tracks smoothly and never clogs up

- All buttons and switches can be set to user's preference

- Mouse scrolling wheel speed is customizable

- Tablet features clear-plastic overlay for tracing

- Tablet pen stand is detachable

- It comes with a great software bundle including Photoshop LE, Corel Painter, and more

Software

I have found a few programs that are reasonably priced and are beneficial to making Web sites. You may enjoy checking out some of these products.

Wildform SWFX

www.wildform.com

A demo of SWFX is included on this book's CD-ROM. This very-easy-to-use and versatile tool makes quick text animations for use in Flash. It is a standalone application that comes with 100 different preset text animations to use as well as to customize. Another 100 presets are available from Wildform's Web site. All this is available for only $19.99.

Figure C.10
Wildform SWFX animation tool.

Xara X

www.xara.com

When you need the power of a full-fledged illustration tool, Xara X is probably the easiest vector program (as easy as Fireworks) you'll ever find, and the cost is incredible for what you get. Download a free trial version at **www.xara.com/products/xarax/**.

You will find the Xara X interface quite intuitive, simple, and easy to navigate. You will be amazed that a program that is so feature-rich and performs so well doesn't have more bloat. Xara's home page, the Xara Xone, has links to tutorials that will get you up to speed quickly, as well as links to online galleries where you will see some of the fantastic things being done with Xara X.

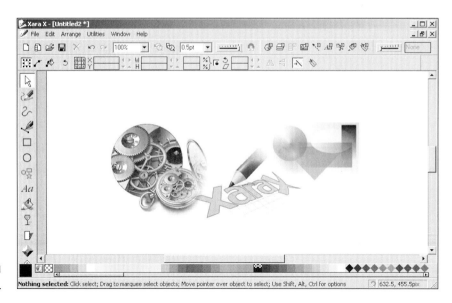

Figure C.11
Xara X illustration tool.

Features

- Vector and bitmap transparency

- Brushes and fills

- Supports pressure-sensitive tablets

- Web design, including automatic HTML and JavaScript production for rollovers

- Realtime antialiasing

- Speed (because of less program bloat, the program responds faster than most)

- Bevel tool

- Realistic shadows

- Feathering, blending, and contouring

- Export to all major formats, including Macromedia Flash

- Dreamweaver integration

What you get for $149 is Xara X, tutorial movies (about 80 of them), introductory movies, 3,000 clipart images, 200 photos, 250 free TT and postscript fonts, and trial versions of Xara 3D 4 and WebStyle. You will also get a link to more clipart available in the clipart gallery on the Web.

SnagIt

www.snagit.com

I began using SnagIt by TechSmith when I received it for writing a review for *Web Review*. I have used it ever since. It was used for all the screen shots taken for this book. You can capture video and text as well, and add sound, annotations, and watermarks. I like the AutoScroll feature, which captures a whole Web page, even the part you can't see. You get all these features and more for only $39.95. You can find a shareware version, which is fully operational, at the SnagIt Web site. If you'd like to see the full review I did about the product, go to **www.webreview.com/2000/12_22/designers/index03.shtml** (if you don't want to type in that long address, just go to **www.webreview.com** and type "Joyce Evans" into the search box).

Camtasia

www.camtasia.com

Camtasia, another product of TechSmith, was used to produce the movie tutorials for *Fireworks 4 f/x and Design,* and is included on this book's CD-ROM. I used the AVI option instead of TechSmith's special TechSmith Screen Capture Codec (TSCC), because using the TSCC would have required you to make an additional installation to be able to view the movies. The TSCC makes the movies smaller, which tempted me to use it, because I could have fit more movies on the CD. But by using regular AVI format, you can view the tutorial movies in any AVI player.

EZ Motion

www.beatware.com

EZ Motion is made by Beatware; you can download a demo at **www.beatware.com**. The program contains dozens of templates such as animated banners, buttons, and other graphics. You can use them as is or customize. A library of graphic objects is also available, including 3D and 2D objects, animated objects, designs, gradients, and images. You can do more than just simple animations such as movement and fades; you can animate text on a curve, change font size, outlines, and fills, as well as shearing and spacing. You also can change the size, shape, and opacity. The elements remain editable. EZ Motion sells for $99.99.

Images

You probably have seen the names "Comstock" and "Hemera" many times throughout this book. Both companies graciously provided images to be used for the exercises and projects. Not only did they make them available to use as samples, but they also have allowed copies in low resolution to be included on this book's CD-ROM so that you can practice with the same images that are used in the exercises and projects.

Hemera Technologies

www.hemera.com

A demo including 500 free Hemera Photo-Objects is included on this book's CD-ROM. These images are ready to be added to any document you are working on. They are on transparent backgrounds and ready to use. If you've been doing the projects, you have used many Hemera Photo-Objects throughout this book, especially in Chapter 2.

The interface that you use to access the objects is very easy to use and is quite impressive. After you install the application, you open the program and an image browser opens. You can scroll to find images, but with 50,000 of them (if you purchase the package), that could take forever. You can search for the items you want. When you locate something of interest and click it, you will be told which CD-ROM to insert. With the Hemera Photo-Objects 50,000 Premium Image Collection, you get eight CD-ROMs and a manual. The package has 80 categories, and now the 50,000 Premium Image Collection is available for both PCs and the Mac, all for $84.99.

DGUSA.COM (Dynamic Graphics)

www.dgusa.com/

Dynamic Graphics has a clipart service with illustrations and royalty free photos. You can get the images on a CD-ROM each month with a print magazine called *Concepts & Designs*. It has tutorials on how to perform techniques using Dynamic Graphics images to produce a variety of different media pieces. I found the magazine very useful and inspirational. It provides a great starting point in the design process for those of us who are "layout challenged." The CD contains both color and black-and-white versions of the images.

As a subscriber, you also have access to images online for only $10 per image. You can get the images via a download or via the mail. Dynamic Graphics will also do a custom image search for you.

Dynamic Graphics has two different services: The Clipper monthly subscription has more images as well as photos and is $74.95 a month. The Designers Club subscription is similar to the Clipper except it has fewer images and no photos; it is $54.95 a month. Both subscriptions include a pictorial index and a print magazine of tutorials and ideas. For more information, check out the Web site at **www.dgusa.com/**.

Clipart

In the design forums and newsgroups I participate in, people are always looking for free clipart sites. I have listed a few that are not free but good. The reason I have not listed any of the free sites is that most of the free sites don't have good clipart and are really scams to get your email address or to falsely inflate the number of hits a site gets to sell more advertising. For a more thorough discussion of this topic, be sure to read an article that Fred Showker of *DT&G Graphic Design* magazine (**www.graphic-design.com**) wrote. You can find the article at **www.60-seconds.com/articles/129.html**. It's a bit of research Fred did about the "free" clipart sites. As with anything you read, do your own research and draw your own conclusions. Fred has provided you with the steps he took when doing this research; that article is at **www.60-seconds.com/articles/129b.html**. If after reading these articles you still want free clipart, just use some of the links from Fred's notes.

Some good news may be on the horizon, though. As a result of Fred's article, Graphic-Design.com is already getting responses from private illustrators who are providing images. Check at this book's companion Web site (**www.je-ideadesign.com/fireworksbook.htm**) for updates and, with any luck, a new resource of illustrations. So far, the best recommendation that I can make is to use the Hemera Photo-Objects and to subscribe to Dynamic Graphics.

Stock Images

Stock images are decent quality images that can be downloaded and/or are available on CD-ROM. Comstock sent me several of their CD-ROMs to use for this book, so I am most familiar with their service, although I've heard good things about EyeWire as well.

Comstock Images

www.comstock.com

An additional CD-ROM, from Comstock, is being shipped with this book. Comstock has included a CD-ROM with over 12,000 "comping" images. (Comping images are sample files that are free to use for layout ideas and presentations to clients. If you use the image for other than comping purposes, you must purchase it.) There is also a section in the browser listing all of the discs available.

EyeWire

www.eyewire.com

EyeWire has a lot of resources if you have the time to search for them. You can access photos, illustrations, audio, type, and more. You can purchase these items in different ways—including buying individual images or even a CD-ROM of images.

Digital Cameras

A digital camera is a great way to obtain the images you need for Web pages. The cameras available today are even suitable for print work, but they are more than suitable for Web design. The cameras listed here are those that I personally have used and tested. They are not the highest-priced versions because, frankly, you don't need the top of the line for Web work. Of course, if you were going to use the camera for high-end print work or very large printed pieces, you would need a camera with higher resolution.

Kodak

www.kodak.com

Besides taking great pictures, this camera is extremely easy to use. This 2.3 megapixel camera has resolutions of 1,760×1,168 (High) and 896×592 (Standard),

Figure C.12
The Kodak DC3400 digital camera.

and image quality settings of Best, Better, and Good. You can print up to 8×10-inch prints with the high resolution setting.

The learning curve is less than half an hour (based on my family). This camera is the one my husband and kids grab when they want to take photos.

Don't let the ease of use fool you, though, because this camera is also powerful. It has an LCD screen to view pictures taken, an autofocus lens, different lighting settings, different flash settings, and even a 3x digital zoom. The pictures taken don't require a lot of time to set up. If you want to, you can make a few adjustments for the lighting and distance, and you are ready to shoot.

I like the fact that it's easy to use, but I also like that I have control over the lighting, flash, and zoom.

> **Note:** If you want to save on batteries and don't want to buy an adapter, I highly recommend getting a card reader. They are wonderful. I found one for only $25 (prices vary), and you simply put the CompactFlash Card in the reader. The images are almost instantly available on your hard drive. Delete them from the card, and you are ready to shoot again.

Nikon

www.nikonusa.com

The camera I have is a 2.11 megapixel with a resolution of up to 1,200×1,600. The first impression I had of this camera right out of the box was that it felt like and looked like a "real" camera. What I particularly like about Nikon cameras is the control I have over the White Balance. I also have noticed that the background detail is better than with some of the other cameras I've used. This is probably because of the Nikkor lens, which has a reputation for being a top-notch lens. Another thing that makes this camera a good value is that you can add additional lenses to it. The lenses that you can add are Wide-Angle, Fisheye, and Telle Converter.

The learning curve for CoolPix is a bit steeper than for some other cameras because of all the options you have. The LCD is easy to see, and I like the Autofocus feature as well. This camera provides a lot of bang for the buck.

A good place to look for a Nikon camera is on Pricewatch. I found the Nikon CoolPix 800 for as low as $459 (**www.pricewatch.com**). The price may be lower when you read this. Nikon has released a new version, the CoolPix 880, that has brought the price down for the 800 version. But if you are doing primarily Web work, you won't really need more than the CoolPix 800 camera provides.

Figure C.13
Nikon CoolPix 800 digital camera.

Books

The books listed here are either currently available ones that I recommend or those that I know are going to be published.

Fireworks

Fireworks books come in several categories. This book, *Fireworks 4 f/x and Design,* is an intermediate- to advanced-level book with a focus on design. Books for absolute beginners also are available, as well as reference books that are designed to be used by users of all levels. Another category is the studio-type book, which showcases the work of many designers and provides inspiration and ideas as well as some instruction.

Beginners

Sandee Cohen. *Fireworks 4 for Windows and Macintosh: Visual QuickStart Guide.* Peachpit Press, 2001.

This book is designed to get you up and running fast. If you're a beginner, this book is perfect to help you understand all the features of the program without any long-winded paragraphs. Author Sandee Cohen has also added loads of helpful tips and explanations for those who are totally new to Web design. The book also contains a special chapter called "Compared to Photoshop" to help those who work with Adobe Photoshop. Finally, the book explains how Fireworks integrates with Macromedia Dreamweaver and Flash.

Reference

Joseph Lowery. *Fireworks 4 Bible.* Hungry Minds (formerly IDG Books Worldwide), April, 2001.

This reference book is a wonderful resource, and anyone serious about Fireworks should own it.

Intermediate to Advanced

Joyce J. Evans. *Fireworks 4 f/x and Design.* The Coriolis Group, 2001.

Fireworks 4 f/x and Design is the only Fireworks book in this category that I'm aware of.

Studio

Linda Rathgeber. *Playing With Fire.* Hungry Minds, April 2001.

This book is a take-off of the Playing With Fire Web site. Because it's a new book, all I can tell you is what the author told me. It's a studio book with tutorials taken from the Web site and contributions of other designers.

Dreamweaver

I would like to mention a couple of Dreamweaver books that will be published near the time of this book's pub date. If I don't make specific comments, it's simply because I haven't seen the title in question.

Beginners

Greg Holden and Scott Willis. *Dreamweaver 4 Visual Insight.* The Coriolis Group, March 2001.

I haven't seen this particular book, but I have reviewed other *Visual Insight* books. They are a wonderful resource for beginners. Every step is accompanied by a picture and informative text. The ones I've seen have been complete and accurate and laid out in a logical learning pattern.

Reference

Joseph Lowery. *Dreamweaver 4 Bible.* Hungry Minds (formerly IDG Books Worldwide), April 2001.

I don't have this version, of course, but I do have and use the *Dreamweaver 3 Bible.* I have always recommended the Dreamweaver 3 book as *the* reference for Dreamweaver, but I'll have to hold on that opinion for this book until I see this latest version.

Jennifer Ackerman Kettell. *Dreamweaver 4: The Complete Reference.* Osborne/McGraw Hill, 2001.

I have seen only a few chapters from this book, but from what I've seen, it includes information I haven't seen in other books. Jennifer Ackerman Kettell knows her topic and expresses it well. This reference book also contains a section on getting started with Fireworks 4.

Intermediate to Advanced

Al Sparber. *Dreamweaver 4 Magic.* New Riders, 2001.

The *Magic* series of books is geared toward intermediate to advanced users. Although this is a new book, I'm sure it will be a good one. Al Sparber is quite active in the Fireworks forum and runs a very successful Web site. He is extremely knowledgeable about Dreamweaver. Al owns the Project VII Design Web site, which is listed at the beginning of this chapter.

Laurie Ann Ulrich. *Dreamweaver 4 f/x and Design.* The Coriolis Group, April 2001.

I haven't seen this book, but other books by this author were quite good.

Be sure to check **www.je-ideadesign.com/fireworksbook.htm**, the companion Web site for *Fireworks 4 f/x and Design,* for updates, new tutorials, and news.

Appendix D

Gel Button Tutorial

In this appendix, you will make a complex gel button using both vector and bitmap tools. You'll add two different highlights and transparency to produce a great-looking gel button.

Hone Your Skills

If you use the dimensions used in this tutorial, all the settings should be the same for you. You can always resize the button later if you don't like the size used here. If you do alter the size beforehand, some of the blur and brightness settings will need to be altered. You can use the color images, which are included in the screenshots.jpg file in the Appendix D resources folder on this book's CD-ROM (some of them also appear in the Color Section), to help you determine how much blur or brightness to add. The finished button file, as well as the button before it is converted to a bitmap (losing all layers), can also be found in the resources folder for Appendix D.

Gel Button

Gel buttons that appear transparent are popular on the Web. The gel button in this tutorial is one of the better ones I've seen because of its great-looking highlights and transparencies. I have adapted this tutorial based on one that Japi Honoo did. It has been adapted and used here with her permission. If you'd like to see more of her work, go to **www.escogitando.it**.

The purpose of this tutorial is for you to use as many as possible of the techniques taught throughout the book in one project and still produce something that is usable for Web pages. This tutorial is quite long and involved, which is why an appendix is devoted to it. If you are ready to roll up your sleeves and begin this tutorial, then follow these steps:

1. Open a new document (File|New) with a transparent background and a size of 220 pixels by 120 pixels.

2. Select the Rectangle tool and draw a rectangle to cover the whole canvas. In the Fill panel (Window|Fill), select Solid and a color of medium gray (#999999). In the Texture box, choose Line-Horiz 1 at 100%.

3. You are now going to make the button shape. Click the yellow folder icon in the Layers panel to add a new layer. In the Fill panel, set the color to white. In the Info panel, set the Height and Width to 50, and place the circle in the center of the canvas and to the left. Select the Ellipse tool, hold down the Shift key, and drag a circle.

4. Guides will help you make this button, so if the rulers are not visible, choose View|Rulers, drag a guide from the top ruler to below the circle you drew, and then drag another one on top of the circle. With the circle selected, choose Edit|Duplicate. Move the duplicate to the other side of the button (see Figure D.1).

5. Select the Rectangle tool and draw a rectangle between the two circles. Place the starting point of the rectangle at the halfway point of the left circle and drag it to the halfway point of the right circle. Check the

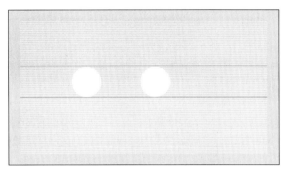

Figure D.1
Two circles in preparation for a button shape.

Height of the rectangle in the Info panel; it should be 50, like the circles. Shift+select each circle and the rectangle, and choose Modify|Combine|Union to combine the shapes into one. In the Info panel, change the overall size of the button to a Width of 150 and press the Enter/Return key.

6. In the Layers panel, double-click Path and name it "Shape". Then, click the right-pointing arrow in the Layers panel and select Duplicate Layer, Before Current Layer. Double-click the duplicate and name it "High-light" (see Figure D.2).

7. Select Shape in the Layers panel. In the Fill panel, click the color well, type in the Hex #283C78 (or any color you'd like), and press Enter/Return. Check in the Fill panel and be sure the texture is set at 0%; it probably is still at 100% because of the texture you added to the background. You won't see the color added just yet because you have the duplicate layer on top.

8. Select Highlight in the Layers panel. In the Info panel, set the size to a Width of 130 and a Height of 20, as shown in Figure D.3.

9. With the Highlight layer still selected, select the Rectangle tool and draw a rectangle over the entire highlight for the mask. In the Fill panel, choose a Linear fill and the Black, White gradient preset (be sure

> **Note:** This part of the tutorial could be done much faster by selecting the Rounded Rectangle tool, setting the Roundness to 100 in the Object panel, and dragging the button shape onto the canvas. This method wasn't used here because I wanted to include the preceding techniques for your practice.

Figure D.2
The Layers panel with the first two objects named.

> **Note:** The size in Step 8 will vary if you are using different dimensions for your button. Size it so it looks like Figure D.3.

Figure D.3
The Highlight layer.

the Texture is set to 0%). Change the direction of the gradient by dragging the round handle up and the square handle down, as shown in Figure D.4.

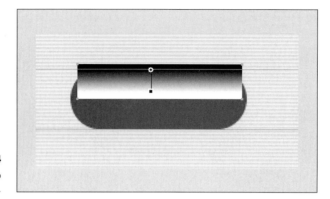

Figure D.4
The gradient applied to the highlight.

10. Shift+select the rectangle and the highlight that has the gradient over it. You can select from the Layers panel, if you'd like. Choose Modify| Mask|Group As Mask (see Figure D.5).

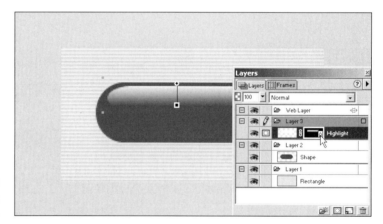

Figure D.5
The highlight with a mask applied.

11. If your highlight doesn't look like Figure D.5, then click the pen icon in the Layers panel next to your mask icon. You can now drag the gradient handles to adjust the gradient. See the Color Section to see the highlight or the color pages that are included in the Appendix D resources folder.

12. In the Layers panel, click the yellow folder icon to add a new layer, Layer 4.

13. Choose the Ellipse tool, hold down the Shift key, and drag a circle to touch the top guide and the bottom guide. Check the Info panel; the

size should be 50 by 50. In the Fill panel, change the Texture to 0%, choose a Radial fill, and then click the Edit button. Click the first color well (on the left), type in Hex #B4E6FA, and press Enter/Return. In the second well, click, type Hex #283C78, and press Return/Enter. Figure D.6 shows the positioning of the gradient and the circle.

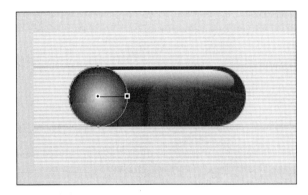

Figure D.6
Radial gradient settings for the circle.

14. Select the Knife tool, place it at the center point of the circle (see Figure D.7), and cut through the other side (bottom) of the circle. Click anywhere on the empty canvas, and then, using the Pointer tool, you can move each half of the circle into position. Place one half at each end of the button, as shown in Figure D.8.

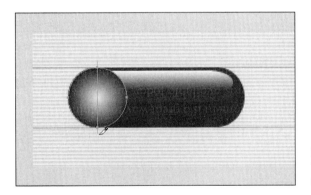

Figure D.7
The position to cut with the Knife tool.

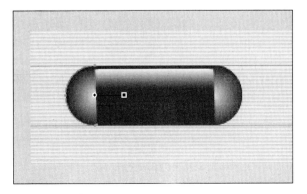

Figure D.8
The position of the halves of the circle in place.

Note: Because this button has been converted to a bitmap, the blur effects in this project will be added via the Xtras menu. If it wasn't converted to a bitmap, effects such as the blur could be added through the Effect panel making them Live Effects; this means they remain editable.

Note: It's easier to position the selection at the very edge of the half circle if you zoom in by selecting the Zoom tool or pressing Z.

15. Select the half circle on the left and choose Modify|Convert To Bitmap. Repeat for the right-side half.

16. Double-click the Marquee tool icon (rectangle), which opens the Marquee tool Options panel. From the drop-down menu, choose Fixed Size, type "2" and "50" for the horizontal and vertical sizes, respectively, and set the Edge to Anti-Alias. Click near the left-side half circle, and a selection will appear that is 2 pixels by 50 pixels. With the Marquee tool still selected, move the selection to the edge of the left-side half circle (see Figure D.9).

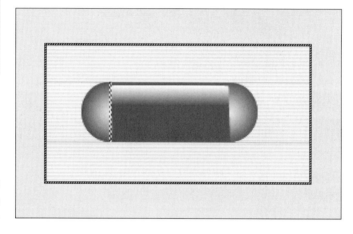

Figure D.9
A very small marquee selection in place.

17. Now you are going to copy the two selected pixels across to the other side of the button. Press the V key to access the Select Behind tool. Check the Pointer tool icon and see whether it has a green box with an arrow. If not, then press V again. You want the Select Behind tool to be active. Press the Alt/Option key and the right arrow on the keyboard. You can hold down the Alt/Option key and hold down the right-arrow key until you meet the other half circle, or hold down the Alt key and click the right-arrow key multiple times. See Figure D.10.

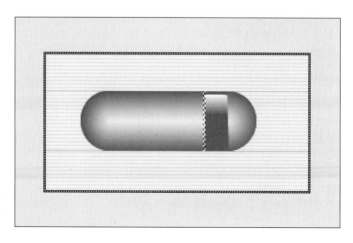

Figure D.10
Copying 2 pixels across the button.

18. Shift+select everything in Layer 4 (default names of Bitmap and Bitmap) and choose Modify|Group. Hold down the Shift key and press the down arrow two times. In the Info panel, set the size of the part you moved down to 140 wide by 40 high. Move this smaller shape to the lower third of the original outline. In the Layers panel, choose Screen from the Mode box (it probably currently says Normal). Your button will look like Figure D.11.

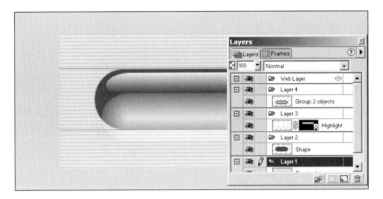

Figure D.11
Gel button with highlight moved down.

19. Double-click the group you just made in Layer 4 and name it "Bottomhighlight".

20. Choose Xtras|Blur|Gaussian Blur. When the dialog box opens saying your vector will be converted to a bitmap, click OK. Set the Blur to 8 and click OK.

> **Note:** If you use the slider in the Gaussian Blur dialog box, you can see the blur effect in realtime on the canvas. If you type in the number, you won't see the effect unless you click OK.

21. In the Layers panel, click the yellow folder icon to add a new layer (Layer 5). Select the Text tool and click the button. Type your text (the name for the button); CaflischScript Regular, bold is used here, with a size of 44 and a color of white. Click OK when you are done making your selections. With the Pointer tool, place the text in position on the button.

22. In the Layers panel, select the mask group in Layer 3 (Highlight) and choose Xtras|Blur|Gaussian Blur. Click OK to convert to a bitmap, enter a Blur amount of 0.5, and click OK. Select Layer 5 and then click the yellow folder icon to add a new layer (Layer 6). Choose Insert|Empty Bitmap.

23. Double-click the Marquee tool to access the Marquee tool options. Change the Style back to Normal, and for the Edge, select Feather with an amount of 50. Draw a rectangle to cover the entire button. Figure D.12 shows the selection around your button.

24. Choose the Paint Bucket tool and select white for the Fill color. Double-click the Paint Bucket tool to access the Paint Bucket tool options. Set

Figure D.12

A selection made around the button using the Marquee tool.

Button Selection

When you select Feather, a rounded rectangle appears around the border after you drag a selection. You want the selection to hug the outline of the button as close as possible. If the selection is inside the button, start drawing the rectangle further away from the button. If you are making a button larger than the one used here, the Feather amount needs to be increased; if your button is smaller, then the Feather amount needs to be decreased to get a selection that is close to the button.

the Edge to Anti-Alias and the Tolerance to 50. Click the button to fill it. Choose Modify|Marquee|Select Inverse. Press the Delete key one time to clear some of the white. Choose Edit|Deselect. Figure D.13 shows the result.

25. Double-click the Magic Wand tool to access the Magic Wand tool options. Set the Edge to Anti-Alias and the Tolerance to 50. Select the center, lighter part of the button. The selection should look like Figure D.14. If it doesn't, deselect, change the Tolerance up or down, and try again.

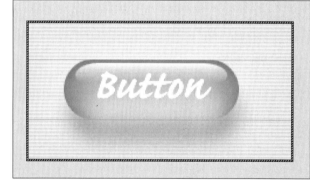

Figure D.13

A white fill added, inversed, and deleted.

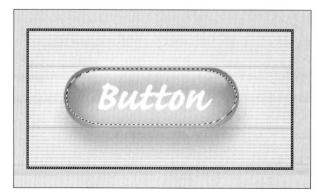

Figure D.14

A selection made with the Magic Wand in the center of the button.

26. Press the Delete key one time to clear some white from the center section. Choose Edit|Deselect. Choose Xtras|Blur|Gaussian Blur and use a Blur amount of 5.

27. To make a shadow, select Layer 4, click the right-pointing arrow, choose Duplicate Layer, and choose After Current Layer. Double-click the duplicate layer and name it "Shadow". Move (click and drag) this layer below Layer 2. In the Layers panel, change the Blend mode to Multiply (it's likely currently set to Normal), and set the Opacity to 75% on the Shadow layer.

28. To produce an image with a realistic effect, you will modify Layer 4 by increasing the brightness. Choose Xtras|Adjust Color|Brightness And Contrast and choose 15 for Brightness and 15 for Contrast. Look at your button—where is the brightness? Is it a bit into the bottom of the text? If not, then nudge this layer up a bit by using the up arrow key. How far to move it up depends on the placement you originally used when you placed the lower highlight.

29. Duplicate the layer with the text on it (Layer 5), select After Current Layer, and rename it "Text Shadow".

30. Select the Text tool, click the Paint Bucket fill color well, and change the color of the text to #283C78. Choose Xtras|Blur|Gaussian Blur, select or type "2", and click OK. Using the Pointer tool, move the shadow to a position you like, using Figure D.15 as a guide. A PNG file for the button up to this point, called gelbeforebitmap.png, is located in the Appendix D resource folder. Use it as a reference if you need it.

> **Note:** Be sure to deselect before adding the blur. If you don't, the edges of the center selection will be distinct instead of blending in with the background of the button.

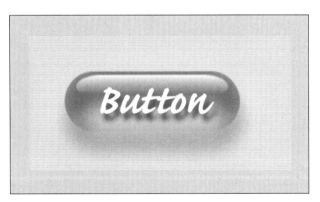

Figure D.15
The button with the text shadow added.

31. You now will remove the editability of the button, except for the background and the text. You first need to lock a few layers. To lock a layer, click the area to the right of the Eye icon (see Figure D.16). The layers to lock are Layer 1, Layer 7 Shadow, Layer 8 Text Shadow, and Layer 5 Text.

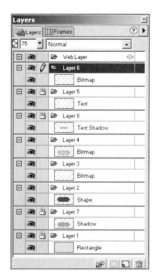

Figure D.16
Multiple layers locked.

32. Shift+select the objects in the layers that are not locked (not the layer names), and choose Modify|Convert To Bitmap. The layers that contained objects that you just converted to a bitmap will appear empty except for one that will say Bitmap. Select that object and choose Xtras|Adjust Color|Brightness And Contrast, choose 15 for both the Contrast and the Brightness, and click OK.

33. Set the layer Opacity of this bitmap to 80%. Figure D.17 shows the finished gel button.

34. If you need the button in another size, choose Modify|Image Size and change it. If you check Constrain Proportions (checked by default) and change either the height or the width, the one not changed will resize proportionately to the dimension you alter.

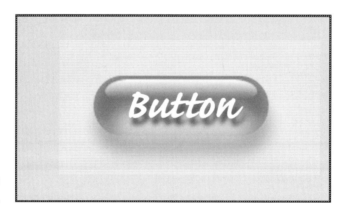

Figure D.17
The finished gel button.

Index

modifying, 31–32

saving as styles, 33–34

tip modifications for, 33

Styles

custom, for pop-up menus, 189–191

saving strokes as, 33–34

Swatches panel, customizing, 39–40

Symbol Editor, making navigation bars into symbols using, 175–176

Symbol Properties dialog box, 201

Symbols. *See also* Animated symbols; Button symbols; Graphic symbols.

copies of, 201

T

Table options tab in Export panel, 164

Tables, roundtrip editing with Dreamweaver, 3

Tabs for navigation, making, 66–67

Tachyon plug-in, 258–259

Target tab in Link Wizard, 173

Text, 19–30. *See also* Editing text.

altering position on path, 23

alternate, 150–151

converting to images, 21

converting to paths, 21–22

editable button symbols with, 178–180

editing in buttons, 174

flipping with paths, 27

with perspective, 28

punching holes using, 50–52

putting on paths, 22–23

slicing, 151

viewing settings for, 28

Text boxes, converting image slices into, 156–159

Text editor, 20–21

Text Editor, baseline shift and, 27

Text-type images, hotspot tools and, 144

Texture, adding to strokes, 34

Textures, adding to fills, 50

Threshold setting in Unsharp Mask dialog box, 251

Tint mode, 14

Tonal range

Auto levels for adjusting, 130

of bitmap images, 125–130

Levels dialog box for adjusting, 125–130

Toolbars, docking, 62

Transforming text, 20–30. *See also specific actions.*

Transform options, 68

Transform tools, 28–30

Transparency

adding to masks, 135–136

for GIF and PNG files, setting, 161–162

Trigger images for rollovers, 181–182

Turn Off Hide Edges option, 114–115

Tweening, 209–213

distributing objects to frames and, 211

of Live Effects, 211–213

multiple tweens and, 210–211

types of, 209

using drop shadows, 212–213

Tween instances, 70–71

Tween instances dialog box, 210

U

Union operation, 85–86

Unsharp Mask dialog box, 250–251

Up state of buttons, 171

URLs, adding to slices, 150–151

User interface, macromedia, 2

V

Vector File Options dialog box, 245

Vector mode, 54

editing tools of, 100–110

Vector objects (images). *See also* Editing vector objects; Paths.

applying strokes to, 55

bitmap images compared with, 54

converting images into, 108–110

hotspot tools and, 144

making images into, 82

Vector tools, 53–75

freeform drawing tools, 71–75

shape tools, 55–71

Viewing. *See also* Displaying; Hiding.

deselecting for, 51

settings for text or objects, 28

If you *like* this book, you'll *love...*

Dreamweaver® 4 f/x and Design
by Laurie Ulrich
Media: CD-ROM

ISBN #: 1-57610-789-2
$49.99 (US) $74.99 (CAN)

Dreamweaver® 4 f/x and Design improves, enriches, and builds upon the reader´s current Dreamweaver skills. Emphasis is made on use of text, graphics, color and special effects including sound, animated gif files, and Flash movies in the book´s chapters. Quick tips are given to format and position Web page content for professional-looking sites. Presenting real-world applications, this book will strengthen Dreamweaver skills and improve Web page design. The CD-ROM included with this book contains all files needed to complete the book´s projects and numerous examples of Web-page layouts.

Illustrator® 9 f/x and Design
by Sherry London
Media: CD-ROM

ISBN #: 1-57610-750-7
$49.99 (US) $74.99 (CAN)

Features new information and projects on styles and effects, how to prepare your images for the Web, as well as other enhanced features. With real-world projects, readers learn firsthand how to create intricate illustrations and compositing techniques. Readers also learn how to work seamlessly between Illustrator® and Photoshop®.

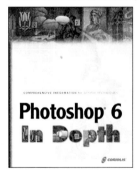

Photoshop® 6 In Depth
by David Xenakis and Benjamin Levisay
Media: 2 CD-ROMs

ISBN #: 1-57610-788-4
$59.99 (US) $89.99 (CAN)

Takes the mystery out of the new Photoshop® functions! Readers will learn layering, channel selection, color corrections, prepress integration with other applications, and how to prepare images for the Web. The linear format in each chapter addresses individual topics, allowing readers to select according to their needs and skill levels. This book includes two CD-ROMs, with three bonus chapters: "Third-Party Filters," "Preparing Graphics for the Web," and "Using ImageReady".

GoLive™ f/x and Design
by Richard Schrand
Media: CD-ROM

ISBN #: 1-57610-786-8
$49.99 (US) $74.99 (CAN)

From basic designs to advanced rollover techniques, *GoLive™ 5 f/x and Design* takes you on a tour of the hottest features of this high–end Web design program. Learn about Cascading Style Sheets, get ideas on how to create eye-catching forms, find out how to build dynamic sites by using today's cutting-edge technology, and then discover how the author builds an entire site using the techniques discussed throughout the book. The CD-ROM contains dozens of demo and free programs, special discounts on memory upgrades exclusive to this book, and original seamless backgrounds for use on your own Web sites.

Flash Forward with Coriolis Books

Flash™ 5 Visual Insight

Authors: Sherry London and Dan London

Audience: Novice to Intermediate Flash™ users

- Fundamentals of Flash™ 5 through a graphically oriented format.
- Projects showing the full range of the product's capabilities.
- Color section illustrating features of Flash™.
- Teaches Flash™ tools and their options, then guides readers to create their own movies.

Flash™ ActionScript f/x and Design

Author: Bill Sanders

Audience: Intermediate to Advanced Flash™ users

- Combines major concepts to show how to create more elaborate, elegant, and outstanding Flash™ 5 movies
- Teaches strategies to integrate ActionScript into Flash™ movies producing desired effects.
- Shows basic algorithms for creating movies not possible without ActionScript.

Flash™ 5 f/x and Design

Author: Bill Sanders

Audience: Intermediate to Advanced Flash™ users

- Newest features of Flash™, with case studies and tutorials.
- Contains advanced topics, including how to use data from external sources, text files, HTML pages, or servers.
- CD-ROM with 50 Flash™ 5 movies in FLA and SWF formats, and trial versions of Flash™, Dreamweaver®, Fireworks®, and FreeHand®.

Flash™ 5 Cartoons and Games f/x and Design

Authors: Bill Turner, James Robertson, and Richard Bazley

Audience: Intermediate to Advanced Flash™ users

- Reveals very beneficial Flash code and authoring source files.
- Learn cartooning with the use of lip-synching with Magpie Pro® and storyboarding in Flash™.
- CD-ROM includes demo versions of Flash™, SmartSound®, Magpie Pro®, and complete authoring files for animation and games, plus numerous games.

Flash™ is the leading vector technology for designing high-impact, low-bandwidth Web sites that deliver motion, sound, interactivity, and graphics. Vector-based Flash™ content downloads faster, is scalable, and boasts higher quality than other graphic formats. The Web experience becomes more attractive and compelling than ever before through the use of Flash™.

Visit us at creative.coriolis.com
Available at book and computer stores worldwide.

Flash-Guru™

The future of Flash training

Founded by **Jon Warren Lentz**, author of the Flash 5 and Flash 4 Bibles, **Flash-Guru**™ is a new vision of Flash knowledge sharing based on the concept of an expert community.

Flash-Guru™ has brought together some of best minds in the Flash world, united in a common endeavor: to develop and deliver a library of superior training materials.

Flash-Guru™ courses are built upon real-world projects by authors who know how to develop course materials for the web.

Flash-Guru™ instructors will develop a broad curriculum of original, compelling, long-form tutorials that cover the full breadth of Flash topics, areas of deep specialization, and the advanced ranges of the integration of Flash with other technologies.

Whether you are an absolute beginner or an accomplished Flash designer, the goal of **Flash-Guru**™ is to provide you with the training you need to take your Flash artistry to the next level.

At **www.Flash-Guru.com** you will get the information and training you need in a hands-on, quality-controlled learning environment.

"Jon Warren Lentz, together with Nik Schramm and Jeffrey Bardzell, has applied the concept of 'learner-centered design' to the creation of a knowledge-sharing web environment that's designed to support the learning goals of the participants, and that's flexible enough to take into account their motivation and lifestyle. The result, Flash-Guru, is a model of instruction that applies equally well to both lone designers and corporate groups." - **(Bill Turner,** author of **Flash 5 Cartoons and Games F/X)**

Flash-Guru, the future of Flash training for IT and motivated individuals.

Starting in May 2001.

What's on the CD-ROM

The Fireworks 4 f/x and Design's companion CD-ROM contains elements specifically selected to enhance the usefulness of this book, including:

- *The tutorial images in the book, arranged by chapter*—The images needed to complete the projects.
- *Tutorial movies*—Demonstrating some of the projects from the book.
- *Commands*—Free commands to use from Brian Baker and Joyce Evans.
- *AutoEye demo for Mac and PC*
- *Photo/Graphic Edges demo for Mac and PC*
- *Xenofex demo for Mac and PC*
- *Eye Candy 4000 demos for Mac and PC*
- *Photo Objects 5,000 Premium Image Collection Trial Version 1.52*
- *Wildform SWFX 1.03 demo*
- *Macromedia Dreamweaver 4 demo for Mac and PC*
- *Macromedia Fireworks 4 demo for Mac and PC*
- *Comstock Images*—Including over 12,000 comping images (on the second CD-ROM)

System Requirements

Windows

- Intel Pentium grade processor running Windows 98, ME, 2000 or NT 4 (with Service Pack 6) or later
- 64 MB of RAM plus 100 MB of available disk space
- 800×600 pixel resolution, 256-color display (1024×768 resolution, millions of colors recommended)
- A mouse or digitizing table
- A CD-ROM drive

Macintosh

- Power Macintosh (G3 or higher recommended), running System 8.6 or 9.x
- 64 MB of RAM plus 100 MB of available disk space
- Adobe Type Manager 4 or later for using Type 1 fonts
- A color monitor (1024×768 resolution, millions of colors recommended)
- A mouse or digitizing tablet
- A CD-ROM drive